RIOTOUS
DEATHSCAPES

RIOTOUS DEATHSCAPES

HUGO KA CANHAM

Duke University Press / Durham and London / 2023

© 2023 DUKE UNIVERSITY PRESS

All rights reserved

Printed in the United States of America on
acid-free paper ∞

Designed by Matthew Tauch

Typeset in Alegreya by Westchester Publishing Services

Library of Congress Cataloging-in-Publication Data
Names: Canham, Hugo, author.
Title: Riotous deathscapes / Hugo ka Canham.
Description: Durham : Duke University Press, 2023. | Includes
index.
Identifiers: LCCN 2022036255 (print)
LCCN 2022036256 (ebook)
ISBN 9781478016953 (hardcover)
ISBN 9781478019596 (paperback)
ISBN 9781478024224 (ebook)
Subjects: LCSH: Pondo (African people)—Social life and customs. |
Pondo (African people)—History. | Black people—Race identity—
South Africa—Pondoland. | Pondoland (South Africa)—Social life
and customs. | Pondoland (South Africa)—Civilization. | BISAC:
SOCIAL SCIENCE / Black Studies (Global) | HISTORY / Africa /
South / Republic of South Africa
Classification: LCC DT1768.P66 C364 2023 (print) | LCC DT1768.P66
(ebook) | DDC 305.89606875/8—dc23/eng/20220927
LC record available at https://lccn.loc.gov/2022036255
LC ebook record available at https://lccn.loc.gov/2022036256

Cover art: Dumile Feni, *The Classroom*. Charcoal and conte
on paper, 229 × 96.5 cm. Bruce Campbell Smith Collection.
Courtesy of the Dumile Feni Trust.

PUBLICATION OF THIS BOOK IS SUPPORTED BY DUKE
UNIVERSITY PRESS'S SCHOLARS OF COLOR FIRST BOOK FUND.

CONTENTS

ACKNOWLEDGMENTS

My mother is present throughout this book. As a protagonist, a facilitator suggesting other protagonists, sitting with me when my ideas ran out and unwittingly planting seeds that drove the manuscript. Deep down, this book is about her. In all my prior scholarship, I have not written about home or emaMpondweni. It is fitting that my first foray into this new writing begins at the place of my birth and with my mother. When other university work threatened to stall the writing of this book, Lusikisiki was a refuge that reconnected me to the people who are at the heart of this text. It is where my ancestral spirits fortify me.

Brett Bowman, Garth Stevens, and Grace Khunou read parts of the earliest draft of this text. Thank you for your early affirmation that I was on to something. Brett has backed me with a rare generosity. My mentor, Bhekizizwe Peterson, steered me toward depth when he pointed me to the ancestral lineage within which I write. When my confidence was dashed, he rallied and gave me a renewed sense of purpose. Jill Bradbury and Bhekizizwe Peterson gave me important space to think about parts of this book at the NEST symposium. In their violence symposium, Karl von Holdt and Garth Stevens similarly enabled the presentation of an early version of what became the final chapter. Zimitri Erasmus and Aline Ferreira Correia, thank you for listening and encouraging me. Nkululeko Nkomo, I appreciate your thoughtfulness and readiness to debate ideas. You are my scholarly sibling. Brendon Barnes's nose for tracing the winding secrets of family lineages helped give form to my own ancestry. Sibusiso Nkomo tutored me on navigating the archive. Mzwa Makhanya saved some of the images that appear in the book. Thank you to the various photographers who allowed me to use their images. Wesley Grimett, thank you for facilitating. Lerato Moroeng provided the financial administrative support that made this book possible. Individually, Rejane Williams, Nomonde Gogo, Vinitha Jithoo, Mpho Mathebula, Sis Pam Mntonintshi, Kopano Ratele, Raygine DiAquoi, Vuyi Mhlambi, Christopher Sonn, Christoph Maier, Katijah Khoza-Shangase, Edith Paswana, Malose Langa, Krystal Klingenberg, Peace Kiguwa, Julio Tavares, Nazeema Mohamed, Tammy Shefer, and Ronelle Carolissen are fellow travelers. Shahnaaz Suffla, Urmitapa Dutta, Devin Atallah, Deanne Bell, and Jesica Fernandez are a community of solidarity. Norman Duncan has long taken bets on me and has followed through with support no matter how busy he became. I can never repay the debt. In a world where time is a commodity and scholars trained in Africa are unseen, I am amazed by how many people responded to my calls for assistance. Jim Reische and Lindsay Frederick Braun do not know me, but they each assisted when I wrote asking for help. At a high point of frustration, on a transatlantic call, La Marr Jurelle Bruce advised me to theorize from where I am. Sarah Grey and Ute Kuhlmann provided editorial interventions at different times of the manuscript's development. The three anonymous reviewers pushed me with a hardness and a gentleness that were informed by a belief that this was a viable project. Thank you for the generosity of time and commitment to ideas.

A manuscript requires critical readers before it becomes a book. I value Moshibudi Motimele's judgment, and I am grateful that she nudged me toward *Pondo Blues*. Khwezi Mkhize's widely read eyes were invaluable for pushing me to read works that became important for this book. I had planned on another book, but Grace A. Musila pointed me to the introduction to Christina Sharpe's *In the Wake*. This gave me permission to write this book. Grace's generosity is a village. She has read each word. Though I take ultimate responsibility for the final text, its lapses, and some of its boundary-testing arguments, this book has the imprint of Grace's generosity. In the course of her iterative readings and our many conversations, I sometimes internalized her astute formulations and evocative turns of phrase. It is a wonderful thing for one's work to be backed with unwavering conviction. Even as I sit in the margins of the global movement of black studies, books and the Twittersphere mean that I have often felt part of an imagined community. The works and words of Saidiya Hartman, Christina Sharpe (who followed me back!), Gabeba Baderoon, Neo S. Musangi, Pumla D. Gqola, Grieve Chelwa, Jayna Brown, Jacob Dlamini, Stella Nyanzi, Keguro Macharia, Tshepo Madlingozi, La Marr Jurelle Bruce, Sylvia Tamale, and Rinaldo Walcott teach me the beauty of living with ideas.

Shireen Hassim plucked me out of obscurity to go on a Mellon-supported fellowship to Harvard University. While there, the Center for African Studies gave me a home base from which to conceptualize this book. There and subsequently, John Comaroff was an early supporter of this project. Mellon funding allowed me to rent a bedroom in the attic of a house in Sommerville. It is from there, in a snowy Massachusetts, that I wrote the first sentences of this book. If the soul of the book is Lusikisiki, the foundation lingers between Sommerville and another apartment in Harlem where I spent the winter of 2016. In New York, CUNY's Graduate Center opened its doors to me, and Michelle Fine, Maria Torre, and Susan Opotow were superb hosts. At CUNY, I felt seen. Anmol Chadda adopted me as his brother in the United States. There is no better host. As I moved toward the finish line, the National Institute for Humanities and Social Sciences (NIHSS) enabled me to spend quality writing time at Centro de Estudos Africanos, Universidade Eduardo Mondlane in Maputo, Mozambique. In Maputo, Miguel de Brito ensured that I had a soft landing. The Oppenheimer Memorial Trust provided a funding boost that enabled the completion of this book in the middle of a global pandemic. My home department, faculty, and the University of the Witwatersrand are key sites from which I work. Of course, the views conveyed in this book are mine and do not represent those of any funders or associated organizations.

At Duke, I worked with the most exacting editor who wanted this book to be its best possible self. She often saw ahead of me and nudged me to look up from where I was. I am grateful for the years of working alongside Elizabeth Ault. Benjamin Kossak worked patiently with me through the final stages of the process. In many ways, this book throws down the gauntlet in relation to where African-based voices can be published, which voices are heard, and under what conditions our voices can travel across the world.

I interviewed a number of villagers for this book. I am grateful to the mostly old people who opened their lives and hearts to me. Their words have shaped this text. I hope to have captured their anguish and their joy. Some died while I was in the process of completing the manuscript. This book is for them but for their descendants too. My neighbors and the villagers whose lives have intersected with mine are in these pages. By focusing on a single place, I wanted to write a book about expansive forms of blackness because the homogenizing narrative jarred with my own experiences of blackness as a village boy. I wanted to provide a portrait of women and queer adolescents as black agents. The people I know as black are old men who have not gone to school. They are not big men. Adolescents teach me to rethink temporality. The old women of my village have always held me close, and they have allowed me to explore a boundless blackness. Readers will encounter horizontal forms of blackness founded on relation and an insistence that no one history or place on the globe has monopolies on blackness. *Riotous Deathscapes* is about place. The rolling hills. The rocky outcrop. The roaring ocean. The flooding river bend and the graves that dot the riotous black deathscapes. The book is forged in this hardness and beauty. I have used the hardness in the content of the book. I have borrowed the form from the beauty that sutures the hardness. *Riotous Deathscapes* is an incomplete portrait of Mpondo life. I hope that those whose experiences I transcribe here will forgive my lapses and any wayward interpretations.

Writing often means that others are shut out. The grace of those I love is humbling. Leaving Johannesburg for Lusikisiki, Mozambique, or the United States is a leap of faith from a place of affection from a small band of people I love. Thank you for always giving me the space to return. Don Andrews and Bongeziwe Mabandla carry me in the quiet moments, and I am assured of their friendship. I am happy they have stayed even as my friendships have thinned out over the years. Mthokozisi, Owenhloso, Kgamadi, Mefana, Kholekile, Mbuso, Kaelo, Plan B, and many others. Eternally, my siblings sis'B, sis'Elain, Mark, Shell, Kinny, their partners and their children. My brother Jo, Keyi, Joseph, Nono knows—I see you. This project has taught me gratitude to my ancestors—both of kin and those I have come to claim, of the human and of the natural world. The Wild Coast. Bhekizizwe Peterson, now a baobab—*camagu*. Claude Ndlovu—in the maddening storms and the silences, *uliliwa lam*.

THIS BOOK IS DEDICATED TO WILLFUL AFRICANS WHO CONTINUE TO THEORIZE AND LOVE—EMAMPONDWENI AND IN OTHER BLIGHTED ZONES OF ABANDONMENT.

River ferry crossing
the Umzimvubu River at
Port St, Johns. Courtesy of
African Studies Map
Collection as well as BC880
Godfrey and Monica
Wilson Papers,
UCT Libraries.

TO BE RELEGATED TO THE MARGINS is to be in a state of being perpetually emotionally charged. Feelings coursing near the surface. Catching feelings. Shackled to emotions. In a defensive posture. Touchy. Surly. Chips on our shoulders. Charged in ways that those who are fully human do not have to be. Charged in ways that surprise others. Seeing into the past and future and connecting invisible but sedimented histories of trauma. Over-analyzing. I write this book from the place of catching feelings. From the chip on my prickly body. From the disorientating vortex of repeated catastrophe and joyful paradox that is the black condition. This book is about amaMpondo people of Mpondoland, but it is also about black people who are subjugated throughout the world.

MPONDO ORIENTATIONS

My mother's life is lived quietly in the former Transkei apartheid homeland, in deep rural Eastern Cape, South Africa. We are generally referred to as the Xhosa people. To be more precise though, we are Mpondo people who speak a derivative of isiXhosa or isiMpondo.[1] In my mother's village of Emfinizweni, electricity arrived in 2006 when she was about sixty-five years old. Piped water is a pipe dream. Her candlelit life has been marked by repeated trauma. In the last few years she has fallen on her back at least eight times. In the first of these falls, in 2011, I was with her. She landed with a thud that fractured three vertebrae in her spine. On this occasion, the two of us were marooned in a flooding valley. At her insistence, I stopped the car that we were traveling in. She was worried that the wheels of the motor vehicle would miss the overflowing and crumbling bridge and we would plunge into the river that had burst its banks. She climbed out of the vehicle and after a few steps in the thick mud, she slipped and fell, landing on her back. The falling rain washed the mud from her face as she lay looking into the weeping sky. Her wet hair clung to her forehead, a forehead whose design inspired my own. Beside myself with fear, I extricated her from the mud. Her mouth froze and her breathing stopped. Desperation struck her eyes. A heart attack, I thought. Leaning into her frozen body, I held her mouth and breathed my panicked breath into her—giving her the air that she'd bequeathed to me before my birth. I would later learn that this was the beginning of heightened panic attacks and not a heart attack. I liken this to the Rwandan condition *ihahamuka*—which means without lungs and is common in the wake of trauma such as genocide.[2] My mother and I did get out of the valley. But faced with roads that jut dangerously out of slippery hills and overflowing riverbanks, my mother lay in bed with a fractured spine for four days over Christmas before the roads cleared sufficiently for us to take her to the hospital. The conditions where people eke out livings in the rural Eastern Cape make black trauma, kaffirization, a quotidian event. My use of the term *kaffirization* is to signal the work of the term beyond the taboo.[3] Its use has always been pejorative. I use it here to point to its unhumaning intent.[4]

In a fall in 2015, my mother was shoved over by a young man wielding a smoking gun at her face. She landed with a thud to her head. She screamed cries that echoed in the distance to signal to my younger brother to escape from the house. Forcing her to the floor, her attacker tramped on her chest, forcing her ribs to yield, until she quieted. Hearing the screams and gunshots, my brother gathered his crutches and stumbled out of the back door, swinging on his single leg. He hid in the garden, and using his mobile phone, he called for help. My mother has screamed for help in agony so many times that her jaws have a way of locking. This is a sign of panic setting into her body. Freezing her. Draining the air from her lungs. Attacking her. Her screams carry memories of her husband, our father, who died young. I was six then, and my brother was a year old. She has been attacked so many times that she sits near windows to scan the road for assailants. Every sound must be accounted for. "What was that?" The remote control resides in the folds of her lap ever ready to mute the television. "Did you hear that?" She no longer watches the news and violent scenes on the television. Violence triggers panic. She flips through the channels to avoid bad news. Her favorite television programs are those whose dialogue she cannot hear. She sits and watches in the darkness late into the night, willing and repelling sleep, waiting for gunshots so that she can hobble away because she can no longer run. She is afraid to fall asleep. The trauma has eaten into her bones and resides in her joints, swelling and crystallizing them with arthritis that makes her body ache and age. Her diminished immune system means that the slightest cold gives way to pneumonia. The large bump on her head has subsided now. Through her snow-white hair, her scalp glistens in pain. She is no longer conscious of pain in her ribs. A pain that would wrack her body with every inward breath she took. Her diaphragm heaving with the movement of her lungs. Crime is rampant. Unemployment supported by neoliberalism's insistence on separating people from land and self-dependence has alienated the youth and is driving them to attack the vulnerable bodies of the aged and debilitated. Young men prowl for money. Raised in a violent historical arc of political, masculinist force, violence is a familiar and ready tool.

My brother, too, knows trauma intimately after multiple encounters. From the car accident that led to his amputation to the stabbing of his abdomen and head and the multiple robberies. Kaffirization is when the doctor does not recognize that a vein needs suturing and applies plaster of paris instead. When the leg becomes gangrenous and the rural hospital cannot do anything about it because it has almost no medical personnel and inadequate medical supplies. When rural life is so cheap that it goes to hospital to die. When it became apparent that my brother's leg was in danger, an ambulance was miraculously found and after a night and ten hours of driving through the rain and mist, my brother arrived first at Mthatha's Nelson Mandela Academic Hospital where he couldn't be helped and then in Durban where he was dropped off at Nkosi Albert Luthuli Academic Hospital. From one Nobel Peace Prize winner and antiapartheid hero to another.

I found my brother unconscious on a stretcher in the emergency department of the Durban hospital. He was unattended while his leg decomposed, because the doctor wanted his next of kin. I was told, "To save him, we need to amputate the leg." Here I was, faced by the literal nonchoice between gangrene and amputation of which James Baldwin (1984) once wrote. The world spun, sweat surged through my pores. My star athlete, twenty-three-year-old little brother whom I had watched learning to crawl and then to walk. And then run like the wind. My brother whom I had cheered as he won all his races at school. I signed the documents and authorized the amputation. Because the gangrene had spread, they cut high. Above the knee. We told him when he regained consciousness. When the phantom pains wracked his body, we coaxed the leg and told it that it was gone. Talking to the (absent) body. Pleading for the brain to catch up to a past that is ongoing. Two years later, the same body and brain had to process stab wounds. Someone waved a car down when they saw him stagger onto the road with his intestines pushing out of his abdomen. In recent years, we have started to worry for his liver, battered by all the drinking. For brutalized young men, drinking alcohol is not a passing relief or rite of passage into adulthood. It is constant because there is no relief for the haunted.

We worry about my mother and brother. We coax them to move to the city where safety can be purchased at a price. They refuse. They are attached to place and land, graves, the river, and the hills that encircle my home. They are disoriented when they are away from the place they call home. The hills enfold them, and the rivers imprison, soothe, and protect. As for me, I witness the deaths and regular brutalization from both near and afar. Sometimes I am at home with my mother. At other times I was in cities such as Cape Town, Durban, and Johannesburg where I have studied and worked. I escaped the fate of most black people that I was raised with because of these movements that have assured a middle-class life of relative safety. I now live in Johannesburg and consider myself to have two homes: one in Johannesburg and one in the village.

Mpondo Orientations

Riotous Deathscapes is the story about the failures of modernity in a place with alternative modes of being that looks to different timescapes and defies death/life binaries. The different chapters suggest that while the incursions of modernity leave devastation in their wake, the Mpondo people make meaningful livings of survivance in the black deathscapes that mark this place. *Riotous Deathscapes* crafts a Mpondo theory. This theory is conceived in the confluence of the natural world and the jostle of oral narratives against officially sanctioned histories. Its components are a constellation of death, life, the ocean, hills, rivers, graves, and spirits. The theory therefore moves against anthropocentric struggles that invest in the human taxonomy of the Chain of Being. Amidst the multiple dyings in Mpondoland are a defiant people whose timescapes root them in a temporality that rubs against colonial time. What emerges is a livingness that points to blackness and indigenous life precariously unmoored from modernity. We witness a hopelessness that does not surrender to helplessness. This is an ethic of black indigenous people. It is a refusal to languish in a state of victimhood but instead craft rampant dying as a way of living. *Riotous Deathscapes* suggests ways of attending differently to black life on the margins. It offers ways of looking askance as a methodology for black studies from the African continent in conversation with those in the black diaspora. To attend askance is to attend queerly, not in the tradition of Western queer studies but in a queerly African way of looking. To be queerly African is to fail at being a self-contained and actualized modern subject.[5] It is to be in relation to multiple others, to eschew the linearity of settler time, and to refuse social formations that are made for Man.[6] To live queerly is to stay in struggle without seeking escape and transcendence. It is to be both black and indigenous, always porous to possibilities of being remade over time. It is to live in the tributary and confluence of varying crosscurrents that signal relation. Oceanic, spiritual, climatic, death, life, erotic, queer. It is to be attentive to emergent geographies of gendered, sexual, transnational, and racial identities that arise in the wake of rupture. *Riotous Deathscapes* charts a course of black life in vast deathscapes. It is a portrait of life among the dead.

This book offers a theory-method of being that I term *Mpondo theory*. The theory is distilled through a meditation and portrait of black life lived in the rural reserve. My transcription shows how people live in the world and in the body. In turn, I examine how the body is enfolded within the natural world, the spiritual, and systemic realms. I engage in a transcription of this theory to provide a portrait of parts of this life by historicizing it in deep time to demonstrate how amaMpondo have weathered colonialism, apartheid, and neoliberal toxins.[7] *Riotous Deathscapes* shows how Mpondo theory both predates these historical incursions and responds to the unhumaning of capitalism and antiblackness while emanating a poetics of relation. Although the theory predates capitalism and offers possibilities beyond it, I see it as conveying a vernacular theory of being in a capitalist world. *Riotous Deathscapes* is a practice of the black public humanities as it traces histories that exist in largely undocumented form. It relies on sources that exist outside of organization and formality. While Bhekizizwe Peterson (2019) describes the black public humanities as knowledges that exist in alternative spaces such as community theater, unions and associations, local savings schemes, mothers' church unions, community radio and newspapers—all of which exist beyond the university and formal archives—I widen this to include inscriptive practices such as orality, the natural environment, ritual, family and community storytelling, and other acts of active remembering and imagining that enable intergenerational sociality and resistance. Similar to Aboriginal practices, I center features of landscape in meaning making.[8] This orthography is not an attempt to make Mpondo people legible to the world as a native informant.[9] Since Mpondo culture is enfolded in opacity, it would be impossible to make it fully legible. Instead, *Riotous Deathscapes* offers a portrait of rural forms of black life that widen current traditions of black, indigenous, queer, and African studies. This meditation offers alternative modes of theorizing refusal and freedom in the midst of overdetermined dying. It offers possibilities for similarly located people seeking freedom in different chronotopes.

Riotous Deathscapes begins by explicating Mpondo theory and its navigational tool—*ukwakumkanya*. It then situates Mpondoland as the focus of this text through a portrait of the cartographies of emaMpondweni. The text's understanding of temporality is then drawn out in a discussion on timescapes. I then move on to illustrate how this theory is embedded within and informed by a number of cognate fields of thought such as black studies, indigenous studies, queer studies, and debilitation studies. Throughout, I signal some key interlocutors in the black world. The introduction concludes with a chapter outline of the five chapters that constitute *Riotous Deathscapes*.

Mpondo Theory

A way of seeing, knowing, being, and living with and against sedimented devastation. Mpondo theory is *Riotous Deathscapes'* contribution to knitting together black and indigenous studies. To explicate this theory, I begin with a key concept that drives this theorization: *ukwakumkanya*. This concept works as a trinity: it is a feature of Mpondo theory, a practice of the theory, and a scholarly method adopted in this book. As a scholarly method and practice of Mpondo theory, *ukwakumkanya* enables the book to stage a meditation and portrait of black life in the rural margins. In what follows, I begin by sketching the coordinates of Mpondo theory through the practice of *ukwakumkanya*.

I lift my hand and shield my eyes. In isiMpondo, the language that I first spoke as a child, this action is *ukwakumkanya*.[10] Creating a shadow in order to illuminate. Shielding one's eyes in order to see far. The paradox of creating light by blocking the sun's glare. *Ukwakumkanya* is to block out distractions and draw into sharp relief. To throw shade or create a shadow over the face. It enables tunnel vision in order to focus the gaze. *Ukwakumkanya* is to pause. To double take by looking again. Re-figure. Eyes shielded and momentarily closed, one can look into the past. *Ukwakumkanya* is to shield one's eyes in order to attend differently and to consider from another vantage point. This way of looking can also be performative, a pretense not to see. To look blankly or past someone. Looking this way allows us to feign surprise but also to express real surprise. This is a way of looking selectively by adopting a register that enables one to attend anew. By blocking out what one does not want to see, this is a very deliberate way of looking. It manages and orders excess. It invites multiple gazes, which could include direct, oblique, repeated, and stalled looks. It can be a look of refusal expressed through looking askance, looking away, and blocking out. *Ukwakumkanya* is to imbue the black subject with self-knowledge and interiority. It is to look from a place of consciousness of one's place in the world. From the existential fact of the body and the accompanying attributions we have been compelled to learn about being-black-in-the-world (Manganyi 2019). *Ukwakumkanya* is to attend from a place of survival that is coded in the body and intergenerational knowledges. It is an archive that radiates from a deep history. It is a perspective from which to gaze at the world thus bringing it into sharp relief. To look this way is to center the subject position of the looker. If we imagine a deep temporality within which our ancestors are embedded agents, we can imagine that our *ukwakumkanya* is discursively related to theirs and our ways of attending can radiate backward. It is to recognize black indigenous wisdom borne by ancestors and elders. Before us then is a deep history of attending while being grounded in this place. Standing on a jagged rock high above the seething ocean of Mpondoland, how many ships did our ancestors see? What does this way of looking tell us about our history, and how are we figured differently by self-seeing beyond colonial and state-sanctioned narratives? How does rooting oneself on the seashore or black shoals discursively link our history to a global history of oceanic existence that builds anticolonial praxis and is indigenously ordered away from the sovereign claims of the nation-state?[11] What do we see when we look away from the colonial and neoliberal state and instead create *ukwakumkanya*? But seeing is not limited to sight. It is to attend with all sensorial registers. One can scan the sky to divine an approaching storm in the gathering clouds, but with eyes shielded, one might smell the storm approach in the air. *Ukwakumkanya* is to pause and attend through the frequency of the sensorial. Through the method of *ukwakumkanya*, Mpondo theory is a multisensorial experience of life and the world. It displaces imperial emphasis on the visual.

These focused looks, tarrying gazes, perked ears, attentive nose, touches, and attempts to perceive differently are the driving motifs of this text. To center looking in relation is to adopt a phenomenological orientation to the world. *Ukwakumkanya* is the mnemonic map. It serves as a memory aid and assists us to retain and retrieve memory. In this text, the hill, ocean, river, spirit world, and grave are maps to Mpondo history. I invite the reader to join me in lifting their hand to create a shelter above their eyes and to attend with me through the illuminating shadow. The place about which I write has a riotous landscape of rolling hills, tempestuous oceans, plunging gorges, meandering streams, disappeared graves, and flooding rivers. *Ukwakumkanya* is a grounded way of attending from these sites.

Ukwakumkanya enables a view that is in solidarity with diasporic blackness but that is grounded in place. This is to suggest that Mpondo theory is related to but distinct from blackness in the diaspora. By attending from here, we tarry in an untypical location that is not forged in the transatlantic slave trade. This way of attending is not a counter gaze. Rather, it is a way of looking that enlarges and decenters black studies from overdetermined ways of knowing.[12] In *The Practice of Diaspora*, Brent Hayes Edwards (2009) uses the term *décalage* to describe precisely these kinds of fault lines:

> This black diasporic *décalage* among African Americans and Africans, then, is not simply geographical distance, nor is it simply difference in evolution or consciousness; instead it is a different kind of interface that might not be susceptible to expression in the oppositional terminology of the "vanguard" and the "backward." In other words, *décalage* is the kernel of precisely that which cannot be transferred or exchanged, the received biases that refuse to pass over when one crosses the water. It is a changing core of difference; it is the work of "differences within unity," an unidentifiable point that is incessantly touched and fingered and pressed. (Edwards 2009, 14)

This is central for my own thoughts in figuring Mpondo theory in relation to a global black studies. Mpondo theory is true to this location, but it is a part of something more than here. It similarly enlarges indigenous studies by figuring African indigeneity as sutured to blackness—in one body. It expands black queer studies by grounding antinormative being in African locales and using more capacious lenses to attend to how we queer and are queered.

If I were to diagrammatically represent Mpondo theory based on the foregoing, I'd begin by shielding the eyes to capture a quizzical look that is both oriented to the future and historically focused.[13] The diagram would convey *ukwakumkanya*'s simultaneous vision across sensorial registers. The looker's feet would be firmly rooted on the ground to signal the present but also to stake a claim to place—not of ownership but of belonging here. The place is the natural world of Mpondoland. The views from these shifting spaces are the praxis that constitute the assemblage of Mpondo theory. But the theory also escapes total legibility. It is uncontainable, riotous, and does not invite nor entertain any desire to be fully grasped in one hand.

Like the ocean, meandering river, hill, graves, and spirit world, it is never fully knowable even to those who practice it as a way of life. It is not unlike Tiffany Lethabo King's (2019) shoal—the surfacing of the ocean floor close to the shoreline, whose unpredictability exceeds total mappability and full knowability.[14] Mpondo theory is akin to John Paul Ricco's description of an affective occurrence that is a formative force but is less than an event whose function is traceable as neither cause nor effect. Ricco contends that this affective occurrence "is in this sense inappropriable: incapable of being claimed and owned or made one's own—but it might also be what cannot be expropriated, stolen, or taken away from you" (2019, 22). At its nub, Mpondo theory suggests an opacity and a meditative posture of neutral affect that refuses commensurability precisely because *ukwakumkanya* is about a mode of relation that resists reader's mastery of the theory. The commitment to "contingency, conjuncture, and extemporizing" suggests a posture that is averse to the will-to-possess, to systematizing and mastery (Ricco 2019, 24). This works alongside Édouard Glissant's (1997) duty to errantry—an insistence on the poetics of relation that do not commit to rootedness, possession, origins, or totalitarianism. *Ukwakumkanya* finds resonance in Glissant's poetics of relation as these ways of being are forged in relation to self and the other rather than in forms of dominance and supremacy—for example, in how the Mpondo responded to Khoekhoe neighbors fleeing settler genocide and white and enslaved Asian and African shipwreck survivors who were castaway on the Mpondo coast. Because the Mpondo people have themselves not mastered *ukwakumkanya* since it comes to them like a mother tongue—and they hold it contingently—it cannot be appropriated. Readers of this book may relate to it, but they are not likely to master it because it is not possible to absorb the subjective and ontological interiority of the margins. Instead, my invitation is for readers to inhabit the world that *Riotous Deathscapes* portrays in order to explore possibilities for how we might reconsider modes of living in abandoned zones.

Following the navigational tool *ukwakumkanya*, a second defining feature of Mpondo theory is the place from which we attend. It is rooted in the past through the centering of ancestral knowledges and continuities between the living, the death bound, and the dead. This relation to the dead is signaled in *ukwakumkanya*'s ability to look back while simultaneously looking forward. As the coronavirus advanced on the rural countryside in May 2020, the concept of *ukwakumkanya* recurred in my daily telephonic conversations with my mother. She told me that old folk like her were focusing their gaze with dread on what would be illuminated. For her, *ukwakumkanya* gave a foreboding historical vision. She described how she occupied her sleeplessness with counting the people who'd died during the wreckage wrought by the AIDS pandemic across our villages. Here, her way of attending to the specter of the coronavirus evoked dying and the ancestral. As a way of attending, dreams are also a form of *ukwakumkanya*. Dreams can fill one with a sense of foreboding, uncertainty, or wonder based on what one sees, smells, hears, touches, or tastes. Dreams link us to futures and pasts. *Ukwakumkanya* provides us with a simultaneously grounded and abstract concept of timespace which Vincente Diaz described as "a product of social and cultural formulation and reckoning" (2011, 27). What we attend to therefore is always discursively located. A gaze from the village is a form of grounded theorizing that reckons with what has gone before, what we are living through, and what awaits us.

The theoretical preoccupation of Mpondo theory primarily responds to dual pressures that Mpondo people struggle with. The first is the long history of colonial and apartheid subjugation and how its entanglement with neoliberal capitalist cultures has had devastating effects on this community. The second pressure is how neoliberal capitalist cultures are variously implicated in the many forms of dying and death detailed in this book. Mpondo theory both precedes these pressures and responds to them. The book is organized around a demonstration of the operation of this trilogy— colonial/neoliberal capitalist cultures, dyings and death, and riotous resurgence.[15] *Riotous Deathscapes* therefore articulates a cosmological, lived, and embodied form of theorization into a matrix of meaning-making that spans death and life. It is a theory of being in relation to persons, ancestors, the natural world, life, and death. Mpondo theory has a complicated set of relations to individual capitalist notions of ownership. It favors shared and environmentally conscious use of the land and ocean's resources characterized by moderation.[16] In practice, it demonstrates a collision between different epistemic legacies of individual ownership and communal sharing. This theory responds to capitalist extraction with a defiant declaration that embraces both living and dying to maintain relations to land. The regularity of death and suffering means that Mpondo people have normalized dying into their way of life. This theory begins with death because in the Mpondo life cycle dying precedes living. Since the ancestors that provide meaning for how we live are already dead, the source of knowledge and life is death. To take the dead seriously is to be attentive to the ghostly elements of social life. Avery Gordon (1997) asserts that a confrontation with ghostly elements requires a major reorientation in relation to how we make and conceive of knowledge. Because the land and water are central to how people die, live, and order their lives, my theorizing is grounded in the sociality enabled by the environment, spirits or supernatural, and embodiment. Reflecting on indigenous people on Turtle Island and their forms of theorization, Leanne Betasamosake Simpson contends that "As political orders, our bodies, minds, emotions, and spirits produce theory and knowledge on a daily basis without conforming to the conventions of the academy" (2017, 31). Because theory has come to be imagined as belonging to particular bodies and places, this is an unconventional way to think of it. However, with this text I continue a tradition of insisting that theory is present even among the unhumaned.[17]

By centering *ukwakumkanya*, I amplify the lives of my protagonists and treat their truth claims with the gravity of theorists.[18] I rely on stories, allusions, traces, and residue that I read off surfaces. I am preoccupied with how one accounts for a history that is undocumented in the written form. How does one write when oral and cosmic archives are primary forms of being and where writing is not a customary archival form? Given the marginality and unimportance of Mpondoland and her people to the colonial project, even the colonial archive is unproductive for this project. The archive fails. There are liberating dividends from a failed colonial archive. There is a freedom and license to stick more closely to the voices of the people and the surfaces of this place. I therefore turn to collective memory scripted on bodies, in the lay of the land, in the hum of the ocean, in the familiar sight of young people's despair, in the mounds of earth that cover bodies felled by AIDS and state-sponsored neoliberal violence, and in abandoned schoolgirls' dreams. My method of the black public humanities works in tandem with Hartman's (2008) concept of critical fabulation—a labor that seeks to paint as full a picture as possible of the lives of black enslaved people and other black undesirables.

The form adopted in this text is conscious of Rinaldo Walcott's 2020 Twitter provocation that a core feature of black studies is an abiding commitment to form. This commitment is based on the recognition that traditional disciplines are unable to engage the fullness of black life. Black studies is an alternative space necessitated by the fact that the disciplines have been complicit in the unhumaning of black life. A subversion of disciplinary academic form is central to this break from the disciplines. I embrace this injunction and adopt forms that enable a fuller trace of the contours of Mpondo sociality. Throughout the text, I try to surface what the chosen form reveals about black indigenous life and how the text battles against disciplinary strictures. For *Riotous Deathscapes*, deformative praxis is an investment in coproducing knowledges with Mpondo protagonists. As an insider and coprotagonist who self-references, it is not possible for me to engage with questions of sampling. I make choices as a member of the community involved in coproducing a portrait of villagers. I am not unaffected by the stories that assemble this text. Another expression of deformation is the claim to theorization with the explicit naming of Mpondo theory. This waywardness is a form of marking this work so that it is not conceived of only as data but as theory. As a deformative gesture, this work is not invested in seeking a place at the table of theory.

Instead, Mpondo theory is an emplaced way of responding that draws on black and indigenous ways of being and resisting. It is wary of the generalizing universal eye. The theory intersects with other forms of indigenous theorization. It however centers the features around which Mpondo ways of dying and living occur. Mpondo responses to being unhumaned may cohere with or diverge from similar communities elsewhere on the continent and in the Global South. By focusing on Mpondoland, I gesture to how globalization and neoliberalism have coopted indigenous ideas such as ubuntu.[19] *Riotous Deathscapes* thinks from a place that registers a radically different kind of precarity and (im)possibility. The national and global imaginaries cannot account for Mpondo theory precisely because it is a substantially more difficult geographical and mental place from which to think. While my focus is emaMpondweni, I anticipate that the African village across the continent grapples with survival in the aftermath of slavery, colonial and neoliberal devastation, and ongoing neglect. In response, villagers work against the production of forgetful subjects and insist themselves into history.

To theorize from the African village, I lean on Frantz Fanon's (1967) sociogeny to argue that all cultures are lived locally rather than universally.[20] Sea-level theorization deepens particularity but offers something beyond the particular. Sociogeny works against canonical narratives. This text is about meeting people where they live. The fact that I am part of them and part of elsewhere inflects this meeting. In many ways, then, I am simultaneously self-writing while also writing my coprotagonists. This writing takes seriously the idea that the problems I narrate are socially produced and not inherently a part of the people and the place and therefore unchanging. Sociogeny enables multiple histories that are grounded in community. Since truth is a process of endless recovery and revision (Marriott 2011), this project is attentive to the new truths that are possible and the leaps that villagers take out of an overdetermined history. To see blackness as unstuck from canonical history is to embrace a certain buoyancy from which reimagining can occur. To be in community with the spiritual world is to disrupt teleology, and to resist development is to be out of time with neoliberalism. When villagers resist Western civilization as the only version of the future, they make room for different ontological possibilities. What openings exist and how do leaps through openings potentially take us out of the imprisoning black history of colonialism? The text is attentive to the leaps and ways in which we take flight. Throughout *Riotous Deathscapes*, the co-protagonists, the stories they tell, and the historical figures and events with which I engage point to a fugitive orientation to the world. Read sociogenetically, then, the black state of being in the village is an art of studied refusal with moments of capitulation. Tina Marie Campt (2019) asserts that the practice of refusal is to reject the conditions of the status quo as livable. In her conception, negation is generative for its potentialities of how we might live otherwise. The practice of refusal draws on a black history of fugitive and rebellious existence. Throughout the text we observe different ways in which amaMpondo say no and embrace waywardness in a demonstration of Fred Moten's (2018) conception of fugitivity as an ongoing desire to escape. If desire is a driving impulse for life, the Fanonian leaps in the break produce alternative socialities where ancestors walk among us and where choices are framed more broadly than life and death. In *Riotous Deathscapes*, sociality is death defying. It is driven by an imaginary that takes us to spaces and possibilities beyond death—to what else happened.[21]

Mpondo theory proposes another way of articulating the *being* of being black. Rather than mounting an argument for why we are deserving of being human on the terms of Sylvia Wynter's *Man*, Mpondo theory offers a decentered view of being. Decentered from whiteness and constitutive of the natural, animal, spiritual, and ancestral worlds. In this conception, the beingness of being black and indigenous is not about recuperating the human, dominion, elevation, reason, possessing an essence, or reestablishing an alternative center. It is neither posthuman nor entirely animalist.[22] In this project, I explore what is liberated when we conceive of being as elastic, reciprocal, and unbounded. It is exactly the consignment of the Mpondo to the status of the unhuman that enables this yearning to be both in and outside of the human—to be boundless. Mpondo theory is invested in the indigenous, natural environment and the ancestral. As a people who have remained on our motherland, we are not alienated since our beingness derives from being in place. Our order of consciousness is based on our specific social reality fortified by *ukwakumkanya*. Mpondo theory therefore assembles black being as an orientation that is less about precision but more oceanic. Located but in motion.[23] This portrait of Mpondo life suggests that it is unenclosed.

Cartographies of Mpondo Spatiality

If indigenous spatiality is unbounded and dynamic, mapping has the effect of binding space and rendering it static in ways that enable capitalist claims to privatization. Mpondoland has largely evaded the colonial, apartheid, and postapartheid cartographers' lenses. Almost all cartographies of South Africa move from a great level of detail to a general inexactness with significant gaps on the maps when Mpondoland appears. Indeed, as colonial cartographers were more interested in "the manufactured image of complete knowledge" rather "than gaining the actual knowledge itself," its illegibility became an important subaltern attribute for the Transkei (Braun 2008, 2). The lack of interest in the area and its supposed unknowability means that a sea-level theory—a planetary perspective from below—is how the territory is mentally mapped by its inhabitants, outside of any formal processes.[24] AmaMpondo have always known our world. Oral accounts as well as my own experience clearly demonstrate that we know one hill from another. The pathways of our rivers, the secrets of their depths, and ritual histories are intimate parts of who we are. The ocean's shoals tell us our history in the ebb and flow of the tides. The valleys and spaces between our villages are stories of our lineages that speak to how we relate. Our graves are relational zones with our ancestors.

How do we capture this complexity in a modern cartography whose audience is always external to the area and whose goal is abstraction? If, as Joel Wainwright and Joe Bryan suggest, "mapping indigenous lands involves locating indigenous peoples within . . . a grid of intelligibility" (2009, 155), we may have to ask what the value of a mapping exercise is. How might a work of cartographic abstraction reproduce unequal power relations by erasing complicated interests and historic sets of relations? To continue a line of questioning posed by Wainwright and Bryan (2009, 156), "what are the possibilities, and limits, of this particular effort to calculate the incalculable, to demarcate the indemarcatable"? Given this incommensurability of indigenous mapping and impossibility of capturing the

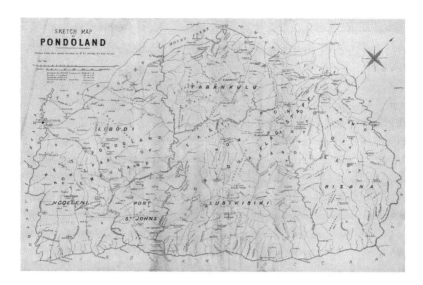

MAP I.1 Sketch map of Pondoland. Courtesy of African Studies Map Collection as well as BC880 Godfrey and Monica Wilson Papers, UCT Libraries.

unmappable, in this project I settle for the recognition of the mental maps that villagers possess about their own land and histories.[25] This resonates with King's (2019) and Glissant's (1997) reminder that nonreducibility is a core part of black thought and black life. Mpondo mental maps honor black indigenous thought because they are constituted of actual knowledge that is uninterested in complete knowledge.[26]

Colonial maps described the Eastern Cape territory as Kaffraria. This term can be loosely understood as the place of "kaffirs." The word had wide and everyday usage in South African history and was used to mark particular groups as subhuman. The Mpondo people counted among those indexed as another variation of fauna. To recognize people and spaces that have long been misrecognized, I refer to the territory as Mpondoland or emaMpondweni.[27] This territory was one of the last independent areas to be annexed into South Africa. When the annexation occurred in 1894, it was with the condition that the land would remain under the control of the people of Mpondoland (Millar 1908). Lusikisiki is the place from which I think this project, but *Riotous Deathscapes* is about the entire territory of Mpondoland. Together with Mbizana, Flagstaff, and Ntabankulu, Lusikisiki is part of Eastern Mpondoland. To the west is the adjacent Western Mpondoland, made up of Libode, Ngqeleni, and Port St. Johns (Hendricks and Peires 2011). Eastern and Western Mpondoland are collectively known as Mpondoland or emaMpondweni.[28] Map I.1 visually represents the spatial location of emaMpondweni. Inhabitants speak isiMpondo and practice customs particular to the region.

In Nguni languages, *pondo* means horn, or it suggests the head. *Mpondo* signifies the plural for horns. Cattle are prized in Nguni culture. George McCall Theal (1886) observed that horned cattle are the principal form of wealth among the Mpondo. But cattle are more than wealth. They are relational animals in significant practices like those of marriage and death. They hint at the rupture of the human and point to a malleability that denotes this form of blackness as simultaneously human, subhuman, and superhuman. Sylvia Tamale (2020, 87) observes that the "epistemic relationship between Indigenous people and nature manifests through their spirituality, clan totems, taboos, ancestral myths, rituals, fables." To be Mpondo is figuratively to be the horns of an animal. The binaries and dualisms of anthropocentrism are exploded by indigenous epistemologies.

Present-day Mpondoland can be read through municipal data sources. According to Statistics South Africa (2020), the Ingquza Hill Local Municipality, made up of Flagstaff and Lusikisiki and bordering the Indian Ocean on the Wild Coast, has a population of approximately 300,000 inhabitants, with nearly 43 percent under the age of fifteen. Only 6 percent of the population is over the age of sixty-five. There are eighty-nine males for every hundred females. Women head 63 percent of the region's households. Approximately 70 percent of the population is unemployed; 2.4 percent of the population has completed school, and only 1.4 percent of the population has post-school education. One percent has access to piped water inside their dwelling. From single digits ten years prior, 85 percent of households now have electricity (Statistics South Africa 2020). The province receives the highest social welfare support as 40.3 percent of all grants are administered in the Eastern Cape (Statistics South Africa 2020). Whereas in the past Mpondoland was a labor reserve for the country's mines, with declining mining reserves, mechanization, and the emergence of more diverse labor sources, migrant labor—which offered more secure employment—has drastically declined. Xola A. Ngonini (2007) reports that 200,000 jobs were shed by the mining sector in the first decade of democracy.

I enter this location with questions that illuminate the contours and interests of this project. What happens when the social order changes or breaks down? Are there connections between the growth of the social welfare system in rural areas and the (im)possibilities of young women? To think about these questions, I hone in on Lusikisiki, my birthplace and home. Like

Zolani Ngwane (2003) writes about his Transkei village of Cancele by fore-grounding the rural homes of migrants instead of the urban centers where they work, I too foreground the rural as the nub of analysis. A postapocalyptic backwater, this place was always a wasteland. It was treated as a reserve for excess bodies. To say something is a reserve is to identify it as off-center, as waiting, queer, and lacking in the essence of the center. A labor reserve is a place of surplus people where there is no work for sustaining life within a capitalist economy. I point to how the logics of segregation and apartheid created spaces of redundancy. In a way, those in urban areas could be both conscripted and abandoned by the capitalist labor economy, but those in the rural homelands were precluded from even entering into that contradictory possibility of racial capitalism.[29] By focusing on the rural, I pursue a dif-ferent path from that taken by Achille Mbembe and Sarah Nuttall (2004) and Xavier Livermon (2020), whose work focused on Johannesburg as the center of theorization. My insistence on figuring rural black precarity is to question modern African subjectivity that tends to assume the charac-ter of the urban. Instead, I point to what we lose when the city comes to overrepresent what being-black-in-the-world looks like.[30] Here, then, I seek to move sideways by shifting away from the givens about racial capi-talism and changing the cartography while still engaging with the long and ongoing effects of colonial modernity and capitalism. I lean on black and indigenous studies to think about place. This locates black and indigenous studies as unsettled and fugitive epistemologies. *Riotous Deathscapes* is a way of returning to the remnants of the colonial apocalyptic explosion and working in the debris. As a mode of sitting with sorrow in the moments of quiet, it might also be understood as a way of living with awfulness.

Multitudinous Timescapes: Cylindrical Epiphenomenal Temporality

Placing Mpondo theory in time requires that we set aside modern tempo-rality and coevalness with settler communities. In place of modern tempo-rality, Mpondo theory demands a longer timescape that is intimately tied to the environment-person interface. Mpondo theory offers cylindrical epiphenomenal temporality. I am indebted to Yvette Abrahams (2000) for her concept of cylindrical time, and I work with Michelle Wright's (2015) formulation of epiphenomenal temporality. Briefly stated, these terms suggest a time that is always occurring in the present. The past, future, and present coexist productively. This recalls indigenous temporalities as sketched by Simpson (2017). To accede to modern time is to accept colonial historization, which redraws the maps, parcels out the land to settler communities, removes people, and retells histories of discovery, founding, and conquest. It reduces black and indigenous groups to the defeated and inherently inferior. To accept colonial time is therefore to flatten complexity and accept myths of nation states. Mpondo theory fills out the nuance and problematizes modern temporality. It offers an alternative way of thinking of and assessing black and indigenous being-in-time while pushing against modern capitalist time (Simpson 2017). What does it mean to center black and indigenous time in thinking about marginal communities? What do we see when the point of reference is not colonial time? *Riotous Deathscapes* offers a temporal frame located in natural and ancestral worlds and the interplay of official histories and oral histories. It reads present events and lives in relation to timescales that defy colonial time. New insights for reading black and indigenous life are illuminated by stretching extant frames of reference. In this conception, temporality refuses stasis and latches on to the movement of social actors.

The risk for black studies, and indeed for black life, is that we can imagine black studies in the Global North diaspora as occupying a current timescale, while black life in Africa can be consigned as stuck in the past and as unworthy of scholarly interest. Johannes Fabian (2014) has critiqued the hidden assumptions of anthropology's study of the other as a denial of coevalness. He terms this *allochronism* to describe being out of tune with modern time. Keguro Macharia (2020, 571) meditates on African "belatedness" to intimate modernity and contends that the ground and place onto which he writes is "around sutures of difficult coevalness, seeking something that might be called freedom." To be an African writer, then, is to wrestle with a "difficult coevalness." The fallacy of peoples who lag behind perpetuates a colonial logic that may see black studies in the diaspora as theorizing while continental blackness may be viewed as constituting anthropological data and as incapable of theorization. Mpondo theory claims different timescales that point to multiple temporal zones and challenge universal conceptions of time. To point to multiplicity is not to reinforce the fallacy of modern time set up against primitive temporality. Instead of binary time, we coexist within multitudinous timescales.

When we figure marginal actors of history at the center, new vistas are made possible. *Riotous Deathscapes* maps a pathway for coming to new horizons of black life. Mpondo theory is born in relation to thinking with indigenous scholars who insist on claiming timescapes that bend and push against colonial imposition of temporality. In placing temporality and the land at the center of theory and practice, I follow Glen Sean Coulthard, who challenges Marxian theorization for prioritizing labor and individual rights before land. Coulthard (2014, 13) contends that "Indigenous anticolonialism, including Indigenous anticapitalism, is best understood as a struggle primarily inspired by and oriented around *the question of land*—a struggle not only *for* land in the material sense, but also deeply *informed* by what the land *as a system of reciprocal relations and obligations* can teach us about living our lives in relation to one another and the natural world in nondominating and nonexploitative terms—and less around our emergent status as 'rightless proletarians.'" Similarly, land as a system of reciprocal relations is seminal to Mpondo existence, struggles, and self-theorization. There are productive synergies between indigenous studies and black life if one considers blackness as expansive rather than closed.

Writing Mpondoland into the Epistemological Horizons of Black Studies

Since Mpondo theory is also a theory of blackness, it follows that this is an important category of analysis. I locate *Riotous Deathscapes* firmly in the tradition of black studies. I am attracted to thinking together with others who value black life by taking seriously Christina Sharpe's provocation that doing the work of black studies in the wake of white supremacy requires us to "tend to, care for, comfort, and defend the dead, the dying, and those living lives consigned, in aftermath of legal chattel slavery, to death that is always imminent and immanent" (2014, 60). To this I add those who live with the residue of colonization, the scorched earth of apartheid, and debilitating neoliberalism. I am drawn to black studies that lean in, care for and tend to black precarity. There is a variety of black studies. One strand insists that we recognize the pleasure of black life and not flatten everything into undifferentiated suffering. And there is another that sees the witnessing of black suffering and death as an ethical imperative for black studies. I am not a proponent of being totally engulfed by despair. I arrive at this orientation because the coprotagonists of this text have taken me here. They live with devastation but they relish life. I am simultaneously invested in the hold and in what Sharpe conceives of as exceeding the hold (Terrefe and Sharpe 2016). After all, everywhere I see black suffering, I am struck by laughter. Sometimes mocking and guttural, but also light, mirthful, and explosive. Is the explosion of laughter not the sound of freedom? To exceed the hold is to be attentive to other things beyond succumbing to death (King 2019). It is to imagine what else occurred at this site of death. It is also to recognize the inseparable relation among black pleasure, suffering, and beauty (Campt 2019). I am drawn to black studies scholars who are oriented toward tending and caring for blackness. I am attracted by their poetic cadence, their readiness to shift when blackness moves, and their commitment to a capacious blackness beyond North America.

This work is not written into a void. To think of black life from here is to embrace N. Chabani Manganyi's challenge first made in 1973 when he contended that the "most important contribution on the black experience will come from Africa" (2019, 1). Here, Manganyi was thinking about the repressive and codified conditions of apartheid. In some ways, he believed that, as a black majority country, South Africa was a modern laboratory for how black experience could be studied as it unfolded to overcome oppression. Steve Biko (2004) made a similar claim when he noted that South Africa had the possibility of showing the world a more human face. Victoria Collis-Buthelezi (2017, 14) makes a case for black studies in South Africa thus: "Moving forward need not require disowning blackness, rather it must entail reckoning with the phenomenology of blackness that renders us in a new epiphenomenal time that does not traffic in the past of black political exclusion, but contends with the present of a democratic dispensation and a cultural and economic order that continues to shape black experience as disparate and unequal."[31] *Riotous Deathscapes* takes up this challenge by adopting a black studies with an epiphenomenal temporality that collapses time to make meaning of black people's ongoing present. However, while black studies in South Africa would necessarily have marked the particularities sketched by Manganyi and Biko, this book resists a parochial black studies that sees South Africa as exceptional. This is to suggest that African black studies from this location resonates with black life across sub-Saharan Africa. While I do not want this work to be parochially South African, I recognize that blackness is experienced differently across the continent.[32] In addition, since South Africa has the largest white settler community in Africa, racialized experiences and consciousness are more sharply pronounced here than elsewhere on the continent. Indeed, Africans from elsewhere on the continent who have lived in South Africa observe that they became black in South Africa.[33]

I do not portray amaMpondo as existing in prelapsarian space. Mpondoland is not untouched by history, modernity, incursions of world systems, and the other. Even in its seclusion, I show that its rugged coastline has not insulated it from shipwreck castaways. The abandonment of Mpondoland should be read within Elizabeth Povinelli's framework of *Economies of Abandonment* (2011). She argues that late liberalism is designed to defeat and distribute significance and abandonments in the service of hierarchies of value. She contends that "the nature of social events contribute to the ways that life and death, endurance and exhaustion, and hope and harm are distributed in late liberalism"—and we should be attentive to "how this distribution is made ethically and politically sensible and compelling" (132). Following this and David Harvey's (2018) conception of organized abandonment, it becomes normal and ethically defensible to coexist with blighted spaces whose existence is unremarkable and whose struggles are exhausting and chronic. As a former labor reserve, Mpondoland has been the supplier of labor to the country's mining centers over several generations. As a place of migrancy, Mpondoland may be naturally unspoiled, but it has not been insulated from the toxicity of neoliberalism. Movement and relations with multiple elsewheres mean that we do not escape racialization. As Pierre (2012) deftly illustrates, race is always present in the post-slavery and postcolonial world. It may not always announce itself like it does in the urban cityscapes of South Africa or in the contemporary United States. The global nature of white supremacy presents a total atmosphere that is present everywhere. I am interested in drawing out the contours of white supremacy and how the multiple manifestations of racecraft permeate and are made in the distant place of Mpondoland—a spacetime that is not hermetically sealed but that negotiates a complex autonomy. Both Mahmood Mamdani (2003) and Hannah Arendt (1975) demonstrated that South Africa was foundational to the making of race as a category in modern society through imperialism where the bureaucracy of the rule of law functioned through race. Tim Keegan's (1997) historiography of Cape Town has shown how the foundational moments of colonial settlement, enslavement, and racialization were simultaneously taking place in the Cape Colony as they were in the Americas. Here, the coevality of these locations is apparent. Similarly, by pointing to Cedric Robinson's (2000) notion of racial capitalism, Robin Kelley (2017) demonstrates how racialization has always coexisted with capital accumulation in the colonies, empire, and the New World. Robinson developed the term from its original explanation of

South Africa's apartheid economy as a means of "understanding the *general* history of modern capitalism" (Kelley 2017). Racial capitalism was therefore central to the establishment of modern South Africa. Consequently, it is impossible for Mpondoland to escape the effects of racialization.

In this project, I bring an African village into view of what black studies can look like when we think and theorize blackness from places structured by economies of abandonment. I am inspired by Hartman's (2008) quest to understand African American life and histories of slavery from both sides of the Atlantic. Knowledge about black life on the African continent is framed as African studies and postcolonial studies. Under this umbrella, everything goes. The utility of these frameworks is that they enable complexity. African studies addresses everything from health, welfare, political economy, food security, history, politics, sexuality, and the poetics of being African. However, African philosopher Paulin Hountondji (2009) has argued that the agenda of African studies has been determined by forces external to the continent. Nevertheless, postcolonial studies provides a verdant analysis of life after the demise of colonialism.[34] The generality evades capture and refuses the reduction of being African to race and racialization. But we lose something of the particularity of the black condition that informs our complex African identities. For me, what is lost is both our relation to diasporic blackness and the racialized particularity and varieties of black life on the continent. In this conception, being African should not transcend blackness. The two are not mutually exclusive and could productively be seen as both potentially making and unmaking each other. Black studies would be enriched by a careful engagement with African life. This is part of the project of *Riotous Deathscapes*. What does black studies, being-black-in-the-world, look like from an African village when read in relation to blackness in the diaspora?

Though attuned to various forms of invisibilization, this text is primarily about seeing, listening, and generally attending to each other.[35] To complain of invisibilization is to discount African interlocutors and readers and to valorize recognition of the Global North. To write black studies from Africa is therefore to recognize African scholars and readers while also being in dialogue with a global black studies tradition. Kopano Ratele (2019) charges Africans to prioritize looking from here by not seeing African lives through the lenses of scholars looking at us from out there. I take up this challenge of attending from here, but since I am invested in a global black studies and a way of being in relation to blackness everywhere, through *ukwakumkanya*, my orientation is grounded here but in relation to the diaspora. Another way of saying this is to claim an investment in a black gaze—in the encounter of black thinking across space. Macharia (2016, 186) articulates this observation by signaling "the dissonant intimacies that emerge" as black people create shared ground. This commitment entails particular demands that include acknowledging that African writers exist and that those like N. Chabani Manganyi and Sylvia Tamale have, over time, theorized the black condition. It is also to acknowledge that this text is not written into a diasporic void because Frantz Fanon, Sylvia Wynter, Édouard Glissant, Hortense Spillers, and Saidiya Hartman exceed the contemporary moment of black studies. This lineage of black studies is fecund ground for this project for how, through the practice of *ukwakumkanya*, it helps me to grapple with global and grounded forms of antiblackness, black coevalness, the limits of the human for being-black-in-the-world, and the possibilities of boundless forms of blackness.

Looking Again through Indigenous Studies

Africans are simultaneously black and indigenous. Indigenous studies elsewhere in the world considers native peoples as distinct from settler communities and displaced peoples. My intervention is therefore to untether indigeneity beyond its current theoretical imaginaries and to suture it with blackness. To think blackness from here is to take account of the complexity and dialogic relations of African lives. I draw on a rich body of work by indigenous theorists, including Leanne Betasamosake Simpson, Billy-Ray Belcourt, Glen Coulthard, Michael Marker, and Vincente M. Diaz, in order to surface the temporal and violence defying indigenous wisdoms of indigenous people. To center wisdom is to make epistemic claims that foreground indigenous theorizations of temporality, myth, and cosmology. It is to breach colonial epistemes. Linda Tuhiwai Smith's (1999) example of placing Maori women at the heart of critiques of Western paradigms of knowledge is an important example for *Riotous Deathscapes*. In addition to genocidal hauntings, Gerald Vizenor (2010) insists that we recognize survivance as a core part of indigenous being. I read survivance alongside McKittrick's (2015) black livingness in order to suture indigenous and being-black-in-the-world. From Marker (2003, 362), I learn to assume an authoritative voice when he insists on pushing against the white anthropologist paradigm that disbelieves indigenous voices as "ramblings of the uncivilized mind." Instead, I attend to how black indigenous people narrate in ways that make sense to them. As one of them, I self-narrate in the double register of black indigenous storytelling that I entangle with scholarly discourse.[36] Billy-Ray Belcourt (2015) helps me to think about the placeness of indigenous truth claims and to relocate the decolonized animal in indigenous cosmologies.

I seek an ethical meeting place for black and indigenous studies. Theorist Tiffany Lethabo King (2019) is exemplary for this project's attempt toward bringing black studies into conversation with indigenous studies. She models a keenness to know more than just about one's own death—a drive to touch the grooves, entwining textures and seams of our collective dying and our multiplicity. Her approach coincides with my own theory-method of *ukwakumkanya*. She contends that to think of our common violences "requires a way of sensing that allows moving in and out of blurred and sharpened vision, acute and dulled senses of smell." Using the idea of black shoals in the shallow end of the ocean, King offers a way of pausing, slowing down—shoaling in order to reconsider and interrupt Western critical epistemologies, and then to think of black studies in relation to indigenous or native studies. King describes the black shoals as "a site where Black studies connects land and water. It presents an analytical and geographical site where Black studies attempts to engage Native studies on ethical terms." Thinking about the Northern Hemisphere, King suggests that slavery and indigenous genocide have no edges—they wash into each other. I refashion this to consider the meeting places of African colonialism and its indigenous genocide in relation to survivance in conditions of conquest in the Southern Hemisphere. I interrupt continental common sense by reconsidering relation.

To think about indigenous lives in Africa, I ask: if black people in Africa are simultaneously black and indigenous, how can we craft a black studies that takes both blackness and indigeneity seriously?[37] From this position, indigenous and black studies are potentially mutually coconstitutive. To separate these fields is to bifurcate identities of relation that are inseparable in this context. Even if we were to think of groups such as the Khoekhoe, San, and Bantu as different, they are people whose pasts, fates and ways of dying are intimately connected on Africa's black shoals. Historian T. J. Tallie (2019) points to how settler colonizers in the Natal colony of the 1850s sought to apply a logic of indigenous genocide that was being applied in other settler colonies such as Canada, Australia, and New Zealand. Tallie's intervention is handy for highlighting the coevalness of settler genocidal strategies for those marked as indigenous. To read the black people of Africa as simultaneously indigenous and black is to parse out the ways in which they were targets of indigenous genocidal strategies going on elsewhere on the globe, and racist dispossession, segregation and slavery that fixed on black people. I however depart from Tallie by insisting on the blackness of indigenous African people. I have a third objective that is necessitated by the heterogenous and frontier character of the Eastern Cape as constituted by the San, Khoekhoe, the diverse majority Bantu inhabitants, and early white settlers. The necessity for more expansive forms of blackness and indigeneity is therefore particularly important.

By insisting on ways of attending that are rooted in place—*ukwakumkanya*—*Riotous Deathscapes* conceives of boundless forms of blackness and indigeneity in order to refuse colonial strictures. Creating a fissure between oppressed communities of Khoekhoe, San, and Bantu peoples is to enable a colonial incursion to dictate our ethic of care and witnessing in the present and the future. My understanding of this impossible demarcation is captured by Mohamed Adhikari's (2010, 22) assertion that the San, Khoekhoe, and Bantu-speaking agro-pastoralists interacted with each other in "complex ways which ranged from coexistence, inter-marriage and social absorption, through clientship and provision of shamanic services such as rainmaking and healing, to armed conflict." Conceiving of black people as indigenous is to suggest that black studies and indigenous studies on the continent have to be necessarily different from those in the diaspora where black people are not indigenous. My project is less about claims to first-nation status and essential or pure identities. Instead, I am committed to bearing witness to how they weather this unhumaning and what emerges from it.

The tenacious and mournful hold that amaMpondo have on the land of their ancestors can be seen as a practice of Mpondo theory that recalls other ancestral losses. This requires us to see the Mpondo as not only a parochial people of the Eastern Cape but as a community in relation to black indigenous others who became incorporated into the community. Mpondo theory eschews notions of pure identities and embraces porosity. As a "minor" tribe ensconced between the culturally dominant amaZulu to the north and amaXhosa to the south, amaMpondo are not blinded by parochial ideas of grandeur that come from fetishized purity. They refuse to accede their birthright and they anchor themselves in an identity forged between various Bantu, indigenous, and castaway groups through the long history of this place.

Modernity and its neoliberal offshoots produce queer Africans.[38] This is to say that as refractions of Man and as colonial subjects, marginal forms of blackness will always be waywardly deformed. As I have argued, to blur blackness and indigeneity is already a queer way to be black. In this text, queer means same-sex intimacy and relation, but it also exceeds this. A queer orientation is to be positioned improperly in relation to dominant social codes. It could be conceived of as a turning away from certain social relations and orienting oneself anew in ways that might disrupt these relations. For Sara Ahmed (2006), a queer orientation to the world represents a failure to be proper.[39] This conception provides a pathway for me to apply pressure on the ways in which black rural people fail at being proper. I am attentive to the promise of what emerges from these failures. To be queerly African is to move against coherence and singularities.[40] I take up Ahmed's provocation that we examine queer phenomenology. This is to say, I am attuned to how subjecthood is constituted relative to others. To be oriented away from singularities. T. J. Tallie (2019, 7) makes a similarly compelling case for queering colonial Natal by conceiving of native resistance—moving against colonial order—as queer. He contends: "The customs, practices, and potentially the very bodies of indigenous peoples can become queer despite remaining ostensibly heterosexual in their orientation and practice, as their very existence constantly undermines the desired order." Tallie's concept of *ukuphazama iNatali* is productive for helping us conceive of queerness as embracing multiplicity and exploring spaces beyond sexual orientation and the folds between binaries of resistance and normative orders.[41] However, indigenous scholar Billy-Ray Belcourt (2016a) reminds us that queer same-sex–loving people can easily be exiled and forced into the negative space surrounding *real* indigenous or black people. For Belcourt, "These queernesses exist outside the traditional and the identitarian borders of indigeneity, ones that the past cannot make sense of because they emerge in the most unexpected places." Therefore, while I want queer to be capacious, I ground it to consider the differently queered so that queer Mpondo people become thinkable beings and do not remain as ghostly traces and aberrations of black indigeneity. This is to say that I want the deathscape to be the dreamscape of queer love too—to bring queerness into the fold of blackness.

Like this book is invested in a global black studies, it is committed to a black queer studies that is African but that resonates with blackness everywhere. Omise'eke Natasha Tinsley (2008, 212) conceives of a transnational black queer studies thus: "When black becomes only African American, black queer theory becomes insular; as the crosscurrents between Atlantic and Caribbean, Atlantic and Mediterranean, Atlantic and Indian Ocean are richest in marine life, so they will be richest in depth of theorizing." It is the crossings, inbetweenity, and relationality that *Riotous Deathscapes* is most attentive to. I am attracted to queer as resistance and indifference to normative orders that seek to colonize and control. It is praxis as committed and informed action. For Tinsley, queer is a disruption of violence and it insists on loving that which is supposed to be loathed by "forging interpersonal connections that counteract imperial desires for Africans' living deaths" (199). To insist on love and relation even in the face of death is a queer act that brings blackness into view in new ways.[42] In the practice of *ukwakumkanya*, to be queerly black is to look away from impending death and to embrace feeling.

Learning from Musangi (2018), I think with my coprotagonists and fold our boundless identities into one another in ways that expand and complicate how we are figured.[43] My more capacious use of queer takes its inspiration from Keguro Macharia's (2019) injunction that black queer studies in Africa attends more obliquely and tunes into traces, touchings, and openings. Significantly, my approach is informed by misgivings about the costs of tethering Mpondo theory too tightly to conventional queer framings. I seek to carefully delineate the queerness of Mpondo theory, to ensure its audibility and legibility on its terms, not on overdetermined terms of current debates in queer studies. The particularity with which *Riotous Deathscapes* relates to black queer studies nourishes both Mpondo theory and black queer studies. I suggest that an overdetermined use of queer as legible forms of sexual categories would impoverish Mpondo theory without expanding black queer theory and instead merely confirming its current parameters.

Debilitation in Mpondoland

The histories of colonization, enslavement, and genocide mean that there are spaces where race has determined the course of life, and many of us consequently live deeply racialized lives. Scholars of intersectionality have however cautioned that race never operates alone and that to invisibilize other identity categories is to misrecognize the constitutive nature of being and the complexity with which we live. As in the preceding queering of Mpondo life, I see the critical disability lens as part of the critical race feminist theory that underpins the analysis of the protagonists' narratives and histories that I tell. However, following Jasbir Puar (2017), I read disability as braided with debilitation within a geopolitical zone of slow death that marks particular bodies for rapid wearing down within registers that include and exceed legible disabilities. This expansive recasting of disability signifies its ongoingness in registers "not prone to capture by a consciousness organized by archives of memorable impact" (Puar 2017, 11). Here, disability should not be seen as a nuance or magnifier of race, class, gender, or sexuality. Rather, it is constitutive of the totality of the experience of being and nonbeing of the black subject whose stories occupy these pages. In this respect, I heed the caution advanced by Nirmala Erevelles and Andrea Minear (2010, 128) when they say that disability should not fall foul of the analytic tactic of scholars who "through their unconscious non-analysis of disability as it intersects with race, class, and gender oppression" evacuate the constitutive role of disability. Instead, I adopt an intercategorical approach that sees identity categories not as additive but as socially and historically constituted.[44] I attempt to think of identity categories cognizant of Anjali Arondekar's (2005) caution that we should not import North American–centric ideas of identity when thinking about lives lived beyond the United States. In this regard, sexuality, disability, and other markers of difference should not always be measured against race as a stable register of oppression. In her words, "Buried, in such 'linkages,' is the very mathematical paradox of parallelism that forecloses any true intersection, even as it invites lines of common origin and travel" (240). To think of race, sexuality, gender, and debilitation as contextually and historically situated is to give primacy to place as a practice of *ukwakumkanya*, without closing off the possibilities of movement and connections between geopolitical locales. A pressure point for my analysis is to understand what it means to be constituted of multiplicity. Are the multiplicities represented by dosages of melanin, in one's gender and the fluid configurations of sexuality, in the capacity to feel pleasure as exquisitely as pain, in the limitations imposed by disability and debilitating contexts, in the freedom of the unending hills and the body compelled to dance like it has only ever known love? There is something simultaneously dangerous and buoyant in this capacity for expansiveness. It means that we absorb a lot of the world's cruelty. The effects of brutality and inequality scar our bodies and are debilitating. But our joy is expansive precisely because our multiplicity presents infinite possibilities for pleasure and the malleability of queerness that comes from being at odds with the world's norms.

Black Deathscapes

This introductory chapter is an attempt to trace what I have called death-scapes. Since death is ubiquitous emaMpondweni and we bury most our dead in unmarked graves within the parameter of the homestead, I imagine that the unruly landscape is littered with the dead. Elizabeth Teather (2001, 185) defines deathscapes as "the material expression in the landscape of practices relating to death."[45] My orientation to deathscapes is most aligned to Terence Heng (2018) as I am interested in absent presence—how the dead hover among us in the landscape, in our psyches and rituals. To attend to the dead, I lean on *ukwakumkanya* as method—to attend to matter across life forms and worlds. This enables us to hear ancestors, enter spirit worlds, and commune with animal life. Conceptually and methodologically, *ukwakumkanya* is an openness to be moved by the vibrational charge from the grave. It is central to reading the deathscape.

In chapter 4, I stand on a hill high above my home village and take stock of the dead. Many of them were young and died during the AIDS-dying epoch.[46] But many others died of treatable illnesses in a place where the state is an absentee landlord. In this rogue place where the underresourced hospital dispenses paracetamol for trauma, AIDS, headaches, and cancer, we die easily and endlessly. We are laid in the land that bears the bones of our ancestors. Our spirits hover, our ghosts haunt relentlessly. There are more ancestors than there are people alive. Here death has found a home. We have acclimated to living among the dead. In naming this text *Riotous Deathscapes*, I practice *ukwakumkanya* by pausing on the conceptual scale of the deathscape. A number of questions fill this pause. What does a deathscape look like? What is evoked? What do deathscapes say about the dead and the living? What does it mean to live on a deathscape? What does McKittrick's (2016) black livingness look like when thought of from this conceptual plane? What crosscurrents exist between the dead and the living? What does the gravesite offer as a theoretical site of being? What does the deathscape convey to us about those living among the remains of the dead? If keening from a place of fungibility is a form of sociality at the graveside, what can we learn from black screams? In applying pressure on conceptual deathscapes, my intervention is to see them as tethered to land

and psyche and therefore as present wherever black life is. I see deathscapes as the cartography of the earth but also as levitating spaces in our psyches. As unbounded capsules of memory that we carry with us. I am seized with bringing various concepts that drive this text into a collision with deathscapes and then observing what emerges. To pair deathscapes with riots is to point to the leap in the breach. Throughout this introductory chapter, I have accounted for the ways in which black life remains buoyant even as we die. This commitment to the countless ways in which we die and live is the driving impulse of *Riotous Deathscapes*. My conception of riotous is based on Fanon and Coulthard's insistence on self-affirmation as a prerequisite for enacting freedom.[47] In places that the state has turned away from, self-affirmative cultural practices keep the possibility of freedom alive.

Audience and Aesthetics

Riotous Deathscapes has two publics. The first is less likely to read the book in the short term. However, like slave narratives were not immediately legible to enslaved people, their grandchildren valued them generations later. For me, this public is constituted by the rural protagonists of the book and marginalized people elsewhere. At the level of the register, the book is in conversation with them through its cadence, rhythm, and poetics. The register is a way of thinking at the edge of theory and lyric. It is a language. This project invites the reader to experience and read the text through the lens of *ukwakumkanya*. For this reason, it may not be entirely legible to the second public, which is potentially constituted by a global scholarly readership. I am in conversation with this second public through my citational frames and linguistic register. Both publics are important to this text. To value them both demands a practice and ethic of partial legibility invested in Glissant's concept of opacity and obscurity. To be a native informer who overtranslates for my scholarly audience is to lose my rural community as a future audience. It is to repeatedly eject those who want to see themselves in history. To write exclusively in the metaphors and tenor of my community risks missing my scholarly audience. I live in both worlds and this text is a meeting place for these worlds. As African scholars, the politics of addressivity in the context of epistemic gatekeeping means that we are not often given the space to address our complex worlds. This text attempts to carve a place of congregation for worlds we know too well but are unable to inhabit fully within the academy. By centering Mpondo theory, I am foregrounding the rural protagonists through a scholarly register that does not lose the soul of the village. Mpondo theory and its method and form of *ukwakumkanya* therefore enable me to assemble a theoretical performance in a double register that will hopefully have both sides of the floor nodding in moments of recognition or incredulity.

The writing cadence follows the register of isiMpondo as a language and way of life. The very poetry of the language is its ability to evade capture through its refusal of standardization into the written form. I read the language as an insistence on beauty in spite of hardship and pain. Here poetics can be understood in Stefano Harney and Fred Moten's (2013) conception of the politics of the undercommons. It is a way of exceeding the hold and a practice of black livingness through opacity. Poetics is akin to *ukwakumkanya* as a way of knowing that shifts between looking, listening, and feeling askance, blocking out, facing away. An insistence on black interiority through the embrace of multiple registers. Lewis R. Gordon (2015, 73–74) has observed a similar commitment to the poetic in Caribbean scholarship. He notes that "this kind of writing challenges purities in theory and practice as different, even opposing, elements of writing are brought together for the sake of reality."[48] This method of exploding distinctions was a Fanonian feature of writing when he sought to negotiate the space between the historical and the poetic. Life is lived in these spaces of relation rather than in disciplinary corners. The drama of life and history cannot be captured by a singular way of attending. This project is attentive to complexity rather than clarity and arrival—a *chaos-monde*, if you will.[49] The frequent questions signal this inability and refusal to arrive. The deformative practice and nonlinear sociality of the subject work in tandem to produce a black studies from here.

The envisioned audience of this text is best told through a brief account of Mpondo music and the language itself. Here, I move away from the mostly visual plane and illustrate a more aural dimension of *ukwakumkanya* as an audible archive only accessible through listening askance. Mpondo music and the style of singing are simultaneously beautiful and disruptive. Its call and response is common to a universal blackness and other black musics. However, its multiple interjections signal subaltern capacities that work against transparency. These occur through voice, whistle, claps, and use of hands to ventriloquize voice. Sazi Dlamini (2010) terms this Mpondo vocal polyphony and harmony to signal the multiple simultaneous and independent melodies a single musical piece can have.[50] The music signals an openness and hybridity that combines multiple styles and histories. A key feature of this music is *ukugwaba*, which is a strategy of closing down, muffling, creating reverberations, collapsing into tonal sounds, hums that cut off words, and partially uttered phrases that all appeal to the sensorial and surrender to the nonverbal. The music entails losing oneself to the chorus and folding into the group. *Ukugwaba* begins with some structure and responsorial legible to the "colonial" ear, but it soon collapses into tonal sounds characterized by shifts between tonic tonality to countertonic tonality and a buildup of tonal masses that go to pieces.[51] This is partly achieved through a vocal technique of prolonging the tone with closed lips. Similarly, as a practice of *ukwakumkanya*, isiMpondo is an unruly language that evades writing and produces new grammars and idioms of living in relation. Mpondo children do not read books written in their language. They are taught isiXhosa. There is something tragic in not being taught to read and write one's own language. In the move to create legible postapartheid identities, people have been truncated into larger, more legible groupings and languages. Alongside the official languages are languages and people that occupy unofficial registers.[52] Nondominant groups fall into the fissures. However, the beauty of not pinning down a language means that it remains unruly and unresponsive to discipline and demands of transparency. It grows and is open to influence from other languages. IsiMpondo is not self-satisfied, and connection is more important than the perfection that Glissant describes as a poetics of language-in-itself. It is nonterritorial and evades perfection and capture. Like the music, the language thrives in marginality and the grammars of multiplicities, opacity, and going to pieces.

If Mpondo music and language are invested in the multiple legibilities of *ukwakumkanya*, to describe them requires a strategy akin to the music itself. To show and conceal. Those inside the Mpondo culture recognize the secret and nuance, and those beyond the culture are engulfed in the collapse and tonal maze. Those outside of the culture are part of the sound and are affected by the atmosphere but unable to determine the terms of the singing. *Riotous Deathscapes* adopts an approach similar to Mpondo music. The audience of the text works together with the multiplicity evoked by Mpondo music. I conceive of this audience as my Mpondo interlocutors and those interested in a form of African black studies in conversation with diasporic black and indigenous studies. I am not invested in translation. In this regard, Mpondo theory is queer in relation to the nation state and its global relationality. But notwithstanding these investments in opacity, fear of legibility should not render one mute. To follow the example of the Mpondo technique of *ukugwaba*, one can speak in multiple registers to communicate what is necessary to maintain relation. There is an urgency for this accounting of the ontology of black suffering—of how different life forms exist in a world that has only ever written them out and mistranslated. Mpondo theory unmasks this violence but also tells a story of black survivance and livingness that works against obliteration.

An Itinerary of Riotous Deathscapes

Riotous Deathscapes is both a set of thematically related essays and an argument that builds progressively across the chapters. While the chapters can be read alone, a fuller understanding of events and concepts is elaborated as the chapters unfurl. The chapters are organized in ways that are attentive to the chronological occurrence of the historical events that the text engages. While each chapter explicates an aspect of Mpondo theory, there are overlaps as the theory is enfolded and difficult to parse out into discreet parts. For example, the body cannot be read apart from the spirit, and the hill cannot be neatly parsed out from the river valley from which it arises. Each chapter plays with temporality by moving between timescapes which I term cylindrical epiphenomenal temporality.[53] In addition, each chapter is centered on a wayward ancestral figure and contemporary protagonists. These ancestral figures are cotheorists rather than illustrations. They include Nongqawuse in chapter 1, Nontetha Nkwenkwe in chapter 2, Clara Germana Cele in chapter 3, Sarah Baartman in chapter 4, and Khotso Sethuntsa in chapter 5. With the navigational tool of *ukwakumkanya*, the chapters are organized as follows.

In chapter 1, we explore Mpondoland as a place of crosscurrents between Mpondo people, living in relation to Khoekhoe and San people, and European and enslaved African and Asian shipwreck castaways. At stake here is how indigenous theorization illuminates errantry and freedom dreams across time. Our driving concern is what this confluence and assembling of people teaches us about ancestral relationality. This chapter explicates Mpondo theory by focusing on the tumultuous ocean. It shows how the ocean rubs against the landmass of Mpondoland and how it forces us to grapple with centuries of intimacy between those who arrived by ship and those they found on the seashore. The ocean is examined as a source of conflict, the site of arrival of otherness through shipwrecked castaways, a place of renewal, and for how it produces the possibilities of identities that unsettle hierarchies of being. Here, we explore extant identity making and resurgent views of race purity and racialization. This chapter thinks through a series of questions that are important for interrogating truths that might be more complex than dominant narratives would have us believe. It addresses the following questions: How do I, and my family, figure in the narrative of Mpondoland and what might autoethnography reveal about the longtime production of black subjectivities? What are the traces of the arrival of the Europeans and enslaved Asians and Africans in cylindrical epiphenomenal temporality? What explains the life of the traces long after the colonizer has departed? What are the problematics of not following the winding spoor through the dark tunnel of time? The text contends that we have fractured identities whose cartilage—the rationality that forms us—is worn and fragile. When the rain, sun, and wind—the weather—erases the footprints of conquest, is it possible to piece together a path that might join the dots in the present and future? What is the meaning of time for making sense of devastation? Nongqawuse anchors this chapter as a riotous ancestral figure who collaborated with the ocean to change the course of history. Reckoning with the ancestral is central to the oceanic forces that enable arrivals and departures in shaping Mpondoland and the people of this place. Life and identity occur at the confluence of these forces which give us the tools to think of ways of refiguring black being.

In chapter 2, we are grounded in the rivers of Mpondoland, which connect personhood and the longtime of history. Here we come to understand what it means to be unhumaned but also to be reborn in waters that operate on a queer frequency. We look to the history of Mpondoland to see how people there have always resisted abjection and asserted their being in the face of capitalist imperialist discipline. The chapter dwells on the incessant onslaught against Mpondo bodies and indigenous ways of life. Here, history is my alibi. I begin this history with the sinking of the SS *Mendi*. But the history I lean on is a lived-in history that is given form by the elders I talk to—my coprotagonists. They go back to the revolt on Ngquza Hill and caress it like an old scar.[54] They tell its story to mark an old history of their animalization but also to recall their valor and resistance. I connect Ngquza Hill to other hills that bore witness to black death and resistance. At the base of the hill is the river. At the end of the river is the sea. These are places of healing and fortification where death and trauma are cleansed. Chapter 2 presents an argument that cleansing ceremonies at the river are deeply embodied rituals that are primarily concerned with redeeming bodies that have been marked as deviant by trauma. Fortification crafts a space between livability and the fungible. In this chapter, I build the case for queering Mpondoland as an analytic that opens up routes to black freedom. The chapter takes up the question of how we might recast history to trace queer socialities of refusal. I argue that the history of amaMpondo refusal makes possible the resistance that amounted to the Marikana massacre and other movements such as that against titanium mining and "development" in Mgungundlovu, Mpondoland.[55] But there are prior lineages from which we draw. Prophetess Nontetha Nkwenkwe shows that the bombarded always resist, even after they die. They do this globally through queer gathering in mass assembly. Even as it gestures to the mourning that engulfs this place, this chapter resists any notions that the people of Mpondoland are passive or pathological.

In chapter 3, we move into the present and more recent past and find adolescents reaching for the supernatural to assert black queer buoyancy and refusal in a school system predicated on capitalist discipline, anxiety, and mournful community surveillance. This chapter lingers on the queer preoccupations of this text. As people at the bottom of the hierarchy of the unhumaned, through spirit possession or *ukukhuphuka izizwe*, young women defy societal and market control by finding shelter in multiple worlds and temporalities. I offer *ukukhuphuka izizwe* as a queer formation that enables opacity and errantry under pressure. Clara Germana Cele's *ukukhuphuka izizwe* in the early 1900s points to historical antecedents of liberatory leaps through the breach as queer refusal. Here, motifs of the river and ocean illustrate Mpondo theory through the centrality of these sites for spiritual corruption, cleansing, and renewal. This chapter demonstrates how capitalist desires and consumption play out in the wasteland and hinterlands of the neoliberal market. Dissociative symptoms are read as worlding practices that push against black queer enclosure.

In chapter 4, we deal directly with the graves of the dead, engaging with ancestors and their presence in the landscapes of what were or are enclosures and sites of genocidal hauntings. As a death-defying ancestral being, Sarah Baartman grounds this chapter. Here, an unflinching gaze is cast on the deathscapes of Mpondoland's black enclosures. In order to understand the devastation wrought by the AIDS pandemic and debilitation—the slow wearing down of bodies—on the rural landscape, I lean on *ukwakumkanya*'s sensorial registers to attend to the vibrational frequencies that emit from the deathscape. This chapter pauses on the graves of the dead in order to both demonstrate the reality of our multiple dyings at the other end of neoliberalism, and to illustrate how dying is coopted by Mpondo theory. The chapter theorizes through refusal and indigenous wisdom in order to think of ancestors as formations that defy death.

The supernatural as technology for rural life is the focus of chapter 5. From the vantage point of the hill, we look at vampirism, cannibalism, and the occult as forms of consumption for those who are excluded from the processes of capital accumulation. As grasps for freedom, we conceive of these practices as queering and parodying consumption. In a way, cannibalism and the frustrations that flow from here have some of their roots in the AIDS genocide and colonial violence. The chapter is concerned with how the material remains of the body, both dead and dying, are a means of making meaning of how we live in a global world where the consequences of inequality are most pronounced among abandoned rural subjects. I illustrate that stories of gravedigging medicine men, cannibals, and vampires are imaginative moral frameworks for making meaning of inequality that is always present in migration, development, markets, and consumption. But I also illuminate how these systems of modernity come loose at the seams and fail. By centering Khotso Sethuntsa, I suggest that black subjectivities are made through a long self-referential and refracting history. I return to Ngquza Hill, introduced in chapter 2, and demonstrate how this relates to cannibal and vampire activities that flare and proliferate in the rural countryside. Ultimately, the chapter mounts an argument that black survivance and livingness are tied to famished and queer registers of desire and occult practices.

1 WATCHFUL OCEAN, OBSERVANT MOUNTAIN

Yet every time our skin goes under

It's as if the reeds remember that they were once chains

And the water, restless, wishes it could spew all of the slaves and

    ships onto shore

Whole as they had boarded, sailed and sunk

Their tears are what have turned the ocean salty . . .

The audacity to arrive by water and invade us

If this land was really yours, then resurrect the bones of the

    colonisers and use them as a compass . . .

KOLEKA PUTUMA, "WATER" (2017)

The ocean and the rock face are scripts off which I read our past as a vast deathscape. In this deathscape the dead are forever present, and *Riotous Deathscapes* demonstrates how they are fashioned as a strategy for living. The chapter reclaims a diverse set of ancestors in order to illustrate how Mpondo theory is born out of relation. I suggest that without a written black archive that takes us to a period before colonialism, the crashing ocean shore and ancient mountain rock are surfaces off which Mpondo indigenous histories can be read. Methodologically, I rely on the technique of *ukwakumkanya* to look askance into the past. *Ukwakumkanya* is to attend to surfaces whose folds hold stories that remain willfully ignored or misread. In this respect, I follow Stephen Best and Sharon Marcus (2009, 9), who contend that "a surface is what insists on being looked at rather than what we must train ourselves to see through." But this is more than a historicization of place and people. It is an investment in reflecting a portrait of life through theory making. Based on my own history, I illustrate how the Mpondo people are in part constituted by the indigenous San and Khoekhoe who left their imprint in the mountains and gorges and the castaway bedraggled Europeans and enslaved Africans and Asians who emerged from the shipwrecks on the Mpondoland Wild Coast. This allows for a crafting of blackness in relation to indigenous studies and a form of whiteness that surrenders itself to place and relation. While my family history permeates this accounting, this is a story about the Mpondo people and, by extension, other similarly located coastal communities on the African continent. These accounts suggest that African blackness is always relational.

Since the chapter paints the canvas that becomes the space in which everyday deathscapes occur in subsequent chapters, it reaches further back in history than the chapters that follow. It centers the interior, coastal mountain rocks, and ocean by following the silhouettes of the Mpondo coast and mountainous interior where San and Khoekhoe ancestors lived. It announces the arrival of white and enslaved Asian and African presence in Mpondoland through the shipwrecks that dogged the Wild Coast.[1] While the chapters that follow demonstrate Mpondo theory as relation between ourselves, the dead, and the natural world, here I illustrate how we came into relation with displaced San and Khoekhoe and shipwreck castaways who stumbled onto our shores in the violence of the ocean. By recouping the dead, I tarry on the deathscape that levitates in the ocean's mirages. Since much has been made of the castaways, I am interested in how their hosts—the local Mpondo—responded to them. I sit with those castaways who decided to stay in relation with the locals and observe how they themselves became Mpondo. I contend that this is Mpondo theory in practice. As a descendent of the Mpondo who observed the shipwrecks and those from elsewhere who collapsed onto the shore, this accounting is personal. This history has engendered me and marks me (Das 2007). The chapter is guided by questions that provide an opening toward new possibilities of being. How do we remain open but with a confidence and humility that do not sacrifice the ground on which we stand? What is required of the other in order to be in relation with blackness? What emerges when we cleave together and imagine new frontiers? What alternative histories are made possible when black people's lives are at the center of history making? If the winds that howl along the gorges of the Wild Coast and the hills of the village are harnessed, what insights spring from other ways of listening and how do we craft these to tell a theory of being?

Outside of Mpondoland, people, usually men who do not know me, sometimes call me *mtshana*. In isiXhosa, *mtshana* is not gendered. It is inclusive of niece and nephew and their in-betweens. Those who call me *mtshana* are responding to a trace of something simultaneously familiar and foreign. I could be their sister's child and therefore their nephew. But their sister could have conceived me from a liaison with someone not from these parts. I am therefore from both here and elsewhere. A child of the borderlands. I look at my mother's eyes and read the elsewhere as European. Her eyes signal a trace to this lineage that makes her both of here and of elsewhere. I do not have her eyes, but my sister and two of my brothers have them. They too are marked. They attract other names, and these are not always terms of endearment. *iLawu. Iqheya.* Signaling Khoekhoe or San but wrapped in bruising barbs. But what happens when one leans into these terms instead of renouncing them? To see past the insult is to recognize the accusation that one is being hailed as an indigenous person. It is to look past the hurt of placeholding names that often signal anger at a "foreign" father. Only, my father *is* from here. And so was his father. My mother's parents were from here. Born at the local hospitals of Mpondoland. But one of their parents, my great-grandfather who left his eyes, was from elsewhere. It is he who, many generations later, makes me a nephew. Not quite of this place. But of this place in an out of joint kind of way. And yet, parts of my lineage are ancient to this place. As old as the mountains. After my umbilical cord dried and fell off my infant body, like the man that calls me nephew, my navel was buried in the ground of the rolling hills of Mpondoland. Supposedly rooting me and claiming my place in the soil. However, since I am interested in the trace of things endured, things left in the earth, in the tradition of Hortense Spillers, I face this hieroglyphics of the flesh. What occurs when things surface above ground?

Simultaneously Black and Indigenous

I hail from a clan of people forged in the churning currents of emaMpond-weni. One of my ancestors, a woman called Minna, stumbled off a ship-wreck in the early to mid-1700s on the Wild Coast.[2] She appears to have been a young girl of Asian origin traveling on a ship with Europeans and enslaved Africans and Asians. She may have been an enslaved girl. Years later, she married a runaway slave from the Western Cape and their prog-eny intermarried with the Mpondo people among whom they lived. I am part of the tenth generation arising from that shipwreck and its coastal relations. It is unclear, but the man who passed down my surname may have been a settler. My grandfather was a nephew too. He was also a pa-triarch and he married two wives. I am of the lineage of his second wife. The small house. The matriarch of the small house, my grandmother, was a Mpondo woman. It is from her that my siblings get their long-boned gait. But there is something else that I see in the hieroglyphics of the flesh—the pronounced cheekbones. My mother tells me that her father-in-law sometimes referred to his mother as a Griqua woman. Griqua—of the San. The earliest inhabitants of Southern Africa. The people that European ex-plorers called fauna. My paternal grandfather was short. His name was a commentary on his height—*Mfitshi*. Short one. Short like the Griqua. Like the San. Those who forged a life roaming the subcontinent. A people who left their artistic trace on the caves and rock face of the great Drakensburg mountain range.[3] Those who were hunted like fauna and some of whom are now captured in reserves.[4] The San and Khoekhoe whose language is erased from the linguistic potpourri of this land. The suppressed trace that predated colonialism and the arrival of the ships. This trace can be found in me too. It signals a history of people who related to each other and whose lineage points to this relationality. Openness to our relatedness is opposite to a kind of ethnicity that Hortense Spillers (1987, 66) contends "freezes in meaning, takes on constancy, assumes the look and the effects of the Eter-nal." In Édouard Glissant's (1997) conception, relation moves away from a rhizomatic commitment to the root. There are traces of the Khoekhoe and San in the bodies of the Nguni people of the Eastern Cape and the Tswana of the northern provinces (Jabavu 1962). What is the meaning of this trace for thinking indigeneity and blackness? I am drawn to Vincente Diaz's re-lational figuring of indigeneity. In his oceanic enquiry, he points to a deep temporal and geographic range that is discursive and "queries the line between exclusivist and ahistorical definitions of indigeneity" (2011, 23).

Importantly, Diaz (2015) explodes the walls typically drawn between the human and natural world by pointing us to the mutually constitutive nature of the sea, land, and humans. This relational frame allows me to think about amaMpondo at the center of this project in relation to the Khoekhoe, San communities, and natural worlds. I lean on Glissant's productive conception of relation as central to identity. He asserts that an understanding of how we are in relation is to de-emphasize origins that are conceived of as root or biology. It moves against the center or metropolis in favor of decentered and multilingual conceptions of being. To turn away from the root, then, is to embrace those you come across and to recognize how you are coconstituted by them. Glissant contends that "We 'know' that the Other is within us and affects how we evolve . . . and the development of our sensibility" (1997, 27). To be conscious of the Other within is to adapt your tongue in order to be in relation. Monolingual intent is eschewed when people are oriented toward relation. Like Glissant, black and indigenous scholars Tiffany Lethabo King, Jenell Navarro, and Andrea Smith (2020) center relationality between black and indigenous peoples by suggesting that they are stuck together.[5] I read the Mpondo people as committed to permeability and errantry that enables them to be in community with neighbors such as the Khoekhoe, San, and shipwreck castaways. The ethic that frames this encounter is not one of discovery and conquest but knowing. To know the Mpondo, the Khoekhoe, and the enslaved castaway is to learn of genocide, rebellion, riotousness, and community.

There is much to be gained by acknowledging the genocidal hauntings that San and Khoekhoe communities live with. We gain in building solidarity and mutual recognition of a common violence wrought by slavery, colonial, apartheid, and neocolonial waves of devastation. In practice, Godfrey Callaway (1919) observes that a Mpondomise chief routinely presented the San who lived in a local gorge with goats and bullocks in acknowledgement of the fact that he occupied land first lived on by the San. King, Jenell, and Smith suggest that relationality is not fixed and easily knowable and that we need to work against the idea that black people are already known and indigenous people unknown. To see these groups as incommensurate perpetuates a scholarship and politics that read indigenous and black people in isolation of each other rather than in relation. Relation reminds us of the failure of empire even as it sought to annihilate the Khoekhoe and San. They went into poetic alert and adapted in relation to their new Mpondo neighbors to create a more livable world. To conceive of the Mpondo this way is to think of them as layered fugitives. As fugitives that harbor other indigenous fugitives. Below, I consider three strands of thought from the vantage point of Mpondo villagers. In sitting with villagers and adopting *ukwakumkanya*, I am curious to see what theorizing from here means for both this place and black diasporic studies.

In this project, the utility of the indigenous is in its engagement with marginality rather than claims to firstness or legitimacy of place. I use the concept *indigenous* attentive to its two meanings. The first is the claim that some groups of people inhabited parts of the continent before the migration of Bantu groups who subsequently settled among them (Kipuri 2017; Laher and Sing'Oei 2014). These are termed indigenous people. However, Bantu linguistic groups that are said to originate from the interlacustrine region of central Africa (Chami 1999) are also indigenous to the continent. In this framing, indigeneity may be read as a function of who first lived within a particular region.[6] I am however not invested in contestations over origins. The second and more important meaning for this project is how numerically smaller groups were made marginal and minoritized over extended periods of time. Minoritization occurred through territorial conflicts as a consequence of migration and resource-based conflicts, colonization in the Cape provinces, and postcolonial nation building. Indigeneity assists in pointing to layers of marginality within continental blackness. This is to say that there are groups of people who are omitted, neglected, and treated as surplus in the postcolonial nation state. They are forced to assume minority status within the heterogeneity that characterizes blackness in the African nation state. These exclusionary processes perpetuate colonial fissures, identitarian fault lines, impoverishment, and structural inequality of groups that have been rendered inconsequential minorities. In Southern Africa, we have mostly been unable to imagine an expansive blackness in relation to indigenous communities of the San and Khoekhoe.[7] I posit that the explanation for our failure to imagine and practice a blackness that embraces indigenous people may be informed by the ontological fear of primacy. If we concede that these indigenous communities lived in Southern and East Africa before or even at the same time as the Bantu groups to which we belong, this potentially troubles our orientation and claim to place.

There are a number of controversies that attend to becoming indigenous in Africa.[8] Since all Africans are considered to be indigenous to the continent, claims of indigeneity by some groups is contested. Unlike the United States, Canada, South America, Australia, and New Zealand where indigenous peoples are distinct from settler and formerly enslaved populations, in Africa these distinctions are not as obvious. Continental migration of Africans occurred within the continent and both preceded and was different from colonialism by European settlers. African nation states have seen "original" inhabitants of territories as interest groups that are often at odds with the national identity and agenda (Hodgson 2009). Claims of indigeneity confuse the temporality and legitimacy of the nation and claims to land, natural resources, and belonging. African states hesitate to recognize the existence of indigenous peoples because of the fear that such recognition would lead to moves toward secession, threaten territorial integrity of nation states, and shake already fragile conceptions of a national identity (Hodgson 2009). Indigenous people's existence is generally at odds with the neocolonial nation state that purports to represent all people while primarily concerned with promoting majority cultures. The modern neocolonial state requires compulsory settlement on land and adopts development projects that exploit resources of indigenous minority groups. At the global level, there are strong parallels in the histories of dispossession of indigenous and black communities whose colonization, dispossession, genocide, and enslavement left a lasting blemish in the material and psychological condition of the black world. King (2019) reminds us that these are distinct experiences whose violence of genocide and black fungibility move as one. African thought on indigeneity, however, departs from King's figuring of the Northern Hemisphere. As Africans we are both black and indigenous. These identities move apart and fold together over time and through inflections of the politics of the nation state. Africans have however been minor contributors to black and indigenous studies. Among thinkers committed to African and Caribbean-bound lives, there is a tradition that is most famously represented by Frantz Fanon, Aimé Césaire, and Léopold Senghor.[9] This book seeks to widen this scholarship. With a base in desolate Mpondoland, *Riotous Deathscapes* is an experiment in exploring relationality and porosity in ways that trouble the distinctions between marginalized peoples. In the tradition of King (2019), my project is an effort to dialogue and ethically witness African life and theory in relation to North American and Caribbean scholarship on black studies as well as indigenous scholars. This alternative site of engagement is a potential space for solidarity and points to the deep similarities between groups of people and fields of study that have hitherto been conceived of as distinct.

To collapse the histories of the people of the Eastern Cape to apartheid categories is to eliminate complexity and to tell a colonial history. In taking up Fanon's (1967) challenge for sociogeny—a commitment to grounded histories that do not succumb to colonial myth making—what alternative histories emerge and how is life figured in the breach between indigeneity and blackness? Pushed out of the Southern Cape by white colonial settlers, the Nama, Khoekhoe, and San indigenous groups moved further north and settled alongside groups such as the Xhosa, Gcaleka, Mpondomise, and Mpondo. Harold Jack Simons and Ray E. Simons observe that despite fighting back stubbornly, they were "all but annihilated" (1969, 12). Survivors of the Nama were absorbed into "coloured" communities while "the Khoi were hunted down and killed off like the great herds of wild animals that once roamed the plains" (13). Robert Ross (2017) similarly details how the Khoekhoe fled the exploitation of the Dutch in the Cape. Some moved to the Eastern Cape and were absorbed into the Xhosa and the Griqua. He notes that "there are still Xhosa clans that trace their descent back to Khoekhoe groups further east." (xvii). Ross contends that the identities of the Griqua, San, amaXhosa, and Khoekhoe were constantly in flux. I am part of this flux that gestures to the shifting contours of the decentered human. After a family trauma, when the traditional healer made incisions in my body, he cut where the blood runs hot in order to open me up and expose me to ancestral beings. He opened me to a genealogy of trauma and strength that goes back to the generations that came before. Among these ancestors are ancient Mpondo women, San, and people who mix the blood of these women with those who disturbed the Mpondo seashore. I emphasize relation because even though vast numbers of indigenous people were murdered like game and others succumbed to smallpox, the concept of annihilation discounts incorporation into other groups.[10] This living alongside and incorporation invites a more expansive form of blackness characterized by errantry, relation, and survivance. My ancestry speaks to this expansiveness. In 1878, the Mpondo chief Mqikela supported the Griquas of Kokstad in the revolt against the Cape government. He paid for this relational fealty to his indigenous neighbors when his recognition as paramount chief was withdrawn and his kingdom divided into two—eastern Mpondoland and western Mpondoland (Stapleton 2001). Coloniality has always worked against solidarity and relation between black people.

Eastern Cape historians like Jeffery Peires (1982) have noted that the similarities in the material culture of groups such as the Gcaleka-Xhosa and the "Bushmen" support the historical record that large numbers of these groups lived side by side.[11] Similarly, Frans E. Prins and Hester Lewis (1992) observe that an old Mpondo man recalled that three generations earlier, "Bushmen" had settled next to the Ntabankulu Mpondo territory.

San were respected for their rainmaking skills, and the old man recalled that a local Mpondo diviner had befriended a San rainmaker. Maqhoqha, whose father was a San rock artist, was a first-generation descendant of relations between the Mpondomise and San. She became the official rainmaker of the Mpondomise people. In *A First Generation Descendent of the Transkei San*, Pieter Jolly (1986) similarly writes about the history of the San in the Tsolo region of the Eastern Cape. The deep history of exchange and relationality between indigenous San and Bantu people means that we have come to share common cosmologies. For example, the rainmaker told Prins and Lewis (1992) that the widely used Xhosa expression of *Camagu* to say thank you or to greet during religious ceremonies was borrowed from San people. Similarly, Robert Martin (1837) reported that the isiXhosa word *tixo* (god) is from the "Bushmen" word *tixwe*. The San were believed to have magical charms and understood to be mediators between people, the animal world, and nature. To mediate between worlds is an attribute of Mpondo theory that breaks down the enclosures and hierarchies between spiritual, animal, natural, and bounded human. Prins and Lewis (1992) observe that "Bushmen" were associated with water because they could create rain. They also note the significance of water as a mediator between worlds. Jacklyn Cock (2018) contends that water divinities have the power to influence the direction of their ancestors. As King (2019) reminds us, to think with water, land, and shoals is to embrace fluidity, movement, liminality, here and there, unknowability, and unsettlement. In *Riotous Deathscapes*, I consider the role of waters in arrivals, departures, and creation. I attend to how water cleanses and fortifies the body, and I consider its role as a medium of relationality to ancestors. Water sustains material life and cosmological relation. As a methodological location, landscape and water masses give life to Mpondo theory. Rivers tie the Mpondo to their indigenous ancestors. This signifies the relational practice of blackness seen from here. Beyond amaMpondo, Peires (1982) and Prins and Lewis (1992) observe that southern Nguni people were able to draw their neighbors into social relations of reciprocity. They incorporated groups such as Khoekhoe pastoralists and San hunter-gatherers as well as European and enslaved Asian and African shipwreck castaways through kinship relations such as marriage. This chapter is an apt illustration of these diverse kinship ties, and it demonstrates the confluence of various groups who became Mpondo through this ethic of errantry and black sociality.

With reference to Native Americans, Marker (2003) observes that the dominant narrative of indigenous extinction erases colonial settler culpability and responsibility to the descendants of those killed in indigenous genocides. Similarly, in this context, the suppression of Khoekhoe, San, Nama, and other indigenous claims through a temporal lens that writes them out of history suggests that questions related to land are permanently evaded. We who descend from these groups and others are unmoored by a history that uses colonial temporalities to conceive of recognition and reparations. What does it mean to acknowledge the existence of indigenous communities today? The Mpondo people's long-standing claim to land and place represents a base or mooring. However, the repetitive trauma and neoliberal battering to which they are subjected means they are tenuously in place. This is unlike the condition of African Americans who have been untethered from place and American nationhood. King (2019) contends that "they cannot utter reclamation, recovery, or the resurgence of their personhood or land." The Mpondo index a form of blackness that is closer to indigenous people who insist on claiming their land and ways of life. Their resistance is grounded in certainty rather than baselessness. Like indigenous communities elsewhere in the world, there are historic forms of knowledge within which the Mpondo ground their identities and resistance. In addition to the indigenous relations that constitute Mpondo personhood are white, Asian, and African castaways. I address this next.

Mpondo Whiteness

In thinking about borderlands, I am drawn to Gloria Anzaldúa's and Aida Hurtado's thoughts about theory. Hurtado (2003, 216) contends that "theory should emanate from what we live, breathe, and experience in our everyday lives and it is only in breaking boundaries, crossing borders, claiming fragmentation and hybridity that theory will finally be useful for liberation." My aim here is not to liberate whiteness. But like Anzaldúa, *Riotous Deathscapes* offers an accounting of most aspects of Mpondo identity—Bantu, San, and Khoekhoe who met on the land; and white, enslaved Indian and African shipwrecked castaways whose meeting with the Mpondo was on the ocean shore. In deliberating on white castaways who intersected with my own lineage, I can see how a different kind of white life is possible. Life not saturated in whiteness. My aim, though, is to sit with different forms of blackness enabled by the location of Mpondoland, its expansive oceans and its openness to be in relation. In the service of border crossings and in explicating Mpondo life, I stay at the surface informed by a

Deleuzian curiosity with the folds and "labyrinth of continuity" that is unearthed when the surface is closely examined (Deleuze 1991, 231). But I also delve beneath the surface. To think of the fold as shifting and unsettled we have to conceive of surface and depth as continuous and as spaces for the creation and sustainability of possibility (Pickens 2019). For this, I embrace methodological hybridity in the tradition of the black public humanities as a form of *ukwakumkanya* that is attuned to intergenerational whispers and silenced traces. Hieroglyphics. Flesh as text. Mountains and oceans as textual. These are forms of data that subvert the logic of research but that paint a fuller portrait than we currently have. I think about people provisionally designated "coloured." Not those of the urban imagination who lived in racialized ghettos but those who live black in the rural hinterland of Mpondoland. The person I am describing is an ordinary person who somewhat defies categories because they are not quite "coloured" in how this has come to be understood in South Africa. The person I have in mind is Mpondo in language, culture, and lineage. To borrow Anzaldúa's words from her description of *mexicanos-Chicanos*, the Mpondo of the confluence is "stubborn, persevering, impenetrable as stone, yet possessing a malleability that renders us [them] unbreakable, we [they], the *mestizas* and *mestizos*, will remain" (2004, 1030). This person is Mpondo in a slightly different way, because somewhere in their lineage, someone not quite black left their trace. They represent something that unsettles the narrative of categorization and certainty. But this person is of the underclass. This is an unconventional way of thinking of the overdetermined straight chain of race that predominates race thinking in South Africa and elsewhere. It is an enlargement of blackness. I think about this person whose personhood points us to the relational. In a world where race has become stultified and settled, those designated *abatshana*—nephews and nieces—complicate certainties. *Abatshana* are black, but they lead to a double take. Sometimes they are not black from a distance. But sometimes, everything about their appearance is coded black. Except for some of their names. Beyond Mpondoland, *abatshana* indigeneity is tested through language and questions of lineage. The responses are never quite satisfactory, and they are given the provisional status of nephews. Liminal but black because kaffirization is in their lineage and experience.[12] *Riotous Deathscapes* creates an open script that begins to engage with the marginal because of the profound lessons that it has for the universal well-worn pathways. Like King's (2019) meditation on black-indigenous relations, my project is attuned to a porous changing practice informed by ethical encounter. To avoid crystallization and stultification,

I go along with Spillers (1987, 65), who offers: "I must strip down the layers of attenuated meanings, made excess in time, over time, assigned by particular historical order, and there await whatever marvels of my own inventiveness." What happens when we read history differently? I am reminded of what emerged from the earth when I dug up small parts of my grandmother's yard. Surprises from childhood. Things I had not known. Objects that predated me but that were part of my layered and sedimented story. But even as I dig, I cannot look past the surface, for as Uri McMillan (2018, 11) reminds us, "Surface is not inert, but vibrant, pulsating, and constantly in motion, undulating, like a wall of water." In this excavation, I am not interested in uncovering truth, but I want to sift through the layers that emerge in order to read what has been left behind both on the surface and in the many covered surfaces. Attending in the posture of *ukwakumkanya*, what do I apprehend when I look at the shimmering wall of water? Sylvia Wynter was interested in how the peoples imagined outside of the monohuman claimed their humanity as a relational act. To center the human, Wynter offers that while we must read identities of the underclasses as colonized, not white, black, poor, and jobless, these social markers tell us only parts of the story. In reading Wynter, Katherine McKittrick (2015, 6–7) notes that the marginalized are "instead identifiably condemned due to their deselected *human* status." They are marked as outside of monohuman logic. McKittrick contends that as the living, we must be "imagined as inviting *being human as praxis* into our purview, which envisions the human as verb, as alterable, as relational" and as necessarily dislodging the naturalization of deselection. My great-ancestors left a trace on my lineage, in the shape of my nose and ambiguity in the hue of my fleshy body, my tightly curled African hair. This invites some analysis of Wynter's concept of being human as praxis. My mother's grandparents met in the late 1800s and got married. This was at the height of colonialism in the period preceding apartheid. They were Mpondo and white. While I imagine that the colonial administration would have frowned on this union, the geography of this marriage and life is significant. They lived their lives in Mpondoland. A land neglected then as it is now over a century later. Mpondoland allowed for a demonstration of being human as praxis. In Wynter's conception, my ancestors—black great-grandmother and white great-grandfather—illustrate the doing of the human as verb and as alterable. The white man from somewhere in Europe lived in a wholly Mpondo community and learned to speak isiMpondo in order to be in relation to his family and community. He may have had the foresight to recognize that geography and place change people. The cylindrical epiphenomenal temporality of colonial conquest has shown this to be true. People die, the land remains. This is a different narrative to that of the colonial settler as we have come to see him, imposing his will and forcing everyone to adapt to him. Noni Jabavu's (1962) close reading of colonial King William's Town reveals the nuance of the relations between black and white people. The narrative is startlingly complex. I therefore proceed from an awareness of Mpondo blackness as pliable and opaque rather than finite. It is much more fractal and rippled than it is transparent and complete.

I have not wanted to know about my white ancestor because of my fear that he lived as Man. A plunderer. And he must have, for it was impossible to be white and live otherwise. I do not seek to romanticize the relations between my black and white ancestors. Kaiama Glover (2021, 30) cautions that the valorization of hybridity risks eliding the violent past. She contends that "by reading the *métis*—especially the *métisse*—both as the exotic product of empire's 'colonial family romance' and as a symbol of its more harmonious, less 'Black' postcolonial future," the concept can be deployed to elide a violent past. She suggests that "in this respect, *métissage* risks offering resolution of the colonial past via repression of its originary antiblackness and white supremacy." I do not seek a resolution that erases white supremacy, but I am attuned to what the conditions of relationality enable. *Riotous Deathscapes* takes seriously Jarred Sexton's (2008) critique of the multiracial promise as the great hope for dismantling race and racialization and advancing color blindness. "Race mixture" is neither the future nor the solution. I therefore do not seek to valorize the borderlands or to downplay the power that attaches to racial hierarchies. Rather, I point to the reality of Mpondoland and signal the promise of relationality that does not surrender blackness but that expands it and explodes whiteness. I modulate my critique of purity with Danzy Senna's (1998) criticism of the "mulatto millennium." She observes that multiracial pride has the danger of being ahistorical, neutralizing, and depoliticizing race. The "mulatto" is not new and can exist within racist society. To valorize race mixture can lead to the great escape of forgetting. I do not want new categories of erasure. I want to remember while recognizing Mpondo errantry and its implications for blackness.

As a black Jew, Michael Twitty (2017) confronts his own ancestry in his travels to the old North American South and finds that he is the descendant of a prominent slave owner. He also knows that he is the descendant of Africans off the African west coast. With this knowledge, he does not curl up in revulsion but sits with the knowledge of the heritage that is passed down to him. While my own method resonates with the questions posed by Twitty, his work simultaneously helps to illustrate what Mpondo theory, as a practice of relation, does in the wider world. I too must dig into and reckon with my heritage. In doing this, I recognize the fiction of race as a violent invention of a system of colonial power that maintains superiority and inferiority.[13] I therefore read my colonial ancestry through this prism of domination. From snippets of stories from elders in the villages through which my great-grandfather traveled, I pieced together a story of an old man interested and engaged in the life of the village. He is remembered for working in the fields with a strange way of facing down the hill instead of facing toward the top. He planted fruit trees in the indigenous forests so that anyone could freely eat the fruit. This introduction of domesticated fruit into an indigenous forest mirrors white arrival here. An elder who remembered him told me that the people referred to the trees as Reme's trees.[14] Thinking about creolization, Glissant points to the value of processes beyond the content of the complex mix. He directs us to the "mutual mutations generated by this interplay of relations" (1997, 16). Following Glissant's lead, I think of Geme, his wife Olpinah, and their community as relational beings involved in the practice of a mutual ethics of care. Perhaps he lived as Mpondo and not as Man. I know less about my great-grandmother. This is in part because she died fairly young. But in divining her posture and manner in a family photograph and in the carriage of her descendants, I do not see a woman who believed the colonial fiction of her inferiority. I want to believe that this was not a relationship founded on a system of coloniality. María Lugones (2007, 187) defines coloniality not as racial classification but as "an encompassing phenomenon" that as a system of power "permeates all control of sexual access, collective authority, labor, subjectivity/intersubjectivity." Now, as an adult, I want to imagine that my great-grandparents loved each other in their creation of an alterable lineage. Something open, queer, and defying certainty. Always requiring a double take. I wonder though. Why were all his children given English names when their mother was Mpondo? To be sure, they all had Mpondo names, but those names seldom ended up in their identity documents. However, like Glissant's plantation, those of us tethered to the land and ocean have two names, "an official one and an essential one—the nickname given by his community" (1997, 72).[15] This story is common throughout Mpondoland. This is to say, there are many nephews and nieces. They too are both of here and elsewhere. But *abatshana* are not monohuman.

However, because they evoke uncertainty, they inhabit a place of some scorn. We remind the stultified world of its own fallible status, queerness, and provisionality. We do not escape stereotypes. After all, Wynter reminds us that these often have nothing to do with those that are stereotyped. To be Mpondo is evidence of the unsettled nature of identity and a gesture toward alterability and infidelity to the human.

Shipwrecks and Settlers

The trace of elsewhere is writ large on the hilly surface of the Mpondoland coast of South Africa.[16] The early settlers arrived by ship. Sometimes voluntarily and at other times because they were shipwrecked on the Wild Coast. The remnants of shipwrecks can still be found on parts of the Wild Coast of Mpondoland, a rugged coastline that is not easily accessible by motor vehicle. It is along this coastline that ships were sometimes wrecked when wild winds drove them into sandbanks—shoals and rocks that jut out to sea. This led to some accidental arrivals of white people and enslaved people of Asian and African descent. Some of them remained and made lives in the local villages. Monica Wilson (1959, 167) reads the archive as follows: "During the 16th century there were three wrecks along the Transkeian coast whose survivors left some account of the people they met, and during the 17th century there were further wrecks from which survivors spent several years living with Xhosa people before being rescued." Making lives meant liaisons and marriages between castaways and black Mpondo people.[17] Wilson notes that ships that docked in later years sometimes came across groups of survivors of previous shipwrecks. These survivors lived among and in relation to the local people, and many refused to return to Europe. The trace of the shipwrecks marks the coastline in many ways. One of these is the lineage of the black children of castaways and Mpondo people. Of course, the confluence of multiple influences informs this trace. The trace of the Khoekhoe is apparent in Nelson Mandela's face. The political icon and long-term political prisoner Walter Sisulu's father was white and his mother black. On this coastline, purity is a myth. Thinking of personhood requires shoaling, pausing to consider the complexity of history and relation (King 2019). This is a history made at sea and on land—of those who arrived and those they found here. King (2019, 8) evocatively observes that "the shoal disrupts the nautical and oceanic coherence of Blackness as only liquid and enables other modes of thinking about Blackness that opens up other kinds of potentialities, materialities, and forms." To wrest blackness from the exclusively oceanic is to recognize Africans who did not cross the Atlantic but also to tarry with the rubbings between land and ocean. McMillan's (2018) conception of liquidity and plural selves that signal various modalities of being is a generative prism through which to read how we become Mpondo. This unfurling and changeable morphology is essential to the relational core of Mpondo theory. The interruption of the shoals and the disturbance of the waves with the arrival of the ships is marked in my flesh. But it is not my origin. It does not have primacy over my San and Mpondo heritage. It is a part of it. An enlarging of my personhood. I have spent days on the beach, looking and listening. On a 2019 visit, I heard about the multiple groups that have scoured this area in search of history. Among these are archaeologists who have ventured into the gorges and caves that dot the area. An interested villager told me that the archaeologists have found ample evidence of the San's presence in the caves and the layers of sand dunes. While often suppressed, San heritage is writ large on the shoreline and our bodies.

The *Grosvenor* sunk off the coast of Mpondoland on Sunday morning of August 14, 1782.[18] In Ian Glenn's account, about 140 passengers and crew survived after 15 crew died. The survivors were Europeans, enslaved Indians, and the offspring of these two groups.[19] From Percival Kirby (1954) we learn that only 14 of the 123 castaways arrived at the Dutch settlement, a 650-kilometer walk from Lambasi Bay where the wreck occurred. Various accounts suggest that the remainder of the party was separated, with some dying, others assimilating, and others being rescued. Both George Carter (1927) and Jacob van Reenen refer to enslaved people being castaway on the Wild Coast. To pause on these enslaved people is to imagine a different future for them compared to those enslaved and brought to slavery in Cape Town.[20] For those on the *Grosvenor* and its predecessors, the crash landing on the shoals and rocks was a strike for freedom. The breach in their passage marked their emancipation. The unexpected surfacing of the ocean floor was freedom for them to "finally stand on sand again"—but this time, to stand in their liberty (King 2019, 2). For all those on board, it was a crossroads of new beginnings. Stepping onto the black shoals of Mpondoland marked their leap into the Fanonian breach of possibility. Minna, my paternal great-ancestor, would have been one of those who found freedom in the disaster. Centuries later as I stood on the beach staring at the sand at my feet, I wondered whether the feet of the enslaved had disturbed the sand in a celebratory dance while their white peers had left imprints of trepidation. According to Carter (1927), an expedition by Jacob van Reenen many years later found survivors far away from the Cape, which he suspected to be made up of some survivors from shipwrecks that preceded the *Grosvenor*. Van Reenen observed that the rescue expedition found a nation of "*bastaards*" along the Umgazana River, a tributary of the Umgazi River that was not very far from the site of the *Grosvenor* wreck. Among these villagers were descendants of both white people and "yellow-skinned slaves and Bengalese" (Kirby 1953, 3). Carter's description is instructive:

> Far from the Cape, they came across a village of *bastaard* Christians, who were descended from people shipwrecked on that coast, and of which, three old women were living, whom Oemtonoue the Hambonaa captain had taken as his wives. . . . [We] found that the people were descended from whites, some too from slaves of mixed colour, and the natives of the East Indies. We also met the three old women, who said they were sisters, and had, when children, been shipwrecked on this coast, but could not say of what nation they were, being too young to know at the time the accident happened. We offered to take them and their children back with us on our return; at which they seemed much very pleased. (Carter 1927, 160, cited in Glenn 1995, 5)

Carter, however, concluded that the castaway women subsequently refused to leave, citing the need to tend their crops. For the white people who remained behind, shoaling was the beginning of becoming Mpondo. Nigel Penn (2004) writes that the women said they would leave if they could bring along their children and families, which amounted to about four hundred people. The rescuers demurred. The women's refusal to leave their Mpondo children behind was an act of errantry and a claim to blackness. The practice of refusal can be seen as creating possibilities when faced with negation (Campt 2019). Here, negation would have been to leave one's children and social networks established in conditions of relational openness and generosity. For the women, this was to clasp the possibility of living otherwise. The tribe of castaways and Mpondo locals became known as amaTshomane, which literally means to be in relation—to be locked in friendly relation. The chief was Sango, and his wife was named Gquma after the roar of the ocean. Penn notes that her childhood name was Bess, and she may have been about seven years old when she was castaway from an earlier shipwreck. I have wondered about this clan of amaTshomane and the other of amaMolo to which my great-ancestor Minna belonged. *Molo* is to greet in the Mpondo language. The amaTshomane and amaMolo join the worlds of there and here. They collapse timeplace, water, and land. While

Penn cautions against romanticizing the reception of the castaways among their Mpondo hosts, I elect to lean into this relation. For as exasperating as it may have been, it also points to possibilities that emerge when we find common ground and new footing (Macharia 2020; King 2019). It requires a means of seeing beyond the present and looking askance through *ukwakumkanya*. What leap of faith and taboos did chief Sango break to marry Gquma, a stranger from the ocean? And the enslaved girl Minna of the amaMolo from whom I descend? Did the other unnamed Mpondo women and men who married castaways have to face down disapproving communities? Were my paternal great-ancestor—the enslaved and free Minna—and my great-grandmother Olpinah such errant women who leaped into the breach much like Nongqawuse had before? The seizing of the Fanonian breach is Mpondo theory in practice. It relies on a logic that is out of step with modernity and is guided by being in relation. Studying the genetics of the consequences of this breach in Mpondoland, David de Veredicis (2016) found that up to 69.86 percent of his male sample contained a single line of descent to European and Eurasian ancestors in their DNA. To attend closely is to see the sociality of the Mpondo people and their constitution through relation.

Because feminist theorists insist on a focus on the borderlands, I tarry at the ocean. The seashore creates an opening. A sliver to relatedness. I read this opening as the opportunity to think anew outside the veil of coloniality. Sylvia Tamale, Sylvia Wynter, Aida Hurtado, Gloria Anzaldúa, Grace A. Musila, and Maria Lugones strengthen my conviction for attempting new ways of reading. The opening provided by the borderlands of the tumultuous ocean stages possibilities for newness and new ways of attending to old things. The shoreline is a place of surprise where one may look up and see something bobbing on the water or washed ashore from somewhere else. Rinaldo Walcott (2021a, 2) observes that tides and waves take from the shore to the sea "but importantly, tides and waves, leave elements behind as well, resulting in new and different formations." My project is a preoccupation with what is left behind on the shore. On yet another trip, I went to the ocean in search of this opening. The Msikaba River empties itself into the sea in one of the deepest estuaries in South Africa. Further inland, the Ntafufu River passes by the villages of Lusikisiki and feeds the Msikaba River. In turn, smaller rivers and streams fill the Ntafufu River. It is to these rivers and streams that people and healers go to commune with ancestors. At the deep meeting place of the Msikaba and the Indian Ocean where at least two recorded shipwrecks occurred, I imagined that the ancestors witnessed the arrival. Msikaba and Lambasi beaches are places where the sunken remains of the shipwreck play a haunting tune in the wind. The earliest shipwreck recorded on the Mpondoland coastline was a Portuguese ship, the *São Bento*. This shipwreck predates the *Grosvenor* by over two centuries. The *São Bento* and *Grosvenor* wrecks occurred about eight kilometers apart. A range of cannons, export objects produced in India, and a gold coin found at the site engraved with the name of John III King of Portugal and the Algarve suggest that the ship was wrecked at the mouth of the Msikaba River in April 1554.[21] There is evidence that, like shipwrecks that would follow, the *São Bento* had survivors who went ashore. According to Chris Auret and Tim Maggs (1982), the survivors walked along the coast and were eventually rescued in Delagoa Bay in what is now known as Mozambique. George McCall Theal (1902) observes that the Bantu encountered by the Portuguese castaways owned goats and that these "kaffirs" appeared to be of mixed Hottentot and Bantu blood.[22] I imagine their journey, who they met along the way, and the trace that they left behind on the Mpondoland coastline. What does the trace of these wrecks mean for Mpondo theory?

While the *Grosvenor* shipwreck was neither the first nor the last, it occupies a place of compulsive return laden with emotional investments. Figures 1.1. and 1.2 are excavation sites where people have sought to reach the ship ruins and their rumored treasures. Michael Titlestad and Mike Kissack (2005) note that white writing has saturated the *Grosvenor* with ideological meanings assembled around white alienation. For novelist Sheila Fugard (2002), the *Grosvenor* has come to symbolize white arrival. Their crash onto a rugged, uninviting Mpondoland shore. Permanent castaways. In their analysis of Fugard's novel *The Castaway*, Titlestad and Kissack (2005, 139) describe being a castaway as the "only abiding ontological condition of the settler." The disoriented settler and his purgatorial fate. Far away from empire among wary Mpondo savages whom he seeks to tame. At the moment of the crash, though, the power is inverted. The castaway is disoriented, and the Mpondo is surefooted on her land. But the presence of the other is disorienting. The imagined rape of white women survivors fuels part of the compulsive return to the *Grosvenor* wreck. This rape narrative has been repeated over the years without any evidence in the narratives of actual survivors (Titlestad 2008). Penn (2004) observes that the notoriety of this ship was based on the relatively high number of white women who had been on board. For the English, since survival meant rape, anxiety about the women's survival was reportedly worse than fears about their death. Reporting in England, the *Morning Chronicle* (August 6, 1783) observed: "The

1.1 Site of *Grosvenor* shipwreck at Lambasi Bay, Lusikisiki.

1.2 Site of *Grosvenor* shipwreck at Lambasi Bay, Lusikisiki.

situation of the female passengers who were on board the *Grosvenor* Indiaman, must be the most dreadful that imagination can form, or humanity feel for. The ship was lost upon the coast of the Caffres, a country inhabited by the most barbarous and monstrous of the human species. By these Hottentots, they were dragged up into the interior parts of the country, for the purpose of the vilest brutish prostitution, and had the misfortune to see those friends, who were their fellow passengers, sacrificed in their defense" (cited in Taylor 2004, 181). The colonial rape nightmare is also an unconscious guilt at the rape and plunder of the colonial project. The lives of those found on the shore are never engaged with in the verdant literary inheritance that the *Grosvenor* shipwreck has spawned. Except as rapists and cannibals. However, the diaries of those who survived the shipwreck and told their stories to Alexander Dalrymple contradict the colonial terror: "I cannot therefore in my own mind doubt, that many lives may yet be preserved amongst the natives, as they treated the individuals that fell singly amongst them, rather with kindness than brutality, although it was natural to expect that so large a body of Europeans would raise apprehensions; and fear always produces hostility."[23] Martin (1837) similarly observed the kindness and civility of the people on the Caffre Coast toward shipwrecked seamen. Wilson (1959) reads the journals of castaways who made their way up the coastline to Mozambique. She notes that the castaways describe the hospitality of the local community: "Here lived an old man with his sons and grandsons, who with great surprise and joy received our people, and brought them gourds full of milk" (170). It was therefore possible for white sojourners who stumbled onto the shore to become Mpondo if they decided to stay.

Despite the ample record of kindness, the tale of imagined savagery maintains the tropes of the "caffre coast" that survive today. I want to be the Mpondo native, the "caffre" who was present to witness the shipwreck, and indeed, previous and later wrecks. I am the descendant of the rocky outcrop of the river mouth entering the sea. To be Mpondo is to exist in the confluence of currents. The meeting of cultures. I am the Mpondo witnessing the arrival while simultaneously being one of those on the troubled ship. In reading the large corpus of work on the castaways, I am struck by the scant regard for the Mpondo who certainly witnessed the shipwrecks and granted passage to those who walked through their communities and land. They are again reduced to background. Writing some time after the shipwrecks, Grant Millar describes the Mpondo in 1908: "They are not on average, very tall; and, although not as fine a race as the Zulus, they are stoutly and sturdily built. The great majority of them are known as 'Red Kaffirs' from their custom of smearing their bodies and hair with red ochre. They might equally be called 'blanket,' as a blanket hung from the shoulders is the only garment they effect" (380). I draw a distinction between the shipwreck survivor who integrates with the local community and the one who joins the insular port-based colonial settler community. I am a product of the former. The ochre people. The "Red Kaffirs." There is a lesson here on Wynter's relational human versus Man. My existence means that the Mpondo people welcomed some of the strangers who crashed onto their shores. Those who forsook the root identity and embraced Glissant's errantry, lived and became a part of a Mpondo narrative of reciprocity. Those who loved Mpondo people and learned to speak isiMpondo. The women who Van Reenen's diary reported as refusing to return to England already had Mpondo children and were invested in the outcome of the season's crops. These women are not unlike my mother, who, despite the crime and deprivation, refuses to go and live elsewhere. She too is invested in the season's crops.

If white people who have become South Africans return to the *Grosvenor* with longing and regret, how do black people whose existence is also implicated in the wreck think of the arrival? Koleka Putuma's poem that opens this chapter clearly regrets the wreck of the ships. "If this land was really yours, then resurrect the bones of the colonisers and use them as a compass" (2017, 97). In this challenge, she contends that the colonizers' ancestors are not to be found in Africa. For black people, the arrival of settlers marks dispossession of land. It ushers in colonization and apartheid. But the castaways who remained to be in relation to the Mpondo leave a different legacy. To be clear, this is not always a positive legacy. It does however provide us a queer opening for reimagining ourselves.

In 2019, I returned to the Lambasi community and shoreline to see what a black vantage point would reveal. I did this deliberately, cognizant of the fact that the view of indigenous communities has been obscured by colonial suppression and dispossession. Having read Michael Marker (2018, 462), I was aware that "the power of the experience of being in the place where the story exists" is a transformative methodology and pedagogy. Christina Sharpe (2016) refers to this as knowing the ground one stands on. I returned to the beach which is also the site of the shipwreck and white anxiety. But on this trip, I was in search of local beauty and a black vantage point. This is also to say, I assumed the lens of *ukwakumkanya*. To see past the knowledge of our barbarism—to encounter our own beauty, to commune with the natural world. To attend in *ukwakumkanya*'s frequential register, I watched for what is revealed when we keep still. How does landscape vibrate sonically (Campt 2019)? The shoreline was startling. I held my breath several times. The survival of natural beauty is a testament to our own survival. The stubborn rock face is a reflection of the impervious look of the old woman who squints at the tourists who visit the coast. This beauty points to the failure of colonialism. I walked over to the rocks in search of the trace of the shipwreck, but there is nothing left. The waves gush over the rocks and then retreat to the sea. An endless ebb and flow that once crashed with the arrival of lost ships. The wind was still on my first visit, but it was howling in a black sonic register when I returned two days later. The sand moved like a swarm of bees and whipped against my legs with a wrathful energy. It gathered the waves into a fury. Further up, the thick foliage was unmoved by the wind. I looked at the rocky outcrop and imagined how a passing ship would cope against the fury of this wind. In my mind's eye, I saw the startled castaways stumble onto the sand. I looked up into the hill that cast its watchful shadow over the shore. I wondered if the Mpondo people watched the arrival and what they must have thought of the bedraggled castaways. I wondered at this meeting between my ancestors—those from the water and those on the shore. Reading the frequency of the raging water, I witnessed the silent standoff of those from here and there. Standing at the meeting place recalled King's shoal—a shifting space that requires a new footing and calls on new forms of relation. Remarking on the disturbance of shoaling, King (2019, 4) notes that a shoal requires "different chords of embodied rhythms, and new conceptual tools to navigate its terrain." The castaways who crashed ashore had to find new ways of moving. The white castaways were compelled to change from a gait of mastery to uncertainty, the enslaved castaways were buoyed by the rhythms of freedom, and amaMpondo had to reorient themselves to think of and make room for the other in their midst. In the raging wind, it struck me anew that amaMpondo have long adopted a sociality that makes room. Conceptually, this enables us to shift in place and broaden our relational and theoretical frames.

The people of the sea continue to live in relation to the ocean. On the desolate beach, I came across a father teaching his young son to prepare bait. The Wild Coast is not a capitalist shoreline. It refuses domestication and will not be tamed. The roads are impenetrable. One must stop to ask for directions. In the rainy season, the mud ensnares the motor vehicle, and one must rely on local people to push and guide the vehicle out of the tempestuous coast. The local communities have resisted the highway that they fear will kill relationality.[24] They do not want the supremacy of nature to be overtaken by the capitalist toll-based highway. But things lie in a balance. Government favors the construction of a highway. In my insistence on focusing on beauty, I wanted to appreciate the resistance that this coastline represents. I sat on a smooth rock and listened to the roar of the ocean. It was raining and the water was an angry gray. The power of the ocean and the land struck me anew, and I was certain that this ocean will outlast any highway. It has outlived colonialism, and the shipwrecks have been submerged under water. The salty spray competes with the musty smell of the rock and the thousands of plants and animals that make their life in this ecosystem. A shepherd in an oversized yellow raincoat walked across the estuary. His legs pushed against the confluence of the fresh water from the river and the salt water from the ocean. The meeting place between the castaway and the watching amaMpondo. I wondered how the young shepherd perceives this coastline. Does he look up from the deserted beach and marvel at the natural beauty, or is the splendor only legible to tourists? Is the crash of the shipwreck foundational in his mind, or does his communal narrative stretch back over a longer history that defies white arrival? What freedom fires memories before whiteness? What does one see when the view is unencumbered by whiteness? During my stay at the beach, an old woman told me that I look like her son. She enquired after my surname. My response proved her hunch. She broke into a smile and told me that her mother also had an English last name. The ocean roared and beckoned us, and we looked at it as we talked. She reported that there were many descendants of Mpondo and white people in Mpondoland while she was growing up. Practically every community had them. Many moved to the cities over time. "Where were they from?" I asked. "Here and the ships. It was a long time ago and I do not know the details, but the old people told us that when the people who survived the shipwreck moved inland, there was some mixing. That is how many of us came about and this is why some of us have these surnames." She recalled that her father was from farther inland, but when he met her mother at the beach, he moved here. She laughed at the power of her mother's beauty. I laughed along with her because this story confirms the beauty of this place. In the wake of the ships are not only scenes of subjection because beauty proliferates here long after the ships were submerged in the riotous ocean.

A Time before Whiteness

Is it possible to reach out to a time before whiteness? Like Saidiya Hartman (2008) recognizes her failure to capture the experience of enslavement, I too must concede defeat in this exercise. I reach the ends of the limits of narrative, and I must strain against the archive and the memories of those I speak to. If my being is a consequence of the confluence of Mpondo, Khoekhoe, San, white, and enslaved people who settled on the seashore, is it possible to go to a period before? If the written form came with the colonizing missionaries, what trace beyond the written form can take me to before the arrival? Propelled by these questions, I went to the Drakensburg mountain range where the Khoekhoe and San sought refuge from persecution on the plains. This is the place where they left their most famous trace—their carvings and drawings on the rock face of the mountains.[25] A trace for posterity. An ancient graffiti. The language of the forsaken who nevertheless claim space to assert that they too once lived. This was a self-insistence into being, even when the census insisted that they were "kaffirs." None beings. Of course, the San cannot be found wandering across the ridges of the mountain range. I have certainly not seen them on my visits to the Drakensburg. Nevertheless, I have sat in the stillness of a winter afternoon and wondered. With my hands and eyes in the posture of *ukwakumkanya*, I have stared at the rock face and contemplated what living here must have meant to my San ancestors. I have listened to the registers of the evening wind for a trace of their music. And then I have wandered through the streets of Kokstad where the Griqua, the descendants of the San people, live. Before they became the stereotype for alcoholism, I imagined them as a people with pride as they negotiated treaties to live side by side with various Xhosa tribes in the changing landscape of the precolonial coastline. I remembered the fraternal relationship with Mpondo chief Mqikela. I have walked the streets of Cape Town contemplating a time when the Khoekhoe roamed the avenues with a sense of proprietorship over their land before the Dutch wrenched it away from them. At the slave museum, my imaginative resources failed me. The history of colonialism is one of unequal relation to the other. A crash. However, following Marker (2018, 461), despite the apparent dead end, it is "essential to visit these meaning-soaked sites on the landscape in order to tune one's consciousness to versions of time and space that bring the mythic sense of being into contemplation." Standing at the site of history and feeling the wind on my face as the Khoekhoe did before me, I am able to tune into the frequency of the sensorial. In the posture of *ukwakumkanya*, my hand just above my eyes, I channel a queer archive that evades whiteness.

To the east, south, and west, South Africa is nestled between two oceans—the Indian and Atlantic Oceans. The ships that plied their trade in slavery docked on various parts of the upper east and west coasts of the continent where they traded in human cargo. They docked in Cape Town where some of this cargo was sold. Baderoon (2009, 95) evocatively describes these oceans: "Slavery binds these two bodies of water, but the oceans are also a connecting tissue to memories of a life before and outside of slavery." Like we have to read the rock face where the Khoekhoe documented their lives before conquest, we have to read the ocean as a place that bears our histories both within and outside enslavement and colonialism. We have to recognize the power of the natural world in ordering our lives across these time scales. The story of an Eastern Cape prophetess enables us to think about the ordering power of the spiritual and natural environment in imaginaries of black freedom. Perhaps a Mpondo theory of freedom. The orphaned prophetess was Nongqawuse.[26] She was raised by her uncle where the Gxarha River empties into the Indian Ocean. There are varying accounts for the reasons behind Nongqawuse's prophecy that precipitated the great cattle killing of the mid-1800s. Some attribute it to collaboration between the king, her uncle, and white settlers.[27] Meg Samuelson (2005) reminds us that women are either seen as leaky or as empty vessels, unable to hold a historical narrative on their own without being translated through men. Alice Lakwena of Uganda gained great power by attributing her power to the Holy Spirit (Behrend 1999). This enabled her to lead the massive Holy Spirit Movement that almost toppled the government of Uganda. Similarly, Nongqawuse's believability and legibility are attributable to the supernatural. I am less interested in who may have or did not influence Nongqawuse than I am invested in how the prophecy found expression in the will of the people. The version that derives from the sea as told by Gemma Pitcher (2020) and that of Zakes Mda (2000) is instructive. According to this account, while at the river mouth by the sea near her home, Nongqawuse had a vision of her ancestors, who told her to instruct the Xhosa people to kill their cattle and destroy their crops in preparation for a season of plenty. This vision seeks to restore life to what it was before colonial incursions. Jennifer Wenzel (2009) terms this as anticolonial and acolonial vision that is informed by a radical temporality operating beyond the constraints of linear narratives. In this return to precolonial life, Nongqawuse's ancestors would provide healthy cattle in abundance. In the prophecy, the dead would rise and emerge from the sea and return the Xhosa people to their former glory. This period of wealth and health harkened to a time before the arrival of the white man with diseased cattle which contaminated Xhosa cattle. These precolonial longings are affective and political. They long for a time of black agency before the neurosis and anxiety occasioned by the white arrival. Black women's dreams have always been expansive, and their ability to imagine freedom from the most constrained spaces is evident across black literature.[28] Black women's dreams explode and wreak havoc across different orders of subjugation. Nongqawuse's prophecy is an example of the possibilities of black women's imaginaries set free. As an attribute of Mpondo theory, it is a way of theorizing from constrained spaces. While Nongqawuse's prophecy did not wholly come to pass, the fecundity of this failure generated new conditions of possibility.

Baderoon's (2009) evocation of oceanic possibilities is handy for enabling us to imagine a time before slavery. Nongqawuse's prophecy evokes the sea as both prison and freedom. She believed that the ancestors resided in the ocean. The sea harbors her ancestors just as Sharpe's (2016) ocean is the place where the African enslaved lie on a restless watery deathbed. Based on her vision, Nongqawuse instructed the people to kill all their cattle and destroy crops as a precondition for the attainment of freedom from colonial oppression. While the mass killing of cattle led to great starvation resulting in many deaths, it is an example of a woman-led resistance against colonial subjugation where a mass movement of people sacrificed their livelihood for the ideal of freedom. My reading of the cattle killings is that it was a major step in challenging patriarchy given the central role played by cattle in upholding patriarchal cultural practices such as lobola. This custom requires the man's family to compensate that of the woman with cattle and money in exchange for marriage and relation. If his cattle represent the wealth of an African man, then the consequences of Nongqawuse's prophecy struck a blow at the material representation of male power. Even if only in the wake of the great cattle killing, for a period, there would have to be a renegotiation of the terms of relation and the balance of power. As a leap into the breach of patriarchy and colonialism, what possibilities did Nongqawuse's experiment unleash for young women? In her deployment of *ukwakumkanya*, what did freedom look like? Looking past the devastation of hunger and starvation, what energy emits from the ruins and how might *ukwakumkanya* assist us in reading the reanimation of this vitality in the present temporal fold? Are the revolts that mark

Eastern Cape history legacies of this revolt against settler annexation? Of interest here are the possibilities of sight—hind and fore—enabled by the sea spirits. The sea spirits provide a lens that I suggest can assist us to think about life before the arrival and to contemplate its wake in the present. The conception of sea spirits is useful for thinking through resistance to colonial devastation. In the period of Nongqawuse's prophecy, there was a lot of talk of white settlers being swept into the sea when the ancestors emerged from the Indian Ocean. Wenzel reports that according to the prophecy, the Xhosa would be bulletproof against the guns of white settlers.[29] Since the seashore is the place where the imperialist first set foot, it is also through the sea that they would depart. Nongqawuse was herself imprisoned by the British settlers on Robben Island in the Atlantic Ocean for her role in the deaths of her people in the wake of the starvation that followed the cattle killings. This island has become known as the island to which Mandela and his male peers were banished, but before that, as a leper colony, it had long housed riotous bodies including those of women such as Nongqawuse.[30] It is from there that deviant queers, including the enslaved, lepers, and political activists, have looked across the sea to the land of their birth.[31] Nongqawuse was sent to a watery prison. But enclosures have not succeeded in taming black dreams. The island of the waywardly queer—lepers, dangerous prophets and seers, and political dreamers is now a monument to the possibilities of freedom. The desolate white sands of the island and the cold waters of the Atlantic once held dreams that vibrated beyond the island.

Bhekizizwe Peterson urges us to think of Africa as a place before colonialism.[32] Similarly, Lugones (2007) invites us to think of the human outside of a colonial history that gives us tools of analysis that are saturated with coloniality. History did not begin with the disturbance of the sea and the docking of the ships. In South Africa, black writing begins in earnest in the late seventeenth century. Tiyo Soga, D. D. T. Jabavu, and Sol Plaatje are some of the earliest chroniclers of black life through their newspapers and books. This was at least two centuries after the initial colonial arrival. Their work therefore does not give us insight into the precolonial world. It is through their lamentations of the ills of colonial administrators that we learn about how things used to be. If black writing does not reach as far back as the precolonial, we are left with museums and archives to help us to look backward. Patricia Davison (1998), however, cautions that museums, colonial adventurers, and administrators, whose work is in the archive, present early conceptions of Africa as a mirror of their own power and superiority. Thus the oldest museum in the region, the South African Museum, presents a visual rhetoric that associates the Khoekhoe and the San with nature. Galleries of fossils, birds, and fish evince this. The animalization of the precolonial is in keeping with the logic of the Chain of Being. For Davison, then, memory is deliberately made in the image of those who document history. In her analysis of the display of imagined Khoekhoe and San bodies at the South African Museum, she notes: "The problem is not that human beings are grouped with natural history but that only ethnographic 'others' are categorized in this way" (1998, 145). The function of memory making in the postcolony is therefore a practice in creating binaries. The black all-evil other that is at one with nature and the benevolent white above nature. To work with the limits of the archive, we have to read against its grain. This reading requires imagination and curiosity that goes beyond the archive. I begin with the assumption that all indigenous communities always valued liberty and lived in relation to the land (Simpson 2017). I read anything else in the archive against this view. I imagine the aspirations of the Khoekhoe and Nongqawuse to flow from the love of the land and freedom. When I see how the Mpondo struggle to maintain their relationship to the land, I imagine that they honor their Khoekhoe and San ancestors.

Conclusion: Becoming Mpondo

In this chapter, I have sought to think through the meaning of living in relation within the confluence of multiple currents. The chapter theoretically sutures indigenous Khoekhoe, San, and Mpondo people into a single black indigenous body. In the estuary and the site of the shoal that wrecked ships bearing white people and enslaved Asians and Africans, we find new conceptual tools to conceive of relation. A coming together of the here and there on the terms of the poetics of this place. By attending askance through the wreckage and traces of history from the vast deathscape of Mpondoland, both in the folds of its surface and its depths, I attempted to demonstrate a riotous method for decentering and exploding the monohuman. My aim has not been to valorize hybrid identities but to demonstrate that purity is a myth even in rural outposts. In this case, Mpondo theory is about assembling, absorbing, relating, and buoyancy. It is a fluidity that does not concede itself. It is rooted firmly in place—on the tumultuous ocean shoals and plunging gorges of Mpondoland. At the site of the wreck of the ship against the rock face of the Wild Coast are possibilities that have hitherto not been fully explored. Born of the wreck is a community that sutures lineages and offers new ways of being. My San and Khoekhoe ancestors who sheltered in the rocky outcrops of the mountains and sheer gorges forged community with my Mpondo ancestors. In the aftermath we are all unsettled and compelled to make conceptual room for the other needing shelter in blackness. We are unmoored, relational, decentered, and continuous with the natural world and, as I will demonstrate in coming chapters, spirits.

I have painted a portrait of ancestries forged in the tributary and in the confluence of the Mpondo, the San, the Khoekhoe, the European, and the enslaved castaway who became Mpondo. In the dialectics of the tide. The sea is a place of horror and possibility. I am struck by the openness of Mpondo identity. It is not a proud monument of greatness. It is as open as the sea. But like the ocean, the entry and exit can be violent. Being Mpondo is not contingent on narrowly conceived categories. It requires relationality. This is achieved through language and becoming Mpondo. For those who found themselves marooned on the coast or driven by invading settlers in the south, this meant subjecting the self to the ways of those who lived there. Integrating. In emaMpondweni, the many children that came from the unions between the Mpondo and those who arrived are Mpondo. Open identities offer us pathways to being. Having lived elsewhere, I am struck by how closed off communities of whiteness can be. They repel black people. They enslave. They bestow second-class citizenship. They maim limbs, strip flesh, break bones, and debilitate. In Mpondo communities, white people who came and lived in Mpondoland stumbled off the broken ships bedraggled, tired, and sore. But they were seen and given space to eke out a living among us. The enslaved castaways from whom I descend found a firm footing and grabbed their freedom on the Mpondo shoals. All those who stayed behind and in relation learned to speak isiMpondo and to love their hosts. This is how to become black. This is an alternative history to the grand myths of this place. For all the pulverization from outside, the Mpondo cling to their decentered personhood.

This chapter has insisted on reestablishing relation even when colonialism and deracination sought to make us forget textures of relation that predated colonial incursion. It reimagined the kinds of relation that are repressed by binary languages of the present. Like Macharia (2020), the chapter wondered what sutures we might create to knit and stick the forgotten seams of relation. It thus creates relation intentionally and with care to repair what has been destroyed. Although we cannot return to earlier states, we can search for joy and desire in shared spaces. We nurture relation through communal ritual, tending to shared fruit groves and harvests, and waiting under a tree in the hope of creating conversation with passersby. We create relation by exercising curiosity about those stranded on the shoals and retreating into the hills.

2 FORTIFYING RIVERS

Awu! The finest of Africa was busy dying!
The ship couldn't carry its precious cargo,
It was echoing into the inner circles,
Their brave blood faced the King of Kings.
Their deaths had a purpose for all of us
How I wish I could be with them,
How I wish I could stand with them on resurrection day,
How I wish I could sparkle with them like the morning star.
Let it be so!

S. E. K. MQHAYI, "THE SINKING OF THE *MENDI*" (2017)

Mpondo theory conceives of the river as contiguous with the body, ancestral realm, and personhood. It connects the corporeal and the spiritual. It demonstrates the ecological urgency for decentering the human.[1] This chapter explicates water masses and the river in particular as a dimension of Mpondo theory. Continuing the concerns of *Riotous Deathscapes*, I write with a curiosity about what can emerge when the analytical core is the ignored, the putative backwater. Three events are centered in this chapter. The first is the sinking of the ss *Mendi* in 1917, the second is the story of the prophetess Nontetha Nkwenkwe, who died in detention in 1935, and the third is the Mpondo rebellion of the 1950s that culminated in the Mpondo revolt of 1960. I observe the recent history of subsequent revolts as ripples emerging out of the Mpondo revolt but also from received narratives of ancestral riot and refusal. The ripples include the Gum Tree Rebellion, the Marikana massacre, and the protracted battle against sand dune mining of the Wild Coast. I observe how villagers fortify themselves by imbibing the natural world into their bodies in the wake of communal trauma. This cleansing resists maladies such as melancholia, reorients us to the natural world, and locates us queerly in relation to normative outlooks. Through *ukwakumkanya* as method, I imbue historical events with a queer sociality to point to new conceptual possibilities and to enliven flattened histories. The chapter is about the many ways that the people of Mpondoland resist kaffirization. This resistance is set against the cylindrical epiphenomenal temporality of neoliberal destruction of black life and the overarching thread of the violence of capital. These violences occur—first through the destruction of an indigenous economy to fuel the labor needs of mining, then the contemporary deepening of economic precarity amidst joblessness, poor education, and unlivable wages. This is enfolded in the pressure to consume in a context where consumption power has come to define full citizenship. AmaMpondo have died resisting the neoliberal catastrophe that seeks to separate them from indigenous land. As Mqhayi's poem suggests, even in death there is honor. The Mpondo people have always died with the knowledge that life carries on after death. For them, even death is resistance. Dying is a form of living Mpondo theory.

For this chapter, my data are a reading of the archive in relation to interviews with protagonists in Mpondoland. I observe that all of these related forms of riotousness within the same community dispel any notions of passivity. They lend nuance and complexity to black death and life. But I also demonstrate that there is loss in resistance. The consequences of waves of loss are communal mourning. After great trauma, communal fortification rituals enable shared understandings of events and craft a communal defense against future invasion. I demonstrate how protective rites are part of the fabric of Mpondo theory. The relationality at the center of community rituals is central to the explication of this theory. Since I am grounded in place, my focus is on Mpondoland. However, because Mpondo theory radiates outward with relational intent, the point is always more than a parochial way of attending.

Cleansing and Fortifying: A Ritual Pause

Following a spectacular outbreak of the structural violence that is always simmering beneath the surface—trauma through death, injury, invasion, and anguish—the village men convene in a circle to talk about the trauma. Each detail is worked through sequentially. What happened, who was there, when, how? Understanding is emphasized over blame. But it is robust. Witnesses might also be called. There is a hierarchy here among the men. The appointed community leaders take charge, but everyone has a turn. The gathering or *isikade* will take a few days if it has to. It is here that the gathered men decide that the exposure to violence and death warrants a traditional intervention. A cleansing ceremony. Like their forebears, they believe that when the world inundates the village with stressors, cleansing through channeling ancestors is necessary. And so, the healers are called in to guide the process.

The men gather at the river at midnight. The healers take them through their paces for a few hours until dawn's tentacles bring hints of light to the hills. The fortunes must change. Evil must be expelled and the village must know peace once more. Bitter, dark potions. Licking powders. Grimaces. Razor blades make precise incisions. In the scalp. Lightly. The dark powder is inserted in the incisions. The neck receives two light cuts, shoulders, and arms. Downward strokes. Opening the body to spirits and relation. And then suturing the breaches with medicinal powders of the natural world carried down through ancestral wisdoms.[2] Where the chest meets the neck. Bloodless. The men are fortified in much the same way that the San ancestors rubbed potions into cuts on the body.[3] But before this, the evil must be exorcised. Mixtures must be imbibed. Strong herbs that sear the mouth and burn their way into the stomach. Tasteless herbs to soothe. From mouth to mouth the bottles are passed under the watchful eyes of the healer who sees in the darkness. "Swallow," he urges. "More," he nudges with his feathered spear. The dosages are larger for those who were directly impacted by the violence. Those who were there, whose hands killed, and whose eyes bore witness. He pokes at them with his spear and expects them to shield themselves with sticks. Their knuckles are bruised and lacerated because strengthening means self-defense. While waiting for the fortification to take effect, a low hum begins and it is nursed into a chant, growing into rhythmic clapping, the bass overwhelming the fragile soprano. Mpondo blues. The moon catches night-black skin and bounces off bare torsos. At first, the two healers dance alone, but they are joined by the cousins from the valley. The pace increases and legs lift high. The song slows and the leg movements are replaced by chest heaves and Mpondo shakes. Sticks poking the Transkei night sky. Poking holes into the moon. The dancers are joined by the older men who sway more gently to nurse their aching legs. Two men are retching by the riverbank. The healers pay them no heed. The group of retching men grows and with it the increase in the volume of the singing. When half the men are retching, one of the healers joins them and chants, exhorting the evil to depart. To flow away with the river water. "Take it all out," he urges those bent over. Ancestors are beckoned to look over the village.

Prohibitions must be adhered to. There is to be no bathing. To enhance their efficacy, the medicines must linger on the body. Women must be kept at bay. No sex. No touching. If food is prepared by women, it must be placed on the table and then taken. The mood is somber. Body odor makes everyone irritable. Children long for playful fathers. Sleep is for the weak. Three days later, when the Mpondo moon is high, the men convene at the river again. A lesson on bravery is given. A demonstration on applying protective remedies against police, lightning, and murderers is held. "A bullet does not penetrate the flesh of a brave warrior who has applied these herbs. Don't run away. Do not expose your back." And then the bathing commences. Like their ancestors before them, the men wade in the water and the pungent medicines are washed in the river. They emerge with a feeling of rebellion and invincibility coursing through their veins. This is part of the logic of Mpondo theory—the body can be fortified by ancestral ritual and spirit in order to survive the material world.

Decades earlier, at Ngquza Hill, medicine and fortification abounded.[4] I dwell on the Mpondo revolt of 1960 in order to think about the body in relation to resistance, fortification, and death in the ongoing past. This revolt is also known as the Kongo. In 1960, J. Fenwick, the Bantu Affairs Commissioner of Lusikisiki, asked for a state of emergency to be declared in the region as he needed to curtail the chaos of the advancing Kongo: "It is impossible to administer it [Lusikisiki] under present circumstances and the position is rapidly deteriorating. . . . I recommend therefore that the district be proclaimed in order to (a) restrict rumors . . . (b) to enable those [such] as Segwebo and the witchdoctor Bhambalepe Mbhe to be detained. The latter, together with Segwebe's witch doctor has 'fortified' all those so-called 'warriors' who are taking part in these armed demonstrations; (c) that the disaffected locations be raided on a systematic [basis]."[5] The detention of traditional healers who fortified village insurgents suggests that the apartheid state was threatened by the ritual fortification of villagers. The fortification of warriors is an old ancestral tradition where indigenous wisdom is appealed to through what indigenous scholar Leanne Betasamosake Simpson (2017, 192) refers to as embodied resurgent practice. She suggests that "the generative and emergent qualities of living in our bodies as political order represent the small and first steps of aligning one's life in the present with visions of an Indigenous future that are radically decoupled from the domination of colonialism and where Indigenous freedom is centered." While fortification is often read as backward superstition, through Simpson we might see it as embodied political practice where we refuse colonial respectability by embracing backwardness and freedom from the tyrannies of modernity and violent orders of capitalism. Bodily fortification was a prominent strategy of resistance during the Kongo revolt. As we will see, it stretches back past the Kongo to the frontier wars against British forces, and forward to Marikana, their in-betweens and futures.[6] Remarking on the Kowie River, Jacklyn Cock (2018) states that because the Xhosa believed in the sacredness of the river, Xhosa warriors purified themselves by bathing in rivers before battle. The fortification and purification river scene that I paint above is an example of a practice that is central to the personhood of Mpondo people. Ritual rites connect the body with other worlds inhabited by the dead. The sociality of the living is intimately tied to the ancestral. Koleka Putuma (2017) captures this in a stanza of her poem "Water":

> We have come to stir the other world here
> We have come to cleanse ourselves here
> We have come to connect our living to the dead here
> Our respect for water is what you have termed fear

To think with the river is to locate myself downstream from indigenous ancestors whose sociality with the river predates my own. The river enfolds me into a long lineage of black and indigenous being. I drink and bathe in ancestral wisdom. I "stir the other world" at the river.

As a part-time but long-time villager, I do not have firsthand experience of the preceding river scene. Those who do have been sworn to secrecy. Part of being a man here is to keep manly things within a closed circle. The sacred is not for consumption. This applies to the sacred rites of circumcision too. When boys evolve into manhood. Even my brothers will not tell me about the goings-on at the river. Since women are excluded from the river ceremony narrated above, they speak more freely than the men. In the same way that the secret is not mine, it is not theirs. The women whom

I speak to inform me that there is a lot of singing. The clash of sticks re-verberates across the valley. One can hear the men from the river. There is medicine. The men come back weary. They stop eating fish and they have other prohibitions. I recognize the similarities to the accounts of spirit possession detailed by Luvuyo Ntombana and Siphiwo Meveni (2015). Here, too, healers and the possessed do not eat fish. It is impure. It is a weak spot. We are returned to the sea. What bitter truth has the sea borne witness to that even its fish are tainted? Do they swim with the ancient devil whose residence is under the waters?

The preceding fortification scene is based on innuendo and given flesh through evocations. What are the ethics of writing about that which re-fuses to be re-presented? And how does one write without feeding into scripts of barbarism and further production of abject subjectivities? I take comfort in Aimé Césaire's (1972) reminder that the barbaric Negro is an invention of the European. As a stereotype myself, I do not know how not to feed stereotypes. But my project here is to illustrate resistance and renewal through unruliness. To figure the river. I know enough of village life to speculate. I know the feeling of a razor blade making incisions in my body in order to make me stronger. To keep evil at bay. When trauma threatened to overwhelm my family, a healer was summoned. Some of my evocations flow from this experience. My arms bear the scars from searing razor blades. I am protected by dark potions used to suture the incisions in my forearms and scalp. When I evade danger in my life, I trace the inci-sions with my fingers. I imagine that villagers whose loved ones died with the 1917 sinking of the ss *Mendi* had to go to the river. I imagine that they too bore the inscriptive incisions that line my arms. I think with Elizabeth Grosz (1994) who sees the body as an inscriptive surface. She notes that with the act of scarification, the subject's body is bound with the social collective. The scars in my flesh are thus not only mine; they also belong to my community—living and dead. They bind our collective vulnerability and signal our mutual and ancestral protection. As political orders, they open us up to relation with each other and close us off to the pathologies of capital and colonialism. They enable our collective resistance to ongoing kaffirization. The body is thus "a public, collective, category, in modes of inclusion or membership" (Grosz 1994, 140). In the moment of inscription, my body becomes social. Here the body is relational in a way that is consis-tent with Mpondo theory. Through my fortified body coursing with ances-tral rivers, I attend with the wisdom of indigenous inspired *ukwakumkanya* and bypass danger and the toxins of capital.

Fortification rituals and related prohibitions are practiced throughout the continent. For example, three accounts that are engaged here give insight into the similarities of these practices across space. Referring to the rebel battles with the state forces in the Democratic Republic of the Congo, in the novel *Tram 83* Fiston Mwanza Mujila observes, "They brought a witch doctor up to the front line with them, and observed all sorts of prohibitions supposed to render them invulnerable: sexual abstinence of unlimited duration, no bathing, or eating beef, or wearing shoes, and so on" (2014, 14). In her spiritual crusade against the Ugandan state, Alice Lakwena instructed her soldiers to observe a host of prohibitions in order to assure their victory (Behrend 1999). She reportedly fought bullets with spells aided by ancestral spirit mediums. Heike Behrend (1999) observes that the Holy Spirit Movement was a magical war. Lakwena faced a rational technical mode of warfare with Holy Spirit Tactics that included magical acts, objects, and substances like water, stones, and oil. She blurred religion, magic, and science. In fights against invading criminals, gangs, and rivals from other villages, my community has similarly resorted to magic, religion, and the science of guns. Sometimes these are combined in ways that relate to the specific local peculiarities facing communities. They however borrow across place as is evident in Henrietta Moore and Todd Sanders's (2001) continent-wide study of occult practices. The peculiarities of practices follow the logic of local theorizations of life. Mpondo theory therefore domesticates practices to inform local logics. The irony is of course that even while many cultures exclude women from ritual practices, historically and in the present, African women like Alice Lakwena and Nongqawuse have been at the forefront of the world of war and ritual prohibitions. Sylvia Tamale (2020) reminds us that these prohibitions crafted in the lived experiences of women are generally ways of maintaining harmony with the natural world and averting exploitative relations with the environment. Since the consumption of fish is a common prohibition, I speculate that it is partially informed by the preservation of fish species.

The body is centered in fortification. Consuming fish is of consequence. Incisions in the skin that are filled with herbs are constitutive of worlds. In this conception, the body is able to protect life, thus exploding the mind-body dualism of Descartes and anthropocentrism. Grosz (1994, 8) notes that Cartesianism "refuses to acknowledge the distinctive complexities of organic bodies, the fact that bodies construct and are in turn constructed by an interior, a physical and a signifying view-point, consciousness or perspective." Therefore, there are limitations in seeing the body and its mis/behavior as simply conditioned or socially constructed. It is more productive to understand it as having a hand in worlding. Harriet Ngubane's (1977) conception of Zulu cosmology in relation to the body is instructive here. The body is neither an instrument nor a tool for capital as labor or for patriarchal ends. It is also not exclusively for communication or signifying some deeper message to the world. This is to say, it is not a transparent medium conveying a knowable interiority to the external world. For Grosz, flattening the role of the body is to deny it agency—"its constitutive role in forming thoughts, feelings, emotions, and psychic representations" (1994, 10). Limiting the body serves to ignore its role as a creative and generative space between the social, the biological, and the natural world of plant and animal life. Bibi Bakare-Yusuf (1999) points to the importance of seeing the body as a corporeal, material, and fleshy presence so that we engage it as more than representational but as feeling. A host of feminist work focusing on bodily transgressions has displaced Darwin's and Descartes's formulation of the body and monohumanism.[7] This work has returned us to the body. Mpondo theory centers the body's fleshiness and sociality. It connects it to other bodies, ancestors, plant life, and the river. For the Mpondo, then, the body is feeling, open, and relational.

The fortified Mpondo body is however also a queer body. It is queerly positioned in relation to the modern body. To be queerly Mpondo is to engage modern norms with a healthy dose of skepticism. At times this may require willfully turning away from these and like Billy-Ray Belcourt (2016b) writes in the context of native studies, embracing the sociality of savagery.[8] For example, fortification is to give up in statecraft, policing, and nationhood. It is to assert an ageless relational independence under the guidance of the dead. While Mpondoland is a blighted deathscape, there are moments of acute freedom in Mpondo life when it turns away from respectability and coloniality. Since the Mpondo people did not have much formal schooling and all its attendant disciplinary strictures that create colonial subjects, we make for bad colonial subjects who fail at modernity. For later generations that have gone to school—albeit, largely inadequate schooling—we adopt the received wisdom of our ancestors who wore their bodies with a studied indifference and confidently spoke their language beyond the hovering presence of settler superintendence. I am often surprised when other Nguni cultures describe isiMpondo as a coarse language and our manner as stubborn. But when I reflect on these attributions, I gain some insight into what they mean. We are queer because we appear not to care—we walk out of step with modernity. Our commitments are to surviving on the land of our ancestors and we are less enamored with a demonstration of fluency in the genres of late capitalism. We fail spectacularly at being modern subjects. But our failure keeps us true and free. In ways that resonate with the embodied resurgent practices of the Nishnaabeg people of Turtle Island, living in our bodies is not difficult since we are always already queerly aligned because we remain close to our indigenous ways of being. When we live in our bodies, we are not making overt political claims, but our indifference to the colonial panopticon has a political effect.[9] This nonchalance frees us from a debilitating double consciousness that Simpson (2017, 192) conceives of as a "politics of distraction" that requires indigenous people to always respond to "the neoliberal politics of the state." Therefore, if amaMpondo are queerly aligned, it is because our very bodily presence is a strange affront to modernity and the neoliberal state. It points not only to the failure of neoliberal politics but to possibilities of living indifferently in the rubble of the devastation while rooted in the knowledge of Mpondo theory and its ancestral certainties. We have the ability to attend askance even in relation to accepted wisdoms of neoliberal development. This in turn emboldens us to say no when capitalism flashes fool's gold in its efforts to separate us from ancestral land. Grounded by the vision of *ukwakumkanya*, we can look past the distractions that are hurled our way. However, as becomes apparent in chapter 5, not all of us are indifferent to capital. Young people in particular often attempt to access its spoils even in the necropolis. But as people who are wholly debilitated, the good life of capital accumulation is impossible for us. We fail while trying even when we turn to occult means. The theme of fortification is taken up in the engagement with the sinking of the ss *Mendi*.

Queer Waters: The Sinking of the SS *Mendi*

If white South African studies is haunted by the sinking of the *Grosvenor*, black South Africans are preoccupied with the ss *Mendi*. What conditions would convince 21,000 black men, including some chiefs and priests, to board ships heading to Europe taking them to the First World War? A world that had spurned them. A war that was not theirs. In 1917, the ss *Mendi* took sail from Cape Town en route to France with 882 on board to join the British troops fighting in the First World War (Grundlingh 2011). Acquiescence to participation in the war effort was tied to the possibilities of freedom, as the black elites believed that the British would, out of gratitude, relax their colonial grip on black people. They would be greatly disappointed. Out of fear that their government allowances would be cut, some chiefs convinced their subjects to enlist. Others were paid for each recruit they were able to convince to enlist (Willan 1978). During a 2017 interview with an old man about the Ngquza Hill revolt of 1960, his narrative took a sudden turn toward how black men were sometimes tricked onto ships and taken off to European wars. "They would gather Mpondo men together with promises of jobs. Instead of driving them to where they promised, the men would find themselves on the coast where they would be bundled onto ships and taken to fight for the British. We fought in foreign wars without any consent." Therefore, the crew on board the *Mendi* may not all have voluntarily participated in the war effort. This echoes forward in time to the sugarcane laborers to whom I refer in chapter 3.[10] Echoes back to the West African coast where others were sold into slavery to service Caribbean and American plantations.

Brian Willan informs us that the men who boarded the ss *Mendi* had been enlisted for noncombatant labor duties. In service of. Cleaning after. Digging for. Laboring. Building roads, docks, quarrying, loading, unloading, forestry. The South African white public and their political representatives had opposed the enlistment of black soldiers for direct combat out of fear they would fight against white men. Knowing that their own privilege was based on racist ideologies, the white public feared that direct combat would suggest equality in status—from animals to human. This would place them on an equal footing with their white European allies (Willan 1978). Sol Plaatje (1982, 282–83) recounts the white anxiety through the following excerpt from the *East Rand Express*: "The empire must uphold the principle that a coloured man must not raise his hand against a white man if there is to be any law or order in either India, Africa, or any part of the Empire where the white man rules over a large concourse of coloured people. In South Africa it will mean that Natives will secure pictures of whites chased by coloured men, and who knows what harm such pictures may do?" This anxiety sought to maintain black people within their assigned frame as subhuman. Against the wishes of most white South Africans, black soldiers were dispatched by the thousands to France. One dispatch was done through the ss *Mendi*, which departed from Cape Town on January 16, 1917, and headed into the frigid Atlantic carrying mostly African cargo as so many ships had done before. After more than a month at sea, on the morning of February 21, 1917, a large cargo ship, the ss *Darro*, traveling at high speed, crashed into the *Mendi*. The damage to the *Mendi* was significant, and the ship rapidly began to sink (Grundlingh 2011). The *Darro* did little to save the drowning men. They watched the men drown in much the same way that the Italian ship *Libra* would do nearly a century later as African immigrants drowned in the Mediterranean. Reporting for the *Guardian*, Ben Quinn (2016) asserts that over 5,000 Africans died in the Mediterranean in 2016 alone. Europeans continue to watch black bodies sink into the oceans. As Christina Sharpe (2016) contends, black bones line the ocean bed. We might connect this line of bones to a long temporality that Rinaldo Walcott (2021b) has conceived of as the "long emancipation"—a thwarting or interdiction of black freedom. I connect the ss *Mendi* to this tradition of long emancipation, a time of unfreedom.

I tarry on the story of the ss *Mendi* in order to think about water masses in relation to black people. Willan (1978, 20) reports that black people who returned alive from the First World War were received with incredulity. With specific reference to Jason Jingoes, a black man, he notes: "The reason for the incredulous welcome given to Jason Jingoes on his return home from France in 1918, so he says, was the 'superstition that no black person could cross the sea and return again.'" But as Putuma (2017) asks, is it superstition to be wary of the sea when it has wrought death, disappearance, and banishment for Africans? What of the common stereotype that black people across the world are generally unable to swim and are afraid of deep waters? When so many of us drown. Walcott (2021a, 64–65) similarly observes that "reverence and fear and sometimes both simultaneously, characterized our relationship to bodies of water, especially the sea."[11] Reflecting on a similar theme, Putuma asserts that "our respect for water is what you have termed fear." Walcott conceives of the black aquatic to think through the ambivalent relationship between black people and bodies of water. For Walcott, bodies of water are foundationally formative of black subjectivity. As death-bound subjects, we are at once killed and birthed in salt water. Those who arrived and those who departed were reborn on arrival and at departures on the shore. As we learn from Ashna Ali, Pumla Gqola, Gabeba Baderoon, Dionne Brand, and Saidiya Hartman, for black people, death comes by the same means—mass drownings and arrival on distant shores to feed the furnaces of racial capitalism. James Carson's (2006) question—when is an ocean not an ocean?—is important for its allusion to the multiple ways that oceanic water masses are understood across many cultures. I do not suggest that the sea is inherently evil or that black people only fear it. I am interested in the potentialities of the ambivalence evoked by water masses. As I illustrate, black sociality is intimately tied to various bodies of water, and some black communities have more proximal relations to water than others. Rather, I point to those who force others into the ocean as cargo meant to serve the interests of capital and white supremacy. South African ports were places of arrival for enslaved people, but once in a while, black people like those who died on the ss *Mendi* or like Sarah Baartman were taken away into the Atlantic Ocean (Baderoon 2009).[12] South Africa was therefore a place of arrival and departure of human cargo. With all the forced movement of black people, too many black bodies languish in the watery depths of the world's oceans. The explanatory frame of those who deal with spirit possessions is that the sea is where the devil resides. It is where the souls or true selves of the possessed are kept against their will. But, as the great river of life, the ocean also cleanses. Waters can be blessed and used to combat evil possessions. Water masses are simultaneously the prisons of historical trauma and keys to making sense of black possession.[13] The duality of ocean waters is queer. Water masses are an important anchor for Mpondo thought on relation and fortification. Meg Samuelson (2013) provides a useful taxonomy of studies of water masses as either metaphor representing suppressed histories and narratives where the ocean comes to stand in for a material presence that is beyond human comprehension or as passages for transportation and movement across spaces. I am interested in water for its capacity to physically transport people across place, to connect us to ancestors and lineages of indigenous knowledges, and its ability to transport us spiritually and metaphorically. Derek Walcott (1986, 364–47) captures this in his poem "The Sea Is History" with his layered reading of the ocean. The first stanza conceives of the ocean as tribal memory—a repository of black, indigenous, and enslaved people's memories—that refuses suppression.

> *Where are your monuments, your battles, martyrs?*
> *Where is your tribal memory? Sirs,*
> *in that grey vault. The sea. The sea*
> *has locked them up. The sea is History.*

To black people whose histories are absent or willfully miswritten in the archive, the ocean is a reliable vault. It remembers that Africans traveled on sea before the advent of nation states (Ali 2020). Through *ukwakumkanya,* I scour the gray vault for our memories. Like Simpson's (2017) conception of Nishnaabeg intelligence, and Tiffany Lethabo King's (2019) black shoals, for me, water masses such as the ocean and river are a theoretical basis for Mpondo life as their layered and diverse meanings unfold over time and place in Mpondo consciousness. Water masses are central for how we see and how we live. Water is a theory method of *ukwakumkanya*. As I have demonstrated, water is essential for fortification and cleansing. It is a means of historicizing and a method of resistance. Its flow and currents disrupt the monohuman and its linear histories and temporalities.

With the preceding account of water in mind, I return to the discussion of the ss *Mendi*. On board the *Mendi* was Reverend Isaac Wauchope Dyobha, the ship chaplain, who is reported to have famously comforted the black men facing imminent death as follows: "Be quiet and calm, my countrymen, for what is taking place now is exactly what you came to do. You are going to die, but that is what you came to do. Brothers, we are drilling the drill of death. I, a Xhosa, say you are all my brothers, Zulus, Swazis, Pondos, Basutos, we die like brothers. We are the sons of Africa. Raise your cries, brothers, for though they made us leave our weapons at our home, our voices are left with our bodies" (Clothier 1987). Reports indicate that the men arose in a death dance, stamped and sang in unison as the ship sank. While the occurrence of this death drill has been questioned, given the many crossings of black people, we must wonder how many slave ships might have had these dances?[14] Or did they die in chains cramped like so many sardines trapped in fishing nets? What cries of encouragement and solidarity in the wake of their capture? If we attend to this oceanic dying with all our frequential registers—*ukwakumkanya*—what is illuminated? The *Mendi* sank with many of those on board, and others leapt into the cold waters. Since it was winter, some are likely to have died of hypothermia. In total, 607 black men, 9 white men, and 33 crew members died (Grundlingh 2011). About 267 were rescued by the *Mendi*'s escorting destroyer. The remains of the *Mendi* lie on the ocean bed of the British Channel, eleven miles south of the Isle of Wight.[15] We recall other deaths through cylindrical epiphenomenal temporality. For Yvette Abrahams (2000), cyclical time eschews linear conceptions of temporality. It is time that is always present. I think of this as cylindrical time—a time bind where the past, present, and future coexist in productive tension. As in a cylinder, there is an echo that could represent the past, the present, but also the future. I use the concept of cylindrical time alongside Michelle Wright's epiphenomenal temporality. She has observed that phenomenological expressions of blackness occur in epiphenomenal temporality, which is a form of the present or now time "through which the past, present, and future are always interpreted" (2015, 4). For her, the now points to the spatiotemporal gap that is inherent in linear progress narratives. The timeless echo is not unlike the poet S. E. K.

Mqhayi's poem "Umkosi Wemidaka" that rings its heroic myth making about the men of the ss *Mendi* across time.[16] Elizabeth Freeman's conception of queer temporalities resonates with cylindrical time in important ways. She contends that nation-states and corporations want to "adjust the pace of living in the places and people they take on: to quicken up and/or synchronize some elements of everyday existence, while offering up other spaces and activities as leisurely . . . thereby repressing alternative strategies of organizing time" (2010, xii). As a feature of Mpondo theory, cylindrical epiphenomenal temporality flows in alternative, discontinuous ways that disrupt socially sanctioned time. Our oral histories collapse temporalities for present purposes. In recalling through cylindrical epiphenomenal temporality, we think of those who did not return from the transatlantic journey and whose graves are the restless icy waters. What of their families every time they look to the sea into which their kin disappeared? Ghanaians, Togolese, Beninese, Senegalese, Guineas, Sierra Leones, Liberians, Nigerians, Angolans, Mozambicans. Sarah Baartman. The black cargo of the ss *Mendi*. To paint the picture of cylindrical epiphenomenal temporality, the sinking of the *Mendi* is important to the Mpondo people. The paramount chief of western Mpondoland had sent two of his sons to battle on Empire's behalf. Both drowned (Hendricks and Peires 2011). This makes the mass deaths of black men part of the Mpondo narrative and etches it into the collective unconscious of those who live now and those to come. Norman Clothier's (1987) conception of black valor is ours too.

What happens when we punctuate black valor by queering it? Does it resist or does it shift to create space and change form? My definition of queer emerges from Mpondo life but also from a wealth of indigenous and black scholarship by theorists like Billy-Ray Belcourt and Keguro Macharia. It gestures to the nonnormative, emergent, incomplete, evolving, spectral, boundless, and therefore that which is inappropriable by the necropolitical state and global capitalism. It is an orientation to desire and capacious pleasure that evades identitarian folds. But it is also a weeping tree, a river that overflows with the tears and terror of those who've been punished for nonnormative ways of being—the differently queered. Queer is a bottomless refuge that heaves with transgressive energy and fatigue. It retreats and spills over. Queer is a sticky word that I grip reproachingly—it scalds my hands. It fails to sit alongside African blackness.[17] But I do not discard the term because as a free-floating signifier, it provides an opening to be being remade and habitable to Mpondo misfits (Belcourt 2016a).[18] Here I follow Macharia's (2019, 2) example of looking askance at the African archive and tuning into the rubbings and frictions—the frottage that momentarily emerges in the archive. Like Macharia, I embrace the erotic as the ground from which to theorize black being. Since queer Africans are exiled into ghostly phantoms by colonial archives and African patriarchs, I experiment with enfolding the differently queered into indigenous blackness. Macharia begins by provocatively refiguring Alex Haley's *Roots* by tarrying on the frictions between the shackled bodies of enslaved Africans on the long transatlantic voyage to the Americas. This forced proximity in the holds of ships with its grindings and gratings, enables Macharia to "figure these violent rubbings and to foreground the bodily histories and sensations that subtend" his arguments in *Frottage*. In revisiting the ss *Mendi* in the days before it sank to the sound of the stamping death drill, I fabulate a black queer sociality in the small spaces of the ship—its passages, cabins, and showers. To attend to occurrences across a century, I rely on *ukwakumkanya* which enables attending to matter across life forms and worlds, to hear ancestors and enter spirit worlds; an openness to be moved by the vibrational charge from the watery grave and the disquiet of the cattle pen. Through *ukwakumkanya*, I imagine differently queered indigenous blackness into being. A Mpondo man who'd found comfort in the embrace of umZulu. A Basotho who'd shared a bunk with a Swati man. A cabin crew who walked loose waisted across the deck. Furtive eyes brimming with desire after more than a month at sea. Versions of this queer sociality already existed in the enclosed single-sex compounds on the mines on the reef but also in quiet open village spaces (Beinart 1991; Breckenridge 1990). Through a fragment in *Return to Goli*, Peter Abrahams (1953, 98) provides a similar landing space for historicizing queer sociality. Describing the loneliness of the mining compound, Abrahams's narrator tells the newly recruited Dladla: "You will turn to it too, my friend Dladla. As the months pass you will hunger. One night you will turn to me and we will do it. You will see." At the end of the exchange, Dladla tells the narrator, "But it is not natural." The narrator responds, "What is natural, Dladla? Tell me that." Omise'eke Tinsley (2008) has similarly fabulated the erotic lives of enslaved women. Beyond pointing to these archival fragments of queer potential, I do not flesh out the queer intimacies that I imagine in *Return to Goli* and on the ss *Mendi*. Following Macharia once more, I stray from the limited theoretical and restricted imaginative utility of sexual identity categories such as lesbian and gay. I bypass bodies scripted in fixed genders and sexual desire. After more than a month at sea, what queer sociality can we trace from the slate-gray deathscape that is the English Channel?

I suggest that water masses operate on a queer frequency. To queer the ss *Mendi* is to create history for today's differently queered black person who searches for a footing in queer baselessness. I offer that the ss *Mendi* can provide a page that holds multiple geographies and histories. On its deck, the men who drilled on that fateful February morning were from a cross section of the black population. All of us can imagine ourselves on deck in the moments before losing an erotic attachment, a comrade and bunkmate. In imagining this way, with hand hovering over the eyes, we alter the social. The oblique deck offers a shacky patch of shared ground between today's and yesterday's queer. It is a mooring to which we can attach queer erotics—black being out of time in order to read our futures through desire. But since queer resists settlement, like the ss *Mendi* in its final moments, the mooring is always temporary. However, the ghostly deck of the sinking ship may just be enough to provide a moment of pause in order to see oneself reflected in the stormy waters of the English Channel. In the account below, I detail yet another iteration of communal loss and queer resistance through the figure of Prophetess Nontetha Nkwenkwe.

Ancestral Revolts: Nontetha Nkwenkwe

I have attempted to illustrate that resistance always reaches back into itself in cylindrical epiphenomenal temporality. Because I am interested in the kinds of new ideas and spaces that are made possible by returning to our pasts, I linger on Nontetha Nkwenkwe. Nontetha's life was punctuated by the sinking of the ss *Mendi*.[19] She would have been forty-two years old when the ship sank in 1917. I arrive at Nontetha's story at this juncture because she represents an important lineage of oppression and resistance and helps shed light on the Mpondo revolt to which I turn next. Nontetha Nkwenkwe was an Eastern Cape–based prophet with a large following. She was born in 1875 in the Eastern Cape and died in 1935 in Weskoppies, a Pretoria-based asylum. Whereas Nongqawuse who came before her was arrested and banished to Robben Island, Nontetha was apprehended on the charge of being crazy and banished to a distant asylum far away from her followers.[20] Powerful black women who live outside of normative values have historically been made crazy as a pretext for limiting their impact (Mudavanhu 2019). Their very means to power is delegitimized by contending epistemologies of personhood. Therí Alyce Pickens (2019) contends blackness and madness generally implicate each other. If blackness is a prerequisite for madness, then gender is a critical addition to this potent mix. Sloan Mahone (2006) shows that the colonial state in East Africa psychologized religious or cultural manifestations of rebellion by seeing them as manic, neurotic, or epileptic in order to suppress real or imagined opposition. Nontetha Nkwenkwe's dreams and visions were used against her to diagnose her with schizophrenia.[21] Robert Edgar and Hilary Sapire (2000, 34) contend that "the primary concern in confining mad Africans thus was less with 'curing' or alleviating their mental pain than with removing them as a source of disturbance to society as a whole."

As a healer, seer, and prophet who had built a great deal of influence, Nontetha Nkwenkwe was regarded as dangerous by colonial authorities. They feared that she was leading an antiwhite millenarian movement. According to Edgar and Sapire (2000), Nontetha's ability to draw large crowds of black gatherings led to white paranoia. This is the same white terror that erupts when black people assemble in the present.[22] In the next chapter, I press on this subject to argue that anxious adolescents within the school environment

2.1 Statue of prophetess Nontetha Nkwenkwe by Gary Horlor.

similarly terrorize those invested in their control and in social order. Nontetha Nkwenkwe was perceived to be promoting the collapse of class differences and conflicts between missionary-educated and uneducated Africans.[23] For a colonial authority that actively promoted disunity among black people, Nontetha's work became a threat. In addition, South African History Online suggests that Nontetha Nkwenkwe was a potent feminist symbol because of the power that she wielded as a woman leader. The church enabled women to articulate their concerns, and their prophetic role to see into other worlds presented the possibility of heightened standing. Consequently, by the 1920s, "Nontetha had gained immense respect in African society, for she was not only a respected seer and herbalist but also a middle-aged and fully initiated woman and household head" (SAHO 2019b). As a nonnormative person, I suggest that Nontetha Nkwenkwe was a queer figure in colonial South Africa. As a woman and black person, she had remarkable convening power. Her strangeness was a power that caught the attention of colonial authorities. Because of what this power signified about the potency of black women, the state was moved to detain her as it had other queer figures before her. In her case, we might read "schizophrenia" as a queer power of creating multiple worlds of fugitive freedom.

Following her detention, efforts by her followers to free her were unsuccessful and she died in the asylum. During her incarceration she prophesied to fellow inmates and after her death, her church has endured. It is still active as the Church of Prophetess Nontetha (Edgar and Sapire 2000). Through the frequential registers of *ukwakumkanya*, we can see the church as both a mournful congregation and a victorious one. Nontetha and similar prophets are long dead, but people continue to mournfully congregate at their houses hoping to be fortified and healed by their undying spirit.[24] Her statue in King William's Town calls on people to continue to congregate about her (figure 2.1). She is like others who defied death. She is reputed to have died and come back to life. Nontetha Nkwenkwe lives on as a force for women's leadership in generally patriarchal religious spaces. Like Nongqawuse, her life and death are potent symbols of black women's utopian spirit worlds.[25] These worlds enable possibilities unconstrained by patriarchy, racism, and gender norms. The spirit world enables resistance. As a dreamworld of here and elsewhere, it is an agential space for women and other oppressed peoples to imagine alternative futurities of freedom. The opacity enabled by the spiritual realm is an important part of Mpondo theory because of the ways in which it leans on the spiritual to make meaning of life in relation to the ancestral plane where oppression is not possible.

Rural Warriors: The Mpondo Revolt of 1960

While iconic struggles and protests in South Africa have a visibly urban face, across time, there is a strong lineage of rural protest.[26] If we are to understand the Marikana massacre of 2012 and the recent appearance of protests in the quiet hills of Mpondoland, an appeal to cylindrical epiphenomenal temporality may be of value. Govan Mbeki's (1964) *The Peasants' Revolt*, which chronicled the dispossession and revolt of amaMpondo, was preceded by Sol Plaatje whose book of epic proportions detailed the destitution occasioned by the Natives Land Act of 1913.[27] For Plaatje, the very personhood of black people was at stake: "For by law, Natives have now less rights than the snakes and scorpions abounding in that country" (1982, 186). The Mpondo revolt followed the Betterment Scheme of 1947 and the Natives Land Act of 1913. The 1960 protests popularly known as the Mpondo revolts are a fertile archive for understanding how people resisted their kaffirization. They said no to being reduced to having fewer rights than snakes and scorpions. After a number of years of low-level unrest in the countryside, on June 6, 1960, the apartheid security forces descended on a protest against government's plan for rural administration that would see unaccountable chiefs administering villagers on behalf of the apartheid state (Kepe and Ntsebeza 2011). SAHO adds that a contributing factor for the revolt was anger at chiefs who collaborated with the state. "Chiefs were no longer figures in their own right, but were carrying out orders of the central government and imposing them on the Pondo people" (SAHO 2019a). Moreover, the use of land, including that for grazing, would be regulated by the state through the Rehabilitation or Betterment Scheme of 1947 with far-reaching consequences for livestock, food security, and the Mpondo way of life (Ntsebeza 2011). For William Beinart (2001, 134), the introduction of betterment policies and control in the rural hinterland was "the most far-reaching intervention into rural life since annexation." The Mpondo consequently resisted these impositions on their lives through the 1950s and into 1960, when the resistance reached its riotous crescendo. Mbeki's (1964) account of this revolt is that villagers participated in mass protests, burned collaborators' houses, boycotted local traders' stores, and refused to pay taxes. Eleven protestors were killed in Lusikisiki. Jimmy Pieterse (2011) cites the *Cape Times*, which in December of 1960 reported that twenty-two Mpondo were killed, and 363 huts and some stores were burned. The resistance mounted by the Mpondo was a refusal of state-sponsored capitalism that sought to wrest their land from them and dictate how it should be used. However, the suppression led to many deaths, incarceration, and injuries. Then and now, a deathscape. Using draconian apartheid laws, thirty people were sentenced to death. Others were subjected to ongoing harassment, intimidation, and beatings.

Because history is not linear, echoes of the Betterment Schemes of the 1940s when white extension officers and politicians proposed these schemes for the reserves, and again in Mpondoland in the 1950s and 1960s, reemerge in the present. In his 2003 address to the provincial legislature, the ANC Eastern Cape Provincial Minister of Agriculture, Max Mamase, without any sense of irony, pronounced the following: "The communal land tenure system poses a challenge of a different nature. Communal ownership of grazing land interferes with the proper planning of the communal lands. The decision-making process does not facilitate the commercialisation of agriculture. The delay in proper planning of grazing land exacerbates the denudation of this diminishing and finite resource, leading to unchecked soil erosion with grave consequences for future generations."[28] Here the dichotomy between modernity and traditional backwardness is constructed in a way that diminishes communal land ownership and use. Moreover, the history of rural communities' opposition to forms of development that unsettle their relationship to land is ignored. Then and now, state care is state harm. The logic of the reserve operates in ways that are similar to the reserves of Native Americans. Belcourt (2016a, 26) defines the reserve as "part of a dispossessory ethos through which the settler state reifies land as the sign of sovereignty itself, and thus effects political death of indigeneity, decomposing it into nothingness. . . . They [reserves] are borderlands that connote simultaneous possession and dispossession . . . zones of death. . . . It is as if the reserve were a site of complete atrophy, where indigeneity is supposed to waste away or degenerate, where queerness has already bled out." On the one hand, the state promotes customary ownership and custodianship of land while simultaneously describing our management as degenerate and our methods as backward. It greedily desires the minerals in the earth. Our history of survivance, however, means that we will not fully atrophy and our queer disposition may just be the shelter we need to survive and not fully bleed out.[29] Belcourt describes a "reserve consciousness" as a protective factor for indigenous communities. This is an awareness of the deathliness of the reserve. Through *ukwakumkanya*, we have developed strategies for defeating deathliness by embracing it and enfolding it into Mpondo theory—our way of being-in-the-world.

Writing about the Mpondo revolt, Pieterse (2011) reports that the *Daily Dispatch* newspaper was sympathetic to the protestors. The newspaper suggested that Mpondo villagers were being taken by submarines to Russia where they were receiving military training in order to protect their land and way of life. The unruly coastline had remained beyond easy surveillance of the state, and it was not beyond belief that submarines visited the rugged coast. This narrative of Russian intervention in the 1960s USSR period echoes the old cry that the African Americans were coming by ship to overthrow the colonial government of the late 1800s (Vinson 2012). In this earlier period, Wellington Elias Buthelezi, a Zulu man who changed his name and pretended to be African American, was a key protagonist. He opened a number of Universal Negro Improvement Association (UNIA) schools and churches in the 1930s, especially in the Nqamakwe district of the Eastern Cape (Vinson 2012). The schools and churches encouraged the belief that Africans in the diaspora had overcome enslavement and would come and help to overthrow white colonial rule. The grasp of UNIA philosophy was extensive and reached into rural spaces where it was refashioned to the fantasies and needs of the people. The Mpondo drew on these narratives to bolster their opposition to external control of their lives. An elder that I spoke to in May 2017 seemed to recall that German and Soviet Union planes came to Mpondoland to assist in the protests against the apartheid government. Here we observe how cosmology, the oceans, myth, and everyday life come together to enable resistance narratives for indigenous people. Mqhayi had similarly immortalized the black death occasioned by the sinking of the SS *Mendi*. This layering that we bring to world making is an important part of Mpondo theory. Through *ukwakumkanya*, this is an ability to see far into a past that is repurposed in order to live a more bearable present and imagine a future of black freedom.

The sea that had facilitated the arrival of oppressive colonizers would also be the path to salvation. Prophetess Nontetha Nkwenkwe had also given life to a circulating narrative when she told her congregants that a foreigner from across the seas would assist in bringing salvation. In the instance of the African American return, Garveyism was an important inspiration in South Africa and beyond.[30] The descendants of those stolen from the continent would be Africa's liberators. Referring to the early twentieth century, Robert Trent Vinson (2012, 106) observes that "various African prophets in the Rhodesias, the Belgian Congo, Nyasa-land, and Southwest Africa predicted that African American liberators would arrive via airplanes, ships, and motorcycles, even coming from underground, to expel colonial whites and reinstate African independence." Cold War hostilities between Western governments such as the United States and United Kingdom that generally supported the apartheid state, and the Russians and Cubans who were invested in overthrowing capitalism together with Soviet-trained, exiled ANC activists, meant that Russian and Cuban support was a ready explanatory framework.[31] In Lusikisiki, during the trial that followed the Ngquza Hill revolt, people testified that leaders had indicated that the Russians would be the new government of Mpondoland after the white apartheid state was defeated. They noted that the Russians were not white but rather an ancestral reincarnation meant to rid them of traitors and enforced white leadership (Fidler 2010). Solidarities, real and imagined, emboldened resistance efforts. The duality of the ocean is consistently drawn on as simultaneously ushering oppression and freedom in its endless ebb and flow. For both prophetesses Nongqawuse and Nontetha, the ocean can also serve as a conduit for the arrival of departed ancestors. It can both vanquish and cleanse. In Mpondo cosmology, the salt water can heal and cleanse bad omens.[32]

I draw a relationship between Mpondo activism against the Betterment Scheme and politicization and unionization in the mines. T. Dunbar Moodie (2011) argues that the Mpondo laborers brought a spirit of activism and mobilization to the mining belt and urban centers. This enabled them to agitate for the collective rights of employees. I draw on this relationship to posit that the predominance of protestors from Mpondoland at Marikana and the subsequent massacre can in part be informed by this history of activism against abjection by colonial and apartheid authorities. Nongqawuse can also be evoked as an early ancestor of resistance. If the ocean is the low point, the hill is the high point. In addition to the sea and river where cleansing ceremonies are held, the hill is a place of defense against invasion. I return to the hills of the Mpondo revolt. Protestors are reported to have found refuge in surrounding hills including the mountains Nongulwana, Ndlovu, Ngquza, and Nqindilili. The elders with whom I spoke about the revolt informed me that committees were formed on the hills and strategies for protest and other actions were devised. King (2019, xiii) similarly illustrates the elevated place of the mountain and tree in indigenous life by recalling that it "served as a meeting place between two nations; a place of encounter, shared breath, speaking a rhythm, flow, and exchange between two peoples." For black and indigenous people, the hill is a place of relation. The importance of the hill together with other parts of the natural environment in African cosmology is observed by Anthony

Kanu (2013, 541) in his contention that "the African universe is made up of myriad of spirits. And these spirits have their abode on mountains, hills, rivers, seas, oceans, trees, roads, markets, caves, brooks, lakes and forests." The Nazareth Church in KwaZulu-Natal conducts open-air sermons, and its most holy location is Mount Nhlangakazi (Becken 1968). As an African indigenous church steeped in African cosmologies, the mountain serves as an abode of the spiritual. The retreat to the hills of Mpondoland during the revolt can therefore be understood in relation to Kanu's conception of the African universe and King's place of relation and shared ground.

Roger Southall (1983, 113) captures the events of the Mpondo revolt by observing that "police reinforcements were brought in, and on 30 November 1960 a state of emergency was imposed across the entire Transkei. The authority of the chiefs and headmen was expanded; people were subjected to draconian repression, and even to call for a boycott became illegal. This was followed by mass arrests and the incarceration of some 5,000 people. Eventually, 30 were sentenced to death; nine of these were later given reprieves." How do we sit with the terror of being arrested and then sentenced to death by hanging? How do we do this not as a historical footnote but as a viscerally embodied experience? The protagonists that I interviewed in the villages of Lusikisiki are old people who were young men and women at the time of the Ngquza Hill revolt. Through them, I imagine what it must have been like. In the late 1950s and 1960s, modern weapons such as guns would have been rare in rural reserves such as Lusikisiki. The elders in my village told me that insurgents threw sticks at police helicopters and wielded domestic weaponry such as machetes. The villagers were no real match for the state forces armed with modern weapons including large military trucks, aircraft, and guns. The protestors posed more of a threat to other villagers who were seen as traitors and informers. The arrest and sentencing to death of thirty men was therefore a drastic action meant to discourage unrest and resistance by rural dissenters.

I imagine then how those arrested were transported first to local prisons and then on the long trip to Pretoria. This is a journey that many had made before and after Ngquza Hill. Prophetess Nontetha was one of those who made the trip. Driven from the King William's Town magistrate courts where she was first incarcerated and then to Pretoria's Weskoppies asylum. Bantu Stephen Biko's battered and brutalized body was driven in the back of a police jeep before he was killed in an interrogation chamber in Pretoria, the capital of death. In my mind's eye, sutured between Nontetha Nkwenkwe and Steve Biko, I see the Mpondo men, bound and huddled and bumping along the gravel road that I know so well. I see the snaking route through the rolling hills. Family members left behind perhaps suspecting that they would never see their fathers, sons, lovers, husbands, and neighbors again. The vehicle would have kicked up a trail of dust before finally stuttering onto the tar roads of the then Natal province and eventually reaching Pretoria. And then, on an ordinary day at the hangman's, twenty-one Mpondo men step through the trap door and fall only to be caught by a noose around their necks.[33] Did the Mpondo men find comfort from knowing that they were alongside their brothers? And if we must always maintain the possibility of a queer sociality, perhaps some of the men were lovers? Belcourt's (2016a) heartbreaking account of queer erasure and the impossibilities of queer love in blighted places like indigenous reserves is an important intervention for giving us pause to courageously imagine possibilities for the erotic and living as differently queered. At the gallows, did the Mpondo men make the connection to their ancestors who danced the death drill on the ss *Mendi* only three decades before? Many years after the men were killed, Solomon Mahlangu would hang from the Pretoria gallows and utter his famous last words, "My blood will nourish the tree that will bear the fruits of freedom. Tell my people that I love them. They must continue the fight."[34] In the moment of vanquishment, reinvigorating one's death is a queer hopefulness that enlivens death and defeats its finality. A triumph of freedom over a murderous regime. I wonder what the Mpondo men's words were to each other. Was there an orator among them who spoke the words of the ss *Mendi*'s death drill? Or were those last moment's silent reveries filled with visions of the rolling hills, the riotous ocean, and hearths of Mpondoland? The men were buried in paupers' graves in areas surrounding Pretoria. They would only be repatriated to be reburied on Ngquza Hill on June 6, 1998, thirty-eight years later.[35] Like Sarah Baartman. Like Prophetess Nontetha, whose limbs were eventually returned home.

In 2017 and 2018, I returned to my village curious as to the elders' recollections of the Mpondo revolt of 1960. I began by sitting down to talk to two old men who repeated a story I would hear often in subsequent interviews with elders. One of them pointed to the Zalu Mountains and the hill above the Mbayi River and reminisced about the events of 1960. We looked at the mountains and hill as he spoke. "I was an adolescent boy of cattle herding age at the time. People of this village would gather at Zalu and discuss strategies against chief Botha Siqcawu and the white police. They would stay on the hill night and day going through protective rites with medicine men." He recalled that without modern weapons of their own, they hoped the medicine men would make them invisible or bulletproof against the guns they knew the state police would use against them. Emboldened by the protective rites they had undergone, they flung sticks and stones at the helicopters when the police came. From our own village, an elder recalled that Mthembu and a number of villagers were captured and imprisoned during that period. Having read Thembela Kepe and Lungisile Ntsebeza's 2011 analysis of the riots, I asked what the reasons for the revolt were. Another man told me that he worked in Tongaat on the sugarcane fields of Natal but clearly recalled talk of the Kongo. In his view, the Kongo was an ANC-affiliated politics of liberation against apartheid. I pressed on and asked, "Why here in Mpondoland where there would have been very few white people?" Another old man responded that white people in Mpondoland were largely traders who subsequently left, but the primary contention that led to the revolts was unhappiness with land policies that required people to move from ancestral land in order to reorganize grazing. This localized protest about land was also a movement against capitalism and its attempts to kill rural subsistence farming and economic independence in order to create surplus labor to service the booming mining industries in the north of the country. Ultimately, in my village, the land rezoning measures were ignored.

In appealing to magic for their protection, villagers know that the supernatural is embodied. Mpondo theory wrestles with life and death as battles that unfold on the physical and spiritual body. Ancestors live beyond death. Since the spiritual and supernatural are key resources for living in rural villages, it is natural that cultural knowledge of magic and supernatural powers would be marshaled to defend against forces that seek to destabilize villagers' relationship to the natural world. Knitting everyday life to the spiritual realm is an example of Mpondo theory in practice. This bolsters a core belief that ritual and ancestors are protective factors that preserve Mpondo life against the onslaught of external evil forces. For Leslie Bank (2004), the state has historically been a force of evil for villagers. Taxation, control of land use, limitations on which animals to keep, forced removals from ancestral land, undermining traditions, neglect, and escalation of crime were all evil. Charmaine Pereira and Dzodzi Tsikata (2021) similarly provide a comprehensive account of how the state and capital have colluded throughout the continent to extract resources and remove people from productive ancestral lands. With reference to Qumbu, Benson Dyantyi (1960) complained that the forced removal of people from villages into fenced-in areas that would become overcrowded reminded him of how people had to leave

Sophiatown for Meadowlands in Johannesburg.[36] My grandfather and his family were forcibly moved from KwaDiki to KwaChandatcha as a consequence of the betterment land policy flowing from the Bantu Authorities Act No. 68 of 1951. The history of violent coercion by the state and other invading forces has meant that rural populations appeal to ancestral and embodied magical powers to defend themselves from the state. The body is tethered to the spiritual and natural world. In accounting for the Mpondo revolt of 1960 (to which I add Marikana and the men referred to above), Allison Drew (2011, 75) notes that belief in magic and witchcraft was rife and people repeatedly engaged in cleansing rituals to eradicate evil spirits. She further contends that amaMpondo "rebels saw their movement as a purifying force to cleanse society of corruption and evil and used prayer and magic rituals and medicines to empower themselves." By using nature and African cosmological beliefs against the state, the people practiced what Grace Musila (2020, 24) termed a "countering of colonial cultures of nature" to illustrate how nature can be channeled against oppression as a cleansing force for good. Nongqawuse too saw the ancestral call to kill cattle as a societal cleanser. This appeal to memory, fortification, cleansing, and the spiritual through natural mediums such as water, plant matter, and seclusion on hills is a core attribute of Mpondo theory. As a practice, it sustains life where death is writ large.

From Ngquza Hill to Marikana: The *Koppie* and the Bones of the Dead

In Marikana, the *koppie* was seen as a place of retreat, planning, fortification, and spiritual engagement.[37] In a place of little hope, traditional medicines have historically provided some comfort to miners. Writing about the history of mining, Jonathan Crush (1994, 318) contends that most miners believed in "the power of traditional medicine to afford guidance and protection, good working conditions, and promotion." Echoing the events of Ngquza Hill, Mount Nongulwana, Ndlovu, and Nqindilili hills, during the 2012 mining protest in Marikana, medicine men are reported to have fortified the protestors against injury even if shot at by police. The *Mail and Guardian* reports: "On Tuesday August 14, . . . hundreds of strikers on the *koppie* were being given rites to keep them safe by the sangoma's two sons" (Davies 2015b).[38] The hill is where villagers go to ask for rain, protection, refuge, and forgiveness (Tamale 2020). Hills are a place of watchfulness where one can look to sea and witness the sense of impending danger. In an old practice of Mpondo theory, ancestors watched from the hills and saw the arrivals of colonialists by way of the sea. According to Wiseman Mbambo (2000), Ngquza Hill's symbolic significance for the riotous protestors derived from its connection to ancestors whom they hoped would guide them through a difficult time. Like the Kikuyu saw Mount Kenya as the place of the gods, Mpondo ancestors were close to the hills.[39] In Marikana, the *koppie* served the role of home to the mountain committee in the same way that Ngquza Hill and other high points had served as the high ground for resistance during the Mpondo revolt fifty-two years earlier. The parents and grandparents of the men killed in the Marikana massacre may themselves have gathered on the hills to revolt against the injustice of the apartheid government's plans for their ancestral land and the capitalist undertow of the mining industry. This echoes the Khoekhoe rebellion and retreat from the coast to the mountains with the inland march of the colonizer.[40] Like indigenous Indians have sacred centers, the sacred places of the Mpondo are the hill, river, ocean, and grave. The latter is the physical connection to the ancestral realm. For Vine Deloria, "The center enables the people to look out along the four dimensions and locate their lands, to relate all historical events within the confines of this particular land, and to accept responsibility for it. Regardless of what subsequently happens to the people, the sacred lands remain as permanent fixtures in their cultural or religious understanding" (2003, 67). As a practice of Mpondo theory, the people return to the hill at the possibility of danger in order to convene, strategize, and resist. They return to the river to cleanse and fortify themselves after battle and violence. They gather at the grave to commune with the ancestors. The ocean is the sacred place for communing with the spirit world. These parts of the natural environment provide the balance necessary for life and mediating the relations between the dead and those who live. These are fundamentally queer ways to live and die. They defy temporality and urge us to make space for world making that resists the powerful sway of colonial modernity. To insert ancestral herbs into one's bloodstream to fortify oneself against police brutality is to live in queer hopefulness and colonial defiance. Crucially, when state machinery penetrates limbs, kills, and maims, the Mpondo remain unshaken in their beliefs in ancestral providence. This Mpondo steadfastness is a queer liberatory project that refuses capture. It turns the fractured bones of state violence into black valor. When death is embraced, absolute defeat is not possible. This insistence in attending queerly is verdant ground for a liberatory politics.

When the miners gathered on the Marikana *koppie* in 2012, they were revolting against white capitalist state-sponsored violence and exploitation. To observers who did not know the significance of the hill, this was a queer gathering of mad natives. Fortifying the body against the might of the police was a queer gesture. But there is a native logic to Mpondo queer enactments. By withholding their labor, they hoped to compel the employer to recognize the indispensable role they played in accumulating wealth for the London-based shareholders and South African elites.[41] But the protesting miners were shot at and killed by police officers in ways that echoed how older villagers had been killed by apartheid police during the Mpondo revolt in 1960. The killing happened in the veld and on the high ground of the *koppie*. Figures 2.2 and 2.3 below are an illustration of the dispensability of black life in cylindrical epiphenomenal temporality. The memorialization captured in the pictures gestures to long memory and a queerly mournful resistance to annihilation. The graves form a deathscape and mark the hills as ancestral grounds for generations to come. The cluster of graves troubles the landscape and centers the dead. To draw on Baderoon (2004b), the knowledge that we possess of the dead transforms the picturesque into a deathscape. To disfigure the landscape thus is to orientate it queerly by bringing the dead into view. When confronted by the dead, we are compelled to pause and engage the spectrality of the deathscape. We cannot claim not to know antiblack violence.

The Marikana *koppie* is a memorial site to which families and workers return to mark the anniversary of the massacre every August 12. But the bodies of the dead lie decomposing in graves in Mpondoland and elsewhere. After the massacre, families searched for and claimed their dead and buried them close to their homes. The young men murdered in Marikana are now watchful ancestors. The deathscape at Ngquza Hill depicted in figure 2.2 is a more recent memorial that resulted from a repatriation of bodies and the reburial of bones in 1998. I return to the bones of the dead in the coming chapters. For now, I focus on how limbs protest, how they are fortified, and how they become casualties of violence. In an eerily telling illustration, figure 2.4 points to the places of origin of the miners who were killed in the Marikana massacre. The Eastern Cape and Mpondoland in particular accounted for an overwhelming number of those murdered by the police. The pins unmap the Eastern Cape and give us a cartographic deathscape. Cleansing and fortification ceremonies would have had to happen in a number of Mpondo villages after the Marikana massacre of 2012 when 112 were shot down and 34 men killed by police officers (Davies 2015a). Twenty-six of

2.2 Ingquza Hill gravesite and memorial 2021.

2.3 Memorial at the foot of Marikana koppie. Courtesy of Reuters/Siphiwe Sibeko.

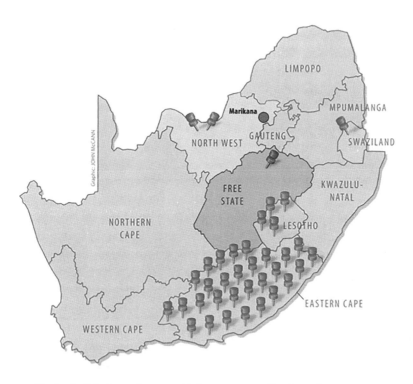

2.4 The dead of Marikana. Courtesy of John McCann, *Mail and Guardian*.

the murdered men were from the northeastern parts of the Eastern Cape—Mpondoland. Niren Tolsi and Paul Botes (2013) tell a tale of devastation in the wake of the massacre by detailing the lives of those left behind by the thirty-four men. They trace the widows and parents of the miners a year after their deaths. The narratives of those left in the wake of brutality and the ravenous capitalist system are saturated in embodied pain. They collapse time and could be the cylindrical wail that ricochets among those who lived in the wake of the Ngquza Hill revolt, Sharpville massacre, Bisho massacre, Langa massacre, Bulhoek massacre, Hope's War of 1880–1881, and the ten frontier wars against the British. They fold into Nongqawuse's revolt, Sarah Baartman's abduction and imprisonment, and those Khoekhoe, San, and Mpondo who watched the first ships flail, sail in, and drop their anchors on the African shoreline.[42]

Jacques De Wet (2011, 2013) details a number of post-1960 and more recent forms of resistance to both state and private business development initiatives intended for Mbizana in the northeastern reaches of Mpondoland. Among these was the Mbizana sugarcane initiative in the late 1970s and 1980s. While the attraction of jobs to an area of high unemployment was enticing, at stake was the loss of ancestral lands and livelihoods from which people would be moved. In yet another iteration of choosing opacity, relying on indigenous wisdom, residents practiced *ukwakumkanya* and looked ahead of the moment. They rejected sugarcane plantations on their land in the same way they had rejected the Betterment Scheme decades earlier. In the late 1990s, there was the so-called Gum Tree Rebellion, which was waged against plans to evacuate settled land that would then be used for commercial forestation.[43] In the logic of the neoliberal economy, ownership of these initiatives largely rests with external corporate funding interests with the promise of small community trusts to benefit the local communities. Pereira and Tsikata (2021) observe that communal land is lost to global capitalism's extractivism throughout the continent. The winner is always big business and communities appear to know this. In this rebellion, the state and South African Pulp & Paper Industries Limited (SAPPI) had proposed renting land from homesteads on which SAPPI would plant trees. Unlike the sugarcane scheme of the 1970s, this would mean that residents would not be required to move and resettle elsewhere. Wangari Maathai (2008) observed this pattern in Kenya and noted that exotic trees often replaced indigenous trees and plants that were the lifeblood of indigenous livelihoods and cosmologies that affirmed the coconstitution of people and nature. While most people in Mpondoland resisted this imposition of external players on communal land usage, some agreed to the deal (De Wet 2011). This led to a resistance that amounted to two weeks of violence in which fourteen homesteads were burned to the ground after they had agreed to commercial forestation. Reverberations of Ngquza Hill, where the houses of supposed collaborators were burned, are apparent here. I read these refusals as an ethical dereliction of the responsibilities to respect development. Even in conflictual situations, amaMpondo might be seen as queerly turning away from modernity and compulsory capitalism.

Following the failure of the sugarcane and forestation efforts, neoliberal interest has shifted to the titanium-rich sand dunes that line this coast. This interest in titanium highlights the decade-long battle between state, business, and the community. The protracted fight against the democratic post-1994 state and big business with multinational reach in the proposed Xolobeni Mineral Sands Project comes against the backdrop of this prior history of struggle against external interventions that threaten land ownership, grazing rights, and people's relationship to the land (Tlale 2020; De Wet 2013). The Australian investor Mineral Resources Commodities wants titanium, and they have discovered that the Mpondoland north coast sand dunes are rich in this mineral. The twenty-two-kilometer stretch of land that they want to mine is a sensitive ecological area that thrives on the indigenous vegetation with high biodiversity (Bennie 2011; De Wet 2011). Modern South Africa is sustained by racial capitalism and an unremitting greed for the abundant natural resources under the soil. Johannesburg was built on the foundations of the gold rush and so were Welkom, Carltonville, and Rustenburg. Kimberly was established around diamond mining. Richards Bay, Dundee, Newcastle, Emalahleni, and many towns in Mpumalanga are coal mining deathscapes. Platinum is mined in Rustenburg and other parts of the North West and Limpopo Provinces. These areas also mine for uranium, chromium, vanadium, and manganese. Without mining activity in the Transkei, the area always served as a labor reserve for distant mining towns. Indeed, by the 1950s, the 1951 census of the Transkei indicated estimates of migrant laborers leaving the Transkei annually at somewhere between 170,000 and 200,000 people (Fidler 2010). The mining of titanium on the Mpondoland coast would mean there would be some local-based mining and employment opportunities. However, the history that amaMpondo have as miners suggests they know how mining has always kaffirized them. Their reserve consciousness or *ukwakumkanya* means they know that mining has consistently undermined their being. With this deep history as part of the Mpondo experience, amaMpondo have constantly rejected mining-based development on their land. Communal relations are built and sustained in relation to the land. This relationality is core to Mpondo theory. To practice Mpondo theory through *ukwakumkanya* is to see far into the past and into the future. On both sides there is devastation. When under threat, the Mpondo reach out to the protective and defensive parts of Mpondo theory—and they riot.

Mpondo Mourning

How do the Mpondo survive in the wake of repeated loss? It is useful to return to Sigmund Freud's (1917) concept of melancholia in order to consider how it expands or forecloses our thinking about black rural life and the waves of loss that the Mpondo have experienced. For Freud, mourning is the emotional reaction to loss of either a loved one or an "abstraction which has taken the place of a loved one, such as one's country, liberty, an ideal" (243). I am more interested in the abstraction here. When loss is not dealt with, it can present as a pathological disposition termed melancholia. This is a psychic explanation for an unhealthy form of dealing with loss. According to Freud, the symptoms of melancholia are experienced at the level of the individual and may include painful dejection, inhibition of all activity, lack of interest in the outside world, and low self-regard. Melancholia may result from both conscious loss (i.e., I am aware of *whom* I have lost) and an unconscious awareness of *what* has been lost. Freud gives us a foundation for where to begin, but I am drawn to Pickens's (2019) wariness of melancholia for its potential to conceptually cannibalize other affective registers of engagement and drown out race in its heaviness. This is despite the utility of Anne Cheng's (2000) "racial melancholia," Paul Gilroy's (2005) "postcolonial melancholia," and the productive ways in which David Eng and Shinhee Han (2019), Sara Ahmed (2010), and Joseph Winters (2016) have expanded the concept of melancholia beyond the individual psyche to understand national and racialized conditions. To work with the mournful conditions of black suffering, I rely on black mourning rather than black melancholia. Mourning is more culturally coded in black life. It has a recognizable surface and a shared interiority rather than a bounded intrapsychic life. Rinaldo Walcott observes that black loss bypasses melancholia. To think of blackness as mournful but not as beholden to grief is to think of blackness in the breach and be attentive to the multiple folds in its surface. It is to see the potentialities of other affects including that of resistance. To resist melancholia is to resist pathologization and to point to the source of the pain. Dionne Brand (2020) characterizes the source as a global state of emergency of antiblackness of pandemic proportions. While mourning is a maddening outcome of oppression, as a chronic negative affect it has a rebellious register that insists on the value of the dead, the importance of ancestors, and it enables a queerly disruptive turning away (Canham 2021). Black loss is attentive to desire for the invention of new selves. Walcott notes that black being rewrites and bypasses melancholia not as stuckness and stasis but as desire, inventiveness, and movement. Similarly, Brand (2012) demonstrates that black loss is about not only dread but creativity and invention. Following Pickens (2019, 16), then, instead of engulfing the range of possible affects, I attempt to read black mourning as exceeding and shifting the available definitions of the human, "specifically how the assumed subject positions of unknowable excess (that is, Black madness and mad Blackness) jeopardize the neatness with which we draw the line between self and other." Since mourning operates in the realms of the here and the ancestral, it breaches self-contained affects.

Using mourning as the register to think about loss, then, what happens when loss comes in waves as in the case of the people of Mpondoland? Can we think of mourning not only as a pathological refusal to let go but also as a mark of the unfinished business of the present? Perhaps, as a past that refuses to let go? What does the mournful declaration of "we want the land" mean in the context of South Africa and elsewhere?[44] What happens when losses are undeclared, and what does that do to the certainty that mourning requires? Can we think of mourning as both personal and communal—a mood that is a shared affect? Can we conceive of mourning as traveling across space and between generations and as producing queer temporalities that defy linearity? I address these questions directly and obliquely across this text.

I begin with the first question that thinks of loss as repetition. This chapter has chronicled an inexhaustive inventory of the losses suffered by the Mpondo. I have shown that some of those on board the ss *Mendi* were the sons and subjects of a Mpondo chief. While the Mpondo revolt of 1960 resulted in the loss of life and exposed many to violence, debilitation, and death, many also lost land through forced removals. My grandparents were casualties of this loss of land. And now, those who live in the cities and recall familial losses of land emanating from the 1913 Natives Land Act mournfully repeat the incantation "bring back the land." However, many of us who long for the lost land are unlikely to return to the places where the land was taken from our ancestors. But we experience a stuckness at this point of loss. Winters argues that there is something productive in recognizing and living from the place of loss. This recognition enables resistance from a place of Mpondo mourning. I contend that there is loss in resistance too. Therefore, even as I demonstrate that the Mpondo have always resisted, there have been both gains and losses. And even the gains exert a toll and have to be paid for. When both the apartheid and democratic states in collaboration with neoliberal capital have repeatedly sought to "develop" Mpondoland through betterment rezoning, tea plantations, sugarcane farming, forestation, and titanium mining, the people have resisted. Through all these iterations of resistance, there have been losses. EmaMpondweni has a residue of loss. Here then we can think of loss as coming in endless exhausting waves. Evoking Lauren Berlant, Belcourt (2016b, 27) asks, "Does resistance always feel like resistance, or does it sometimes feel like bleeding out?" If we think of mourning as communal affect, we can imagine the shroud of mist that constantly hovers over the deathscapes of Mpondoland as a queer mourning heavy with our collective fatigue—our bleeding out. The conditions that give rise to this affect are relentlessly imposed on us. Mourning is the unfinished business. This capacity to remain in mourning points to a queer temporality—to be out of time with modernity but to embrace stuckness because the alternative is vanquishment. Belcourt suggests that to live outside of settler time is to "fall out of that affective life." For *Riotous Deathscapes*, this is to fall out of melancholia's suffocating affects and to embrace a more feral form of mourning. A fanged defensive mourning. We therefore return to worship at Prophetess Nontetha's altar in ways that make rubbish of colonial violence, we fortify ourselves, and we gather strength to fight another day. Our return to Nontetha Nkwenkwe, the death drill of the ss *Mendi*, and the Mpondo revolt is a queer congregation—an assemblage that hums in a mournful frequency of dissent and resistance. My insistence on queering our mourning is a space-clearing intervention for imagining differently queered Mpondo people in the past, present, and future. Through sideways looks, I beckon them to this mournful hearth. Mourning fuels our resistance and advances the ongoing evolution of Mpondo theory as a response to devastation. Thinking with Freud, Ahmed (2010) contends that loss requires a witness to hear and validate the declaration that a loved object has been lost. The declaration of loss by the Mpondo people has generally gone unheard. This is why I have written this book. My intent is to witness the declaration and to repeat it. In this iteration, I summon the queers to hear an inclusive declaration. Without a witness to Mpondo loss, mourning pervades the hills. We retain our experiences of black valor and loss through our oral traditions and we transmit both the losses and victories intergenerationally.

Conclusion

Mourning and resistance are informed by historical and current knowledge that black life is cheapened and commoditized as cheap labor. Resistance to kaffirization is bolstered by the bitter knowledge that miners were shot down in Marikana and the Kongo protestors were hanged. The community of Xolobeni and the neighboring villages of Amadiba do not want their land to be mined. Andrew Bennie (2010) has argued that development discourses have been pitted against environmental concerns without fully considering the livelihood of communities. To this, I add a lack of appreciation of previous resistance to extractivism that undermines African epistemes where people, animals, land, and water masses are interconnected and inseparable (Tamale 2020). In the ongoing court battles with the state, the Amadiba Crises Committee has asserted that they have not asked for development. In a queer counterintuitive move, they have asked international investors to leave their ancestral land. They contend that they have all they need to live. In enacting Mpondo theory as black survivance and livingness, the people of Mpondoland have on several occasions misbehaved by ruining the plans of big business and governments that have run out of ideas. Their revolt continues a thread of anti-extraction movements in rural Africa. Through a practice of grounded theory, they are part of a long lineage that has died saying *no*. And no doubt, there are those who will die resisting human predators in much the same way that Nontetha and the people of Ngquza Hill and Marikana did. As victors and the vanquished, we will continue to resist the waves of violence directed at us. Through Mpondo theory, at river rituals in the dead of night, we infuse herbs into our skin to fortify our bodies, we throw sticks at helicopters, we strategize on the hills, cleanse ourselves in the ocean, levitate and pray with prophetesses, and seek protection from the dead. When we peer into the reflective surface of the river, through *ukwakumkanya*, we see cylindrically into the past and future, and in the ripple, our ancestors hover protectively.

The foregoing is a queer orientation to modernity, and it looks askance at other ways of being normatively oriented. To live with Mpondo theory is to surrender to queer failure—a refusal of settler colonialism and capitalism. Recognizing that differently queered people have been invisibilized and bled out of history, this chapter insisted a boundless queerness into being. Through Belcourt's reserve consciousness and *Riotous Deathscapes'* *ukwakumkanya*, the chapter has summoned all the strays of history. Through ancestral ritual at the river and mournful congregation on hilltops where we fortify ourselves and open our bodies to be in relation to other life forms and ancestors, this chapter has drawn out the liquid and hilly dimensions of Mpondo theory. Emboldened by Macharia's commitment to exploring the conditions of black possibility by seeking sustenance where it has been scarce, I returned to the sites of death in order to scour the debris of the SS *Mendi* for queer providence. This is to say, I sought to create shared ground with the queer ghosts of the future, present, and past. *Ukwakumkanya* serves as a ready and able tool to navigate the realm of the speculative from the demonic ground of Mpondoland.[45] By queering timespace, we can return forward to seminal moments of the Mpondo revolt and recreate ourselves at the riverbank. We can swarm in mournful congregation at the homes of prophetesses who repurpose death and live forever.

3 RIOTOUS SPIRITS— *UKUKHUPHUKA IZIZWE*

We perish for lack of diviners
as if every home housed a witch.
We make a big thing of this schooling:
we're swept away in a stream—nothing's left.

NONTSIZI MGQWETHO, "THE STREAM OF DESPAIR,"
IN *THE NATION'S BOUNTY* (2007)

This chapter explores the boundlessness of Mpondo blackness and how it ontologizes beyond limits and linear progress. It illustrates that black ontology does not have a neat coherence and that it is disjunctive. By focusing on the spiritual dimensions of Mpondo theory through an exploration of possession practices among young people, the chapter points to blackness as constituted by unbounded life forms. As Rinaldo Walcott (2021a) contends through the example of black music, and as shown in relation to Mpondo music in the introduction of this text, the disjunctive nature of blackness means that not all parts of blackness can be violently interdicted because it cannot be fully accessed. Possession is one such state of opacity that eludes capture and points to avenues of black queer freedom. In Mpondo culture, the spiritual is undergirded by the ancestral. The possession outbreaks that are transcribed in this chapter are a practice of Mpondo theory—the otherworldly that remains just out of reach of legibility and mastery. In this chapter, I think through possession through the Mpondo understanding of *ukukhuphuka izizwe*, which literally refers to the emergence of multiple worlds in the experience of the possessed person.[1] *Ukukhuphuka izizwe* is a queer formation that opens up multiplicity and moves away from the limits of categories and regimentation. For Mpondo theory, the emergence of multiple worlds is a form of black malleability that draws us out of narrow conceptions of life while also offering avenues of fugitivity from societal surveillance. Since visions, dreams, and gaps in consciousness are common in the spiritual and ancestral realm, this aspect of Mpondo theory might be seen as applying logics that are yet to come and therefore as ahead of present suffering. A gesture to free states. If the otherworldly is an oblique movement away from surveillance and respectability pressures of modernity, then this chapter offers portraits of being that Zikiyyah Iman Jackson (2020) describes as indifferent to the authority of the law. Together with Jayna Brown (2015, 325), I ask, "What forms of sociality and the communal are available for us if we estrange ourselves from the life of our species?" The chapter meditates on the possibilities of this unmooring from the human and suggests that the spiritual both responds to and evades the social pressures and the policing of schools, community, and other agents of modernity and racial capitalism. When we live into our estrangement from the human through *ukukhuphuka izizwe*, we enable riotous possibilities of being.

This chapter is about what the estranged riotous body tells us about the black condition. The central contentions are that adolescent bodies are mapped as prone to deviance. They are a source of social anxiety which in turn generates further social surveillance and pressure. This results in dissociative symptoms, which are then read through the grammar of spirit possession. Since dissociation assumes a single temporal frame and does not account for cylindrical epiphenomenal temporality, its utility is limited here. Adolescent bodies riot in a worlding protest which, in Mpondo cosmology, is the emergence of worlds—*ukukhuphuka izizwe*.[2] The spiritual worlding creates spaces that enable multiplicity, ambiguity, and the ability to talk back. Because bodies are socially produced, they cannot be understood outside of history and culture—the wrestles between life and death occur in the physical and spiritual body. Bodies therefore cannot be seen as only natural biocentric constructs that are unaffected by the world. Bibi Bakare-Yusuf (1999) and Amina Mama (2017) contend that bodies are not only marked and inscribed by social pressures external to them but are direct effects of the social constitution of nature itself. This lack of fixity and the centrality of the social provide an opening to trace how some bodies become deviant—queer. Mpondoland and those unmoored from the human cannot be understood outside of young people. It is toward the young that social anxiety is projected in the form of communal mourning for certainty. Their bodies become signifiers and representations of things. *Ukukhuphuka izizwe* enables resistance against objectification. The following questions are taken up. What do queer bodies do to village life? How do they unsettle and create relation? Seeing this category of person as a problem is to endow them with queerness. If normative codes do not aid in attending to them beyond pathology, one must take multiple looks using a range of sensorial registers—*ukwakumkanya*. Since the possessed adolescents are sexually illegible, we next ask, how do we live queerly outside of our sexual relations? While we cannot set aside our sexuality, in this chapter *queer* includes and exceeds our sexual attractions.

Even as I read young people in relation to the state, I imagine the conceptual possibilities invented when one unmoors marginalized rural people from the political narrative of the nation-state. If we understand young women's *ukukhuphuka izizwe* as local but also as continuous with responses to long-standing forms of global injustice and alienation, we expand and broaden the register of actions deemed as agential. Read as agency against community surveillance, *ukukhuphuka izizwe* might be understood as a practice of queer freedom from the "confines of the human" in ways that point to the instability of the idea of species and that embraces boundlessness (Brown 2015, 325). This chapter suggests that *ukukhuphuka izizwe* is a practice of *ukwakumkanya* that we might comprehend as an insistence on turning away and attuning the senses toward the self. Kaiama Glover (2021) contends that the ethical practice of freedom tends to be in conflict with heterotraditional and heteronormative community. *Ukukhuphuka izizwe* can be read as an escape from community and a move away from the communal. Bearing in mind John Mbiti's (1990) assertion that communities create individuals, it is useful to ask what happens if we don't impose the virtues of compulsory communalism onto Africans? To loosen the communal lens from unity and totality is to allow space for agential expression, to queer disorder, and to run riot against compulsory ways of being. Thinking alongside Mbiti and Édouard Glissant, Keguro Macharia (2015) offers that a move away from totality is to unmake tradition as root identity. Billy-Ray Belcourt (2016b) observes that tradition is unable to imagine queerness into its fixed parameters. Generative questions are raised by those who move against and stand apart from tradition. What does compulsory collectivism elide? Where do free women and queers figure in relation to the communal? How do we take desire seriously when it is subsumed into the will of the community? Who is excluded from the representative *we* of the nation-state? What does it mean to untether women and girls from the roles of mother, metaphor, wife, daughter, and muse? And how do we unmoor men and boys from compulsory heteronormativity? How might we read these refusals as not always necessarily political or even concerned with the successful overturn of a world stacked against them? To riot in this context is to usher in a queer disorder that is not always aligned with a new vision of how things should be or even a more just world. This is not to claim that the revolts about which I write are apolitical. Rather, it is to be further open to more ambivalent and nonaligned individual refusals that favor opacity and deformation—queering. As politically and morally non-aligned, they operate outside of narratives of linearity, borders, and binaries that critical theory and scholarship have come to value. The lives of the marginal unsettle the moral position of righteousness with riotousness. In a world that demands solutions, villagers point to the queer legitimacy of refusal. Following Glover's (2021) formulation of the *regarded self*, those who refuse ask not to be burdened with the obligation to fix things that they have not broken. In their refusal, they look askance and, at times, they avert their gaze and turn away from the noise. The protagonists of this chapter expose the "mechanisms of coercion" that capitalism, heteropatriarchy, the community, and the nation-state depend on for coherence (Butler 2004, 59). In turning away and averting their gaze, they opt out. This refusal is not often transformative or for the common good. Rather, it is about self-preservation informed by an abiding self-love.[3]

Unlike the previous chapter, this chapter attends to quieter forms of refusal. If these protagonists riot at all, it is often a solitary form of refusal against coercive ways of being. But, as schoolchildren's *ukukhuphuka izizwe* outbreaks show, refusal also occurs in concert. These illegible forms of refusal are encapsulated by *ukwakumkanya*—a queerly steadfast insistence on selective attending and refusal to internalize that which negates being. Curdella Forbes has termed this a "sly disobedience" (2014, 24). In my own observation, this slyness is underpinned by a willfulness. Perhaps a refusal to move or to look in the direction to which those in power point. Refusals may appear as random acts of obstinance that may be seen as even working against the self. How might we read the act of turning to alcohol? To purchase hair and beauty products when the food cupboards are bare? To love queerly when loving heteronormatively is so well rewarded? To sing against the chorus even as the choir calls for going along? To grasp at pleasure in the ruins? Through attending in the opposite direction or cuttingly narrowing the eyes at the offensive object, *ukwakumkanya* may be read as counterhegemonic and as a steadfast self-insistence that refuses cooperation and cooptation into the communal and its forms of individual annihilation. Like Glover's "self-centered" Caribbean women and Saidiya Hartman's (2019) willful African American women, the protagonists of this chapter cannot reconcile themselves to available codes and parameters of inclusion. By staying in the margins, then, they choose themselves. This no-win position that sometimes involves being an outcast or living in poverty and underdevelopment is a reality that critical scholarship invested in narratives of progress often turns away from. Those who turn away from popular insurgence might be pointing us to broadened forms of freedom that accommodate a broader range of black livingness. Through Mpondo theory, protagonists insist that extant frames of justice and freedom make room for their waywardness.

The chapter is interested in how adolescents trapped in regimented school settings are driven by errantry's imaginary vision. Glissant (1997, 20) conceives of errantry as "nothing other than the search for a freedom within particular surroundings." The chapter invites the reader to wander along with me in order to see the frenzied bodies of adolescents as Fanon's imaginative leaps out of overdetermined histories of pain, as Hartman's critical fabulations, and as Glissant's errantry. Plasticity, buoyancy, queer cunning, and radical commitment to life are central to the condition of living in Africa. However, as Brown (2015) and Jackson (2016) warn, plasticity is not unbounded but located contextually and historically. It is not a positioning that is universally shared in relation to the material world. The chapter is seized with understanding how adolescent practices of intimacy and escape dissolve gender and create a queer erotic of unsupervised desire. In the radical black queer tradition of Audre Lorde (1979), the erotic is not reduced to sex. The erotic is the ground upon which we cling to desire and from which we theorize.[4] Sexuality can be unmooring from the dictates of modernity. Jared Sexton (2016) advises that the most radical aspects of black politics emerge from a space of "baselessness" which might be understood as a refusal and inability to make claims to anything. Baselessness might also be thought of as the place of explosion and queer world making. The chapter taps into the generative potentials of explosion and baselessness. By opting out of sanctioned ways of being, adolescents embrace queer baselessness. I lift my hand to queerly create *ukwakumkanya* and attend to what emerges from this queer location of baselessness.

The chapter conveys the complex placement of neoliberal capital, its promises, and failures. Capital creates economic precarity, then concedes to a tokenistic welfare child grant, which in turn further triggers anxieties about girls' consuming power. Boys remain by the wayside—mostly uneducated and unemployable. Both watch their futures foreclosing on them in contexts of poor educational infrastructures owing to neoliberalization of education where "good" education is costly and beyond reach. This is an underlying thread that is key to the production of social anxiety, which is then projected onto the young. In order to understand the dynamic tension between kaffirization and the decentered human, pausing on the bodies of the young is instructive. This is because adolescent bodies are vulnerable and occupied with processes of becoming. They open possibilities for thinking about temporality, worlding, and the queerly oriented body. This chapter focuses on four cases: the story of Thanduxolo, said to have transformed into different nonhuman forms; *ukukhuphuka izizwe* outbreaks at school; the exorcism of Clara Germana Cele, a young woman said to be possessed by a demon in 1906; and young men made surplus. Each of the accounts invites us to break with the bounded realm of sanctified modernity.

Boy, Snake, Pig, Fat Cake

On a hot summer midmorning in 2015, I was sitting under a tree with four unemployed young men when Thanduxolo walked by. One of the young men feigned fear, and with much laughter the men launched into the story of how Thanduxolo had turned into a snake.

The transformation had been immediate. "One moment he was a young ten-year-old boy and the next he was a black snake slithering on the floor. Even the napping teacher had joined in when two girls broke into a scream." The tall man from next door started the story, all the while scanning the ground as though afraid that the snake would emerge at any moment. "You remember how Ms. Fazi would sleep in the afternoons," he rhetorically asked. "Everyone streamed out of the classroom in a chaotic exit. But they say that short kid Qawe remained behind. He saw the snake and called the teacher to come and see but she backtracked even further. The snake slithered out the window when one of the other kids came to witness Qawe's sighting."

The young man from lower down the hill took up the story for the second part. I will call him Xola. Already a seasoned storyteller, he looked expectantly at me. "Just as people were suspiciously coming back into the classroom, there was a push from the back and shouts that Thanduxolo had now become a pig. And sure enough, there was a pig lolling about in the ditch near the grade three classroom. Ms. Fazi had retreated to the back of the room and she did not even attempt to quieten the class. Before anyone knew what was going on, Qawe was chasing the grunting pig out of the schoolyard. The rest of the class joined in and soon the entire school was flailing behind the pig." Xola paused his account of the chase and chuckled.

The third man, Langa, picked up the thread of the story. I had known him since he was a toddler. "As the chase gained ground, they neared the trees there at the edge of the road," he said, gesturing without glancing up. "The chant among the schoolchildren was '*uThandoxolo ulihagu*, Thanduxolo is a pig.' I recall hearing older people muttering this like a catchy song for days after Thanduxolo's transformations. But then, mid-chant, the pig disappeared into the long grass and everyone came to a standstill. Out of breath, Qawe had pushed his fist into his burning side. His disappointment turned to excitement and he pointed. And there at his feet, was *igwinya*, a fat cake, freshly fried, warm, slightly burned and hunched on the ground like a toad." Langa stopped when he saw the disbelief etched on my face. "Really. *Igwinya* made of flour and fried in oil." Xola intervened, "The fat cake was taken as evidence. Ms. Fazi asked Qawe to gather it up into a plastic bag and everyone returned to school."

Langa cut into the tale, as though afraid that Xola would omit the interesting part. "Back at school, someone had begun to pray. The fatigued pig chasers quickly transformed into a prayer meeting whose shouts against evil spirits exhorted the heavens. My niece in Thanduxolo's class told me that the prayers warned against snakes, pigs, and *amagwinya*. Thanduxolo's name had rung out across the village as the prayers reached a crescendo. Even I heard them. I saw our donkey's ears stand stock-still, pointing to the heavens like holy antennae. For a while, the village spoke about the incident. Thanduxolo was spotted once or twice in his mother's yard, although he did not attend school for the remainder of the week. But his mother is a warrior. She took him to school on Monday. I wish I had been there to see it. I hear that she summoned all the teachers and told them that they were superstitious and stupid educated people. She warned that she would be unforgiving if they did not protect her peace-loving son, Thanduxolo. She then marched into Thanduxolo's classroom with him in tow and told him to sit down at his desk. And then, she turned and looked each child in the eye. In a low menacing voice, she growled, 'I will wring your neck if you ever bully my son. If I hear anything about snakes, pigs, and *amagwinya*, I will show you a snake.' And then she strode out of the room leaving Ms. Fazi envious of her authority." Langa's eyes concentrated on the hills across the way as he finished the story.

Stories like this are not uncommon in the rural parts of the country, and increasing accounts of spirit possession have been noted in township schools. I recount this narrative to illustrate the vividness and everydayness of people's experiences with what may be considered abnormal or queer. Here, *queer* is used both in its sexual and antiquated reference to strange. Thanduxolo's transformations are queer because they step out of the expected paths. Following Sara Ahmed (2006), we might see Thanduxolo as orienting himself queerly by rubbing against other worlds. A queer phenomenological approach is productive for this analysis as it avoids the imposition of the saturated labels of lesbian, gay, bisexual, or transgender on the stories of protagonists. In the villages of Mpondoland, these terms do not travel well from the Global North and from the city. For this reason, urban-based theorizations of queer life, which tend to be faithful to categories of sexual orientation and gender, do not illuminate my coprotagonists very well. I share Neo Sinoxolo Musangi's discomfort: "Increasingly I am becoming jaded about and dissatisfied with gender categories that seem to expand the possibilities of gender identity while paradoxically cementing and concretising 'new' gender categories" (2018, 411). Villagers are not fluent in the lexicon of LGBTI, but they know strange. E. P. Johnson's (2001) salutary lesson on "quare" studies was based on his attempt to understand queer from his grandmother.[5] I think of my own grandmother who, after she turned ninety, loved to say, "Men are dogs," all the while looking approvingly at her unmarried and childfree daughter. A queer study of the rural requires the suspension of ready tools of inquiry in favor of double looks and multiple readings typified by the gesture of *ukwakumkanya*, the methodological tool of Mpondo theory. Macharia suggests that black and queer do not play well together. He however concedes that "they often inhabit the same bodies in uncomfortable ways" and their rubbing can lead to "pleasure . . . irritation, and even to pain" (2019, 5). To think with this uncomfortable coupling of black and queer is to remain attentive to the sensations and endless meanings that emerge. In the case narrated here, both the story *and* Thanduxolo are queer and outside of the norm. Since Thanduxolo is considered a bit off-center or queer, he is treated as a curiosity and with some fear and suspicion. And because prayer is considered the remedy for queers to be made normal, people pray for him. He is jeered, there is fear and laughter and a sense of the unusual, spectacle, and the carnivalesque. Of course, we have no way of knowing if Thanduxolo did indeed turn into a snake, pig, or fat cake. Here I concur with Grace A. Musila (2015) that this inability to verify truth is not a useful preoccupation. For Frantz Fanon (1967, 64), "When a story flourishes in the heart of a folklore, it is because in one way or another, it expresses as aspect of 'the spirit of the group.'" This makes stories real. What we do know are the reactions to the belief that Thanduxolo did transform himself or was transformed by someone else. Perhaps he was possessed by evil spirits. However, we also know that Thanduxolo compelled the community to move sideways, to pause and possibly to imagine other more disjunctive routes to freedom and worlds of being. Here, queer creates a breach that enables the strange and transgressive within the bounds of the community. It insists itself into the village and claims residence. It makes space for alternative ways of being.

Ukukhuphuka Izizwe: Mourning and Capitalist Discipline in the 2000s

Spirit possession or what I term *ukukhuphuka izizwe* can be understood as one's body being overtaken by external forces stronger than the possessed person. The nature, intensity, and duration may vary across people. Janice Boddy (1994, 407) contends that the forces could range from ancestors to divinities, "ghosts of foreign origin, or entities both ontologically and ethnically alien." Similarly, reporting on possession in the Cape provinces, Luvuyo Ntombana and Siphiwo Meveni (2015, 2) observed that adolescents claimed they "carried in their bodies a superior older entity, which they refer to as '*amaxhego*' (ancients of ancients, or ancestors)." The approach that this text takes on the subject of *ukukhuphuka izizwe* is primarily contextualizing and phenomenological rather than rationalizing or reductive. It is not interested in the worlding episodes in and of themselves but in the world making that they enable. After all, we take an interest in phenomena from the perspective of how we see them from our location and in relation to what they do in our spacetime. In line with much of the anthropological scholarship on spirit possession, I note that possession is pervasive throughout the African continent and that it is central to our meaning-making (Behrend 1999; Cohen 1999; Boddy 1994). I am particularly interested in the waves of *ukukhuphuka izizwe* that routinely sweep through villages. My interest is also in the predominance of young women among those possessed in Mpondoland (Stoller 2014; Bastian 2001; Boddy 1989; Ong 1988). A final dimension of interest in the possessed behavior of adolescents is the association between *ukukhuphuka izizwe*, a queer erotic, neoliberal structural adjustments, and unemployment (McNally 2011; Smith 2007; Moore and Sanders 2001; Ong 1988).

In 2017 and 2018, I engaged in a series of conversations with young people and some mothers emaMpondweni. From black girl studies I knew that the archive on rural black girls would be thin.[6] Talking to people about girlhood in relation to recent *ukukhuphuka izizwe* events was a more productive exercise, and it fit my approach of doing work grounded in place. I began by speaking to two young women who attended the same high school from about 2000 to 2005. They observed that their school was the epicenter of *ukukhuphuka izizwe* outbreaks. They recalled that outbreaks occurred regularly before they attended the school and many times while they were there. The examinations period was particularly notorious, and cries would break out and spread from classroom to classroom. The schoolmates of those who were possessed observed that the possessed did not appear to be aware of what was happening to them. While the adolescents were not an amorphous group, within particular school settings they appeared to move as one in an affective contagion that moved across bodies and space.[7] The young women would begin to scream and in response to any efforts to restrain them, they would run toward the forests in the area. One of the women pointed in the direction of the houses down the road. "You remember Thembi?" I nodded. "She screamed one day during exams. She was taken home in one of the teacher's cars. I don't know what her family did with her but when she returned to school a few days later, she was fine." I asked if any boys ever experienced spirit possession or the emergence of worlds. They told me that they recalled that it was always girls and never boys. The gendered nature of *ukukhuphuka izizwe* gives me pause. I wonder about the burden of surveillance and social expectations that adolescent girls have to bear. In her Nigerian-based study, Misty Bastian (2001) terms this phenomenon of the gendered nature of possession *Nigerian modern magics*. The common feature of these hysteria magics of adolescents is that the young women are subjected to bodily surveillance, control, and discipline. This is particularly pronounced when they stretch gender norms beyond socially sanctioned parameters. They are routinely warned about pregnancy, and when a pregnancy outbreak occurs, they are surveilled. Virginity and promiscuity are the dominant lenses of engagement and categorization.

The collision between adolescent bodies and other world spirits queers time by generating discontinuous and alternative histories (Freeman 2010). Collisions suggest moments of heightened sensation outside of ready legibility—perhaps unsanctioned erotic encounters among adolescents themselves and between them and spiritual forces. The moral panics that adolescent women's bodies elicit intersect with their sexual and reproductive debut, social policies about sex, pleasure, and conception outside of marriage. While social anxiety tends to shut down imaginations, I push against it to consider the avenues breached by queered adolescents. Here, erotic possibilities imbue young women with agency and lead them into worlds of unchaperoned wonder beyond the colonial superintendence of the state and heteropatriarchy. Adolescent bodies are outside of secular time because they often mature before they are socially sanctioned to. In addition, their possession by unknown spirits that are beyond the reach of science and adults is a disobedient foray into an uncharted and queer history of multiple worlds. Along with Elizabeth Freeman (2010, xi), I offer that seemingly nonsequential forms of time "can also fold subjects into structures of belonging and duration that may be invisible to the historicist eye." *Ukukhuphuka izizwe* enhances opacity and enables a turning away that can provide cover from capitalist, parental, and cultural surveillance. I read the period of *ukukhuphuka izizwe* as unaccounted-for time and therefore as queer temporality or an escape into the unknown. Rural adolescents gesture toward possibilities of evading the schedules of neoliberal time. We might see unaccounted-for time as a disorienting queer phenomenology that involves an "orientation toward what slips, which allows what slips to pass, in the unknowable length of its duration" (Ahmed 2006, 566). Folds in time are a form of *ukwakumkanya* that turn the sensorial inward and close off to the communal. Young women can evade the world unaccompanied, or they might escape as a chorus and share the pleasures and frictions that accrue from occupying multiple plains and erotic temporalities. The moments of ahistorical time are discontinuous and asynchronous (Freeman 2010). They occur alongside socially sanctioned temporalities. The asynchronous or cylindrical epiphenomenal temporality of adolescents and *ukukhuphuka izizwe* enable pleasure and fugitive delights in now temporality (Wright 2015).[8] In Thanduxolo's story, it is apparent that discontinuous time can also interpolate others into unchaperoned moments of riotous deviance. For example, when his peers chased the pig across the schoolyard and village, they had entered into a world of disappearing and transforming objects. This is a queer move off the radar of legibility.

Likewise, in worlding outbreaks, the waves of painful/pleasurable hysteria engulf and wash over classmates by moving between and across bodies. Freeman's conception of queer temporalities opens possibilities for thinking about how communal mourning and dissociation or worlding can be figured among the youth of Mpondoland. I expand these ideas here and beyond.

There is some consensus in the literature that *ukukhuphuka izizwe* thrives in conditions of anxiety and moral panic over adolescent women's bodies in relation to sexual and reproductive debut (see, for example, Ntombana and Meveni 2015; Bank 2004; Ong 1988; Sharp 1990). Contradictions, paradoxes, social fractures, uncertainty, and change bring about a nervous energy. High pregnancy rates among adolescent girls (Tugli and Morwe 2013) suggest that the beneficiaries of child support grants in South Africa are largely young, unmarried mothers. While the welfare grant is fairly small relative to the costs of raising children, for the first time young women have a more reliable cash flow than their male peers. With the high prevalence of unemployment among all age categories, young mothers sometimes have more cash than even older members of the community under the age of sixty (Richter 2009).[9] The inclusion of young mothers in the social welfare system has had the effect of queering the social order of rural Mpondoland. Adolescent girls now live in the liminal position of not having children and being poor and dependent, or having children and having some access to cash. For those at school, the benefits of schooling do not promise much since only 2.4 percent of the local population have completed high school and many of these are unemployed. Moreover, owing to the poor quality of education and schooling facilities, the failure rate in grade 12 is frequently the highest in the country.[10] Almost half of the school-going population attend school to fail. Here education does not hold out the promise of gainful employment that it is reputed to have elsewhere (Canham 2017). As Nontsizi Mgqwetho (2007) warns in the opening epigraph of this chapter, by insisting on the modernist values of education, we make much of this schooling and perish for lack of diviners. In addition, having lived through the AIDS pandemic, the young remember how migration to the urban centers turned out for their older siblings, who often returned home to die. The decline in marriage rates related to prohibitive costs associated with *lobola* or bridal price, the freedom of unmarried life, coupled with the ratio of eighty-nine males to one hundred females, suggests that the prospects of living a traditional life are uncertain. All these factors challenge given conceptions of rural life. Dreams are contradicted by socioeconomic realities. Capitalist discipline requires migration to places of employment. However, with the changing social order, the drop in employment prospects, the gendered nature of work, and historical patterns of work have fundamentally altered. Marriage is no longer considered a viable safety net since mining no longer favors Mpondo men, and the depletion of the mining economy means that low-skilled employment is scarce. The adolescents exist in a queer time where given histories and forecasts do not offer a template and sense of certainty.

The young women observe what happens to girls who misbehave. There is heightened anxiety about, and amongst, adolescent girls raised in the village. Daring to dream of alternative lives where one goes to university, acquires a job and financial independence, and makes decisions of one's own is an unsettling prospect because it is so rare. There is no money for dreams. The evidence of hopelessness is pervasive in a world that simultaneously gives them glimpses of neoliberal capital's gratification of all manner of desires conveyed through curated television shows about *real housewives* and social media. These contradictions produce an incredible dissonance and a taut, volatile affective landscape in young people's psyches. *Ukukhuphuka izizwe* produces a dreamful landscape that pushes against hopelessness. Dreaming defies moral orders of patriarchy and dominant rural subjectivities (Bastian 2001). Within both the home and the school, young women are required to possess good colonial subjectivities. Embodied discipline in dressing expectations and regimented practices of hygiene initially formed in the colonial era have carried into the postcolony and are imbued with modern practices of consumption (Bastian 2001). These are the undercurrents that constitute some rural subjectivities. The rioting bodies of young women suggest that impatience, despair, daring, optimism, alternative temporalities, and dreamscapes shoot through their queer bodies.

In order to understand the effects of black mourning on young women, I turn to another account based on interviews with three women. One of these is the mother of a girl who was said to be possessed. This was in the course of an outbreak of *ukukhuphuka izizwe* that traveled through schools in the villages of Mpondoland in the early 2000s. The woman told me that it was the beginning of satanism in rural areas. She latched on to my recollections and embroidered on them. "The kids would go crazy," she said. Groups of them would suddenly act out during prayer time at assembly. They would talk in strange languages, break into seizures, and run about in frenzied performances. "Only prayer could stop them," she said, conviction flashing in her eyes. The sea was a recurring theme. This appears to be where the kingdom of evil is. The kids were being directed from the depths of the ocean. They would dash to the rivers and had to be restrained and prayed for. "There was a lot of possession at the schools in my area," she said. "When they were prayed for, it would emerge that some of them were replicas." In my confusion, I asked, "*Kanjani?*" How so? "The child was a shell. Just a vacant body. The actual child was with the devil in the depths of the sea. The shell or replica would therefore run to the ocean or water masses in search of the real self." This is a literal evacuation of interiority. The constant reference and meaning-making that evokes the ocean is a core motif of Mpondo theory. It is not just a water mass but harbors evil and relief. As a consequence of their unknowability and association with strangeness, I think of water masses as queer spaces that are unsurprisingly grafted into *ukukhuphuka izizwe*. In drawing attention to the queer sociality of oceans, Omise'eke Tinsley (2008) has called Paul Gilroy's black Atlantic, the queer Atlantic. I suggest that water masses are queer not only for their erotic possibilities but for their fugitive potentialities and for the ways in which they push against transparency. *Ukukhuphuka izizwe* further imbues water masses with a queer character of endless world making potentialities. However, the trace of the erotic also permeates waters where young women purportedly vanish. We have no way of knowing what they do when they disappear into the water. We cannot know the feeling states they enter into and how they sate burgeoning desires freed of colonial and heteropatriarchal superintendence.

I am interested in the idea of the replica or shell for explicating queer temporalities. A shell is a new surface off which we might read errantry and opacity. Conceived of as a shell, the worlding adolescent can take leave of linear time and enter into queer temporalities characterized by worlds that evade capitalist orders and ways of organizing. Seen this way, the rioting body prefigures the idleness and unbounded time of unemployment that awaits. Lesley Sharp's (1990) account of possession in Madagascar suggests a similar pattern where the essence of the possessed person is absent while inhabited by evil spirits. This means that the possessed are not aware of what occurs during *ukukhuphuka izizwe*. The process of healing requires those who witness the exorcism to recount the event to the victim. In her account of the cases emaMpondweni, my protagonist stated that through prayer, the real self would emerge and confess by recounting the ordeal. This suggests some awareness of the occurrences during *ukukhuphuka izizwe*. A meta-awareness of both the real body and the spirit. "Children are supposed to be pure," I said tentatively. "They are, but adults use them," she responded. "The problem is that the evil spirit can spread from one child to others. It spreads like an outbreak." Sigmund Freud (1921) observed that acts and sentiments could be contagious and move between bodies within groups. The mother of the possessed girl recalled that doctors and traditional healers could not help. "At that time, only mass prayer worked." Another woman joined the conversation. It happened in Pietermaritzburg too, she told me. "People move in between the rural and the urban." The rural influences the urban and the urban colors the rural. "A school was closed down for a while because the outbreak was uncontainable. Ukhozi FM discusses this quite often.[11] It's the devil's work," the older woman said. While this may well be true or have competing truths that occur as asynchronous and discontinuous times, I point to the possibilities of freedom enabled by worlding episodes. *Ukukhuphuka izizwe* may enable freedoms from various forms of surveillance by making incursions into multidimensional histories. Perhaps adolescents tap into the erotic energy of ancestors such as Prophetesses Nongqawuse and Nontetha. As Ahmed (2006) reminds, we might be able to discover joy in horror.[12]

A newspaper report describes a possession outbreak in eSwatini:

> The affected children, mostly consisting of girls and just a few boys, are seen running and screaming from invisible apparitions that often instruct them to gaze into a nearby pond. In this pond they are shown a list of students targeted by the demons, to whom they run and inform of their discovery. The children claim that they hear the principal's voice in their heads telling them to drink from the school's tap. They see visions, speak in strange languages, and if held down, they writhe and scream in agony.
>
> The outbreak has prompted school officials to call in a prominent area exorcist, Pastor Manana, in an effort to expel the demons from the children. Manana, who performed a mass exorcism ritual in the school hall on Wednesday, had become a local celebrity after expelling evil spirits from the local army the previous year.[13] (Newkirk 2011)

Possessed youth have an impulse to run to the river or pond—presumably the proxy for the sea where their bodies reside and where the devil is. But the river is also the place of ritual cleansing, where ancestral wisdom lingers for intergenerational practice and communion. Water is a recurring motif for making meaning of the queer act of *ukukhuphuka izizwe*. It attaches to Mpondo theory through its reliance on the river and ocean.

Mpondo theory is illustrated through all the foregoing examples, which reflect a constant wrestle with the body, water, whether through flooding rivers and bridges, fortification rituals at rivers, or through evil spirits in the ocean. However, water masses insist on a queer ambiguity and multiplicity and refuse transparency and knowability. The young woman in figure 3.1 below evokes a mood of this opacity. In the preceding accounts, prayer restores the souls to the bodies that emerge exhausted from their ocean prison. Once blessed by being prayed for by certain people, water could be used to subdue *ukukhuphuka izizwe* and restore the souls of the possessed to their real bodies. When narrated by close family, there is an attempt to attribute the deviance to the devil and not to the misbehaving body and its desires. In this conception, the body is non-agential and is a vessel overtaken by the devil through entrapment. Through *ukwakumkanya*, I offer alternative readings that center fugitivity and create a break for erotic escape and errant fluidity. As we will see in the next account, *ukukuphuka izizwe* can be a painful and potentially liberatory experience. With reference to the queer Atlantic, Tinsley (2008, 193) suggests that "fluidity is not an easy metaphor for queer and racially hybrid identities but for concrete, painful, and liberatory experience." I take up this injunction to recognize the pain and pleasure of fluidity.

3.1 The shore break: where the river meets the sea. By Nonhle Mbuthuma.

Possession: A Twitter Performance

While writing in 2018, I came across a Twitter thread about demon possession at school. The thread had gone viral and attracted a lot of commentary. Here, I pause on Ike Ntanzi's account of demon possession at his school. The pictures that accompany every tweet are irreverent, they appeal to popular culture, and the thread petitions humor. Ntanzi is conscious that this story levitates at the borders of this world and that of spirits. He nevertheless appeals for readers to understand his account as a credible experience. He contends that most of his peers experienced spirit possession. In the religious framing of the story, his peers were demon possessed. The story is remarkably similar to accounts of possession I have already detailed. This suggests that there is a circulating lexicon of *ukukhuphuka izizwe*. Worlding can be located within the tradition of African ontology since the body is always in relation to the environment (Tamale 2020). For George Lakoff and Mark Johnson (2008), the mind is embodied in a way that informs our conceptual systems. Since our bodies are sites of struggle between death and life, conceptual systems draw on the relation between our bodies, the spiritual, and the environments within which we live. *Ukukhuphuka izizwe* renders the body conspicuous as an object of social relations rather than as exclusively mechanical (Fraser and Greco 2005).

In the interests of brevity, not all tweets are included in my retelling of the account below. In choosing what I believe is salient, this is my version of Ntanzi's story. The story begins with a school that imposed religion quite heavily on its adolescent learners. Monday and Friday assemblies were reserved for pastors and motivational speakers. In other words, the week began and ended in judgment and religious surveillance but also motivation and inspiration. The visitors would speak for approximately an hour and the restless adolescents were expected to stand still and be attentive.

Some of Ike Ntanzi's @Ntanzike Twitter performance thread is reproduced here.[14]

> Then one Monday morning we had this pastor from those New Charismatic Churches aka *Osindisweni*. He was preaching and kids kept laughing. He stopped preaching and started praying. It was dead silence for a while and then, from the back row came a loud scream. [meme of an African preacher pointing and saying, "You, demon, loose your grip!"]
>
> As a member of the RCL [representative council of learners] committee, I rushed to the scene coz that's what "we're" suppose to do. The girl is

still screaming and fidgeting on the floor while those "older" gents from school are trying to restrain her. I get there and idk [I don't know] what to do. Moghel [my girl] is kicking and screaming. [meme of African American television host Wendy Williams with rounded astonished eyes, covering her mouth]

The same pastor who made moghel scream came back on Friday. He preached and there were no silly jokes this time. Everyone was on their best behavior. He prayed and nothing happened on this day. His entire sermon was on Demon possession even saying gays are possessed. Almost shit myself. [crying emoji]

Monday came and we were told there was no Assembly Prayer that day. First period in class all the RCLs were summoned to the principal's office. We get there and there are 7 pastors in the room. [crying emojis] I went into panic mode. Thinking they're here to pray my gayness away. [meme of a woman with a hand over her mouth]

In abbreviated form, the Twitter thread can be read as follows: A loud scream by an adolescent girl who subsequently appears to have collapsed into a seizure marked the beginning of what would grow into a contagion of *ukukhuphuka izizwe*. The pastor prayed over her until she passed out. With the secret knowledge that he was queer, the narrator was terrified that the pastors would identify a gay demon in him in their attempts to exorcise the adolescents of demon possession. As one of the prefects, Ntanzi's job was to gather learners from grades 9 to 12, as these were the "most possessed." The average age of learners in these grades is thirteen to seventeen. These are the most turbulent adolescent years. It is a queer time. This period is characterized by sexual awakening, puberty, menstruation, pushing boundaries, mood swings, experimentation, heightened surveillance, and anxiety. Adolescents create anxiety in adults. The verdant scent of bodies growing and blossoming. Adults evoke anxiety among adolescents. Among the adults at the center of this anxiety are those invested in maintaining a conservative social order, such as leaders of religion and schools. Ntanzi continues the Twitter thread:

And our job was to ensure that everyone from these grades goes into the main hall. The school security was also told not to let anyone out. So now we're all in the hall, both students and teachers. There's no sign of principal and 7 pastors. [meme of terrified black woman wearing a red wig]

The 7 pastors walk in, followed by the principal who then locks the door. My heart is now in my throat. I am sweating. The pastors introduce themselves and why they have decided to disrupt our day. They tell us they will lay hands on each and everyone in the room. I panic again. [meme of a weepy local actor with the subtitle, "Oh, Jesus."]

Mind you, as all this is happening, I have to pretend I'm okay. Which is why I think gay people are the most talented people ever! Ay we can act mahn! [laughing emoji] . . . anyway. There is chaos all around me. The pastors are attending to the possessed kids who are now kicking and screaming. [meme of exasperated looking woman sitting in traffic]

The others are "healed" of their possession while others are "stubborn." Among the stubborn was my desk mate. [crying emojis] He was even trying to hit the pastors. He was speaking in a language we didn't know. The pastors were now praying over him, my desk mate wasn't giving in. [meme of a woman rubbing her temples, saying, "Wow."]

The preceding Twitter thread and some content omitted from the account is summarized here. After the girl who started all the trouble was delivered of demons, the narrator's desk mate becomes the focus of the story. He appears resistant to prayers, fights the pastors, and (like Clara Germana Cele about whom I write below) he speaks a strange language. He bites his lower lip, is observed to be drinking his own blood, and slithers on the floor like a snake, all the while emitting an evil laugh. These behaviors are seen as satanic possession and invite amplified prayer. In keeping with other accounts of *ukukhuphuka izizwe*, the possessed are riotous and animalized. Surrounded by pastors and his classmates, the demon-possessed boy confesses to evil activities that implicate a number of people, including 40 percent of his classmates and two teachers. There is of course a great deal of performativity both in the telling of the story by Ntanzi and for the young boy who is constructed as demon-possessed. *Ukukhuphuka izizwe* is performative. It relies on an audience and circulating tropes in the environment. It is also embodied. The body acts out. It writhes, sweats, speaks in strange voices, it is vertiginous and experiences nausea. With the heightened scrutiny and demands for confessions relating to accomplices, the terror spreads beyond the individual. Those who are implicated are in turn pressured to perform possession.

Through his Twitter performance piece, Ike Ntanzi gives us front row access to a school exorcism. We have to consider too that Ntanzi's story could be a fictional performance crafted from circulating tropes since many social media users share fictional autobiographies for a variety of reasons. I am however interested in the circulation of these tropes and the resonances they have for so many people. In the account, we get to witness the terror wrought by exorcism and religious deliverance in the face of perceived evil. The contention here is not that religion is wrong, but rather that efforts to police and control bodies that are seen as excessive and queer evoke anxiety and are potentially terrorizing. Recall the earlier account about Thanduxolo from my village. After his return to school, he was regarded with suspicion and fear. In the case of the possessed boy of Ntanzi's account, after his return to school, he is moved to the back of the class and, like Thanduxolo, regarded with fear. Obliquely oriented bodies fail to walk in straight lines. They revolt and are then further ostracized.

I reached out to Ntanzi to request his permission to use parts of his Twitter thread. He consented.[15] His accounts are remarkably similar to those from my own village. Ntanzi contends that, in his experience, girls were generally more susceptible to demon possession. For him, girls are lured into satanism through hair products and cosmetics. Why is there anxiety evoked by young women's interest in hair and body products? I suggest that it is anxiety about modernity, changes to the social order of certainty and patriarchal control, but it is also a fear of young women's bodily adornment and what it signifies about sexual awakening. It terrorizes boys and men. But it also evokes fear among older women who contemplate the possibilities of young women's sexuality and what it might mean for the boys and men in their lives. In my village, young women should not wear trousers during a storm because they could attract lightning. Men are potential victims of young women's seduction. It is not a stretch then to suggest that cosmetics are satanic. Satan possesses young women's bodies through cosmetics. Young women's bodies are always simultaneously threatening and vulnerable. The surveillance imposed on adolescent bodies manifests in rituals like virginity testing in rural communities.[16] But possession bears queer possibilities. As the chapter has contended, *ukukhuphuka izizwe* introduces inaccessible openings into history and queers temporalities. In their "failure to be proper," the adolescents mine other worlds and temporalities that defy moral orders and heightened surveillance (Ahmed 2006, 533). They harvest ancient queer energies in a process that Freeman conceives of as time binds. I consider these energies as emitting from sedimented historical mourning of ancestors but also from current pressures of modernity and surveillance. Since unaccounted-for worlding time of multiplicity might also be pleasurable, we might conceive of *ukukhuphuka izizwe* as an erotic connection between ancestors and adolescents. A liberatory impulse against the intolerable present.

Ukukhuphuka Izizwe and Dissociative Worlding

Dissociation or what I have termed *worlding* is a central condition of all accounts of possession here. Building on the combined oeuvres of Donald Winnicott and Phillip Bromberg, David Eng and Shinhee Han (2019, 121) define dissociation as "the loss of capacity for self-reflection, the inability to process emotionally charged mental conflicts, and the disconnection of the mind from the psychesoma as a (paradoxical) defense to preserve a sense of selfhood and continuity." For them, the inability to reflect meaningfully on psychic pain creates an artificial separation between the thinking mind and pained psyche. I go along with Eli Somer's (2006, 215) more expansive and culture-bound definition of dissociation when he observes that it is an experience "in which there can be at least two independent streams of consciousness flowing concurrently, allowing some thoughts, feelings, sensations, and behaviors to occur simultaneously or outside awareness." This description is queer as it points to the possibilities of simultaneous and innumerable temporalities that psychoanalytic accounts overlook. It aligns to my conception of *ukukhuphuka izizwe* as a queer formation. Significantly, Somer contends that the higher prevalence of dissociative states outside of the Global North might suggest that the psychological state of dissociation might convey something more than psychopathology, including normative idioms of distancing or disavowal from some experiences. Here, our task is not to make a clear delineation between Western notions of psychopathology and Third World culture-bound conceptions of dissociation. Instead, I signal the continuities between these frames as bleeding into each other rather than as mutually exclusive. Importantly, the dualities and ambiguities enabled by worlding are central for my conceptualization of Mpondo theory—a way of life that sits with multiplicity in both generative and unproductive ways. The chapter extends on this work in order to consider the *ukukhuphuka izizwe* outbreaks described by Ntanzi and my other protagonists.

In addition to the pressure and surveillance on adolescents, I have previously stated that the waves of loss experienced by amaMpondo can be said to induce pervasive mourning that is passed on intergenerationally. Moreover, the related anxieties of adults are misdirected at adolescents and the consequences are *ukukhuphuka iziwe*. These prohibitions and expectations run alongside and in contradiction of adolescents sexual awakening, a secular popular culture and state, challenges to patriarchal traditions and culture, mass failure in the schooling system, and the sham that capitalism rewards those who work hard. They live with failure and in failure. In this context, dissociative worlding can also be seen as a defense and a queerly creative means to maintain personal, communal, and familial continuity and a sense of selfhood in the face of the emotionally charged mental conflicts that emerge in relation to the contradictions that adolescents navigate. The consequence of these unreconciled differences between their reality and the imposed version of reality is dissociative worlding. Somer contends that in addition to an individual quandary, dissociative syndromes communicate societal tensions among different age groups, between sexes, or between religious leaders and ordinary members of society. The emotional collapse that comes from these tensions manifests in *ukukhuphuka izizwe* contagions that run rampant in schools. The schoolyard has a large concentration of anxious bodies and is the pressure point for these psychic riots. It is the place where things come to a head. In this context, exorcism and prayer reinforce social pressure and exacerbate the conditions that give rise to *ukukhuphuka izizwe*. Rather than casting the psychic energy produced by dissociative states as exclusively pathological, I suggest that the energy generates queer flight across spacetime.[17] Queer flight enables escape from surveillance, but it also opens avenues of communion with ancestral others with similarly unfinished business. *Ukukhuphuka izizwe* connects ancient hurts and ecstasies with ongoing traumas and desires for freedoms in ways that complicate linear temporal frames. A crucial intervention here is to complicate possession in ways that recognize its liberatory impulse as a Mpondo leap into the breach.

My emphasis on the erotic as relation can be read with Douglas Hollan (2000, 546–47), who views dissociation among the possessed as behavior that draws them back into "dialog and interaction with the community, rather than leading to alienation and estrangement." This reading points to the relational possibilities of *ukukhuphuka izizwe*—not only with ancestral worlds but with community. I am however less strident in the critique of alienation among the possessed because I believe that they are also communicating a deep-seated sense of alienation against dominant conceptions of moral authority. This alienation belongs to both the adolescents and their alienated ancestors. We can therefore understand the rioting body as unbounded in time and form. It is constituted of dualities and multiplicities. What does it mean to have neoliberal anxieties in a time of mass unemployment and indeed unemployable youth who will probably never access the formal economy? How do these anxieties order the psychic life of young people? The untenable psychic predicament of following in the footsteps of their parents, on the one hand, and, on the other hand, of being successful modern subjects in a world of supposedly endless opportunities is distressing. In a landscape of failure, both options are not possible. My conception of failure is not to suggest that the youths will lead failed lives but rather that they are likely to fail at being "good" traditional rural subjects and at being modern fully employed and self-sustaining adults within the failed neoliberal economy. They are more likely to be part of the failed welfare system than they are to be employed. Neoliberal failures are felt most harshly in the quiet hills of Mpondoland.

Casting Out Demons: Exorcising the Wayward

Taking up Tinsley (2008), Musangi (2018), and Macharia's (2019) invocations, I focus on obscure black histories and read them as queer and imaginative archives of black life. Specifically, I turn to the story of Clara Germana Cele (1890–1913). Her brief life is recorded from the perspective of European missionaries, but it has received almost no critical attention. Cele was a young woman who in 1906 was reportedly possessed by evil spirits.[18] While Brian Levack (2013) provides a version of this story, there is unfortunately no complete account apart from one put together on Wikipedia. This account is based on various sources, some more reliable than others. Some of the account is reproduced here. Cele is said to have experienced her first episode of possession when she was a sixteen-year-old orphaned schoolgirl at St. Michael's Mission, in Umzinto, Natal, South Africa (Young 2016; Levack 2013). She was Zulu speaking and of mixed race parentage. She reportedly entered into a pact with Satan, and this caused her demonic possession. Clara Germana Cele later revealed this information to her confessor, Father Hörner Erasmus. In an account written by a nun, Cele was able to speak languages of which she had no previous knowledge. This was also witnessed by others, who reported that she understood "Polish, German, French, Norwegian, and all other languages." The nun reported that Cele demonstrated clairvoyance by revealing the most intimate secrets and transgressions of people with whom she had no contact. Moreover, she could not bear the presence of blessed objects and seemed imbued with extraordinary strength and ferocity, often hurling nuns about the convent rooms and beating them up. Young (2016) reports that the exorcism was witnessed by six priests and monks, fourteen nuns, and one hundred and fifty inhabitants of the mission station. The nun reported that the girl's cries had a savage bestiality that astonished those around her. About Clara Cele's voice, an attending nun even wrote:

> "No animal had ever made such sounds. Neither the lions of East Africa nor the angry bulls. At times, it sounded like a veritable herd of wild beasts orchestrated by Satan who had formed a hellish choir."

> The girl, according to some, was said to have levitated five feet in the air, sometimes vertically and sometimes horizontally; when sprinkled with holy water, the girl is reported to have come out of this state of her satanic possession.

> According to a *Lutheran Pastoral Handbook*, one possessing these symptoms is an indication that an individual is truly possessed, rather than suffering from a mental illness. Consequently, two Roman Catholic priests, Rev. Mansueti (Director of the St. Michael's Mission) and Rev. Erasmus (her confessor), were appointed to perform an exorcism on Clara Germana Cele; this deliverance lasted for two days. During the exorcism, Clara's first action was to knock the Holy Bible from the priest's hands and grab his stole in an attempt to choke him with it. At the end of the exorcism, it was said that the demon was forced out and the girl was healed. (Wikipedia, n.d.)

In this account, it is apparent that Clara Germana Cele is constructed as a riotously queer body that is so evil that her story has traveled for over a century. On this journey, the account has gathered myth and evocations. She was an orphan raised in the care of nuns at a mission station. She is saved from her orphan status by the missionaries. However, black girl studies scholars such as Dominique Hill (2019), Corinne T. Field et al. (2016), and Relebohile Moletsane (2007) teach us to read black girls attentively since their lives and voices tend to be suffocated in the archive. There is no account of Cele's parents' death or the whereabouts of her extended kin. From Sol Plaatje (1915/1982), who wrote at this time, we know that mass dispossession, displacement, and early death were the order of the day for black people. In this moment, a different kind of mourning would have been heavy in the air. In addition, nothing is said about the conditions and disciplining strictures within the convent. In other words, the conditions that produce volatile erupting bodies are silenced in favor of a redemptive narrative where missionaries save a young black woman from being totally eviscerated by evil and a background of scandalous miscegenation. Cele was however not alone in her possession. According to Young (2016), during her second exorcism in March 1907, two girls—Monica Moletshe and Engelberta—also made a pact with the devil and were exorcised. Like the girls of Mpondoland's riotous eruptions a century later, the girls of Umzinto moved together. In the face of an archive that has failed the young women of Umzinto, like M. Jacqui Alexander (2005) and through *ukwakumkanya*, I look beyond the factual in order to reconsider the worlds of Cele, Moletshe, and Engelberta. As queer subjects of modernity, I suggest that we imagine these young women as aspiring to freedom under pressure of religious institutionalization and colonialism. Analogous to the adolescent women who riot against societal and school surveillance, Cele, Moletshe, and Engelberta might be read as a troika of women who enter into a queer pact. They riot in unison, disorient temporality, grasp at pleasure, and queerly upset the triumph of good over evil. While we are told that Cele's exorcism was successful, Young indicates that she had another episode of *ukukhuphuka izizwe* a year later. This time she was accompanied by Moletshe and Engelberta.

Looking beyond the factual enables a queer imaginary that authorizes us to think of the young women as sexual beings who invest in erotic flight within the confines of a colonial Catholic mission station. If we dare, we can consider them as a threesome who took pleasure where they could. In this way, we might see them as jumping in Fred Moten's (2003) phonic break—narrow spaces of freedom crafted in spaces of black subjugation. Perhaps they generated and shared pleasure with each other and with a lineage of women who were denied desire before them. If we attend on a queer frequency, we may feel the reverberations of desire echo down the corridors of time. We too are invited to leap in the queer breach. In this conception, the queer formation of *ukukhuphuka izizwe* enables brief sojourns of fugitive frictions and unknowable intimacies that leave adolescents exhausted when they reemerge into this world. We imagine the fatigue and disorientation that follows these sojourns and exorcisms. Perhaps the disorientation that follows a dream. Maybe a postcoital sensitivity that leaves the body heaving and vibrating with the aftershocks of pleasure.

Boddy's (1989) contention that possession should be located within the social and historical setting of a society is significant. She claims that the phenomenon is a political and moral position for thinking about and acting on the world and young people's relations to it. The periods of outbreak point to extant societal tensions and entanglements between the past, present, and future. Barbara Glasson's (2009) concept of the spirituality of survival connotes the turn to metaphysical power or spirituality when people are traumatized and failed by systems. Importantly, Young (2016) suggests that Cele's eruption should be interpreted in relation to her animistic culture rather than the demonic. Reading Cele in relation to animism and failed systems compels us to recognize her sexual abuse by an older woman within broader structures of colonialism, patriarchy, oppressive religiosity, and the arrangements of death that rendered her an orphan.

The recorded accounts of Clara Germana Cele's *ukukhuphuka izizwe* give us a sense of evil of overwhelming proportions, so bad that she levitated horizontally and spoke in many different European languages. Ntombana and Meveni (2015, 4) describe a holy or ancestral possession in ways that are remarkably close to what the nuns witnessed as evil possession in Cele. In their words: "When one is being baptised in the spirit, there are expected signs such as speaking in unknown tongues, making a loud noise, falling down in the spirit or jumping or running inside the church." Ntombana and Meveni further describe ancestral possession by *amakhosi* in the Eastern Cape and KwaZulu-Natal as characterized by *ukugquma* (the growling sound of a lion before it attacks) or *ukukhuphuka*. Therefore, while Cele's symptoms are described as evil possession that are forced out through exorcism, Ntombana and Meveni's account suggests that they may have been a superior force of her ancestors speaking through her. Again, this enables us to see the possibilities of queer temporalities where riotous energies feed off each other across temporal planes. What does an *ukwakumkanya*-inspired vision reveal about riotously queer ancestors and the rioting bodies of adolescents today?

Taking our cue from Jackson (2020), if we look queerly past the demeaning intent of animalist attributions, we are able to conceive of Cele's sonic and visual performance at her exorcism as an illustration of the unsettling of the human and a dismantling of the hierarchies between the human and natural worlds, and spiritual and animal worlds. This reading is one that coheres with the investments of Mpondo theory—an insistence on being tethered to other worlds not as plasticized fetish that is both "everything and nothing," but as buoyant, speculative, and freedom bound. It enables necessary feminist thought experiments in the form of radical conceptions of subjectivity. If the individual is not entirely legible, it can never be fully imprisoned. Cele kicks against the figure of black women as the nadir or limit case in the thin line to the animal. She cannot be entirely owned and through *ukukhuphuka izizwe* imagines other ways to be. To think about the place of the animal differently, a decolonial animal ethic that follows the logics of indigenous cosmologies is important (Tamale 2020). This allows us to work with nonspeciesist and anticolonial animality (Belcourt 2015). Like animals refuse domination, Clara Germana Cele fiercely resisted her own domination. Far from positioning animals as evil and available for subjugation as the nuns suggested, Billy-Ray Belcourt reminds us that they occupy a sacred space in the ceremonial world, they enable the creation of the earth and are therefore not available for human domination. However, since animal rights activists have not accounted for the ways in which animals have been used against indigenous and black people, Belcourt (2015, 9) contends that "animals must first be excised from their colonized subjectivities to be subsequently re-oriented within ecologies of decolonial subjecthood and re-signified through Indigenous cosmologies." To re-signify animals is to unsettle speciesism and collapse the Chain of Being. As a decolonial orientation set within indigenous cosmologies and the breach that is the black imagination, Mpondo theory is invested in dismantling boundaries between the natural world and the putatively human.

The Adolescent Woman as a Riotous Queer Body

As I have repeatedly observed, adolescent girls serve as shock absorbers for rural communities in flux. However, if we linger with adolescents' congregation around a nervous sexual energy as a time bind that concentrates in the schoolyard, we are presented with a new line of thought beyond anxiety.[19] As a fold between childhood and adulthood, adolescent menstruation presents as a possible counterpoint to modernity. Seen as a stalled moment just beyond the grasp of adulthood, this period of menstruation congregates young women's bodies around "unproductive" blood, and this queer meeting of bodies unbinds an energy of resistance, pleasure, anxiety, solidarity that reaches toward spasmodic time. The painting in figure 3.2 points to the duality of adolescents. The queer temporality made possible in this possessed congregation reaches back and taps into the residual energy of other riotous bodies of young women over multiple temporalities in Mpondo history. It also reaches sideways in communion with bodies of similarly marginal bodies elsewhere. This contention signals the multiple possibilities enabled by queer dispositions and ways of attending askance. It illuminates what is made visible when we attend differently and when we slow down to perform a quizzical review of things we know in particular ways.

On a hot summer's day in November 2019, I struck up a conversation with a neighbor. Like most conversations at the time, we began talking about the weather and bemoaned yet another delay in the season's rains.

3.2 *Pondo Women with Aloes* by Alfred Neville Lewis. Courtesy of Denver Hendricks and Strauss & Co.

The woman entered into a resigned monologue. "There is no way we will not have a drought when girls are walking around stark naked. You must have heard about my relatives and their daughter across the way," she said, pointing to the neighboring village perched on its own hill. I knew the family well. The old woman of the home we were talking about had known my great-grandfather. She had died a few months ago. The naked girl was her great-granddaughter. The woman continued. "She had moved to live in the *mjondolo* [shanty town] outside of Lusikisiki town. She was spotted walking around naked in the neighborhood at night. There is a rumor that she takes women lovers and has a snake. The snake helps her to make love to the women." I listened on. "There can be no rain when the gods have been shamed by these young girls. We and our herds will die of thirst. The rivers are practically dry." She meandered from the dry river beds back to the young woman. "But her family fetched her one night. A group of her male relatives fetched her and found her naked. They captured her, beat her up thoroughly to make her regain her senses, and brought her back to her father's home." She pointed at the village again. A tree waved back at us from the village. "But her father would not let her into his house with her demons and snakes. He made a cleansing mix with *intelezi* and they doused her naked body to wash off the demons.[20] She stays home now. I think they are watching her closely so that she does not escape." My neighbor fanned herself to move the still air and to indicate her irritation at those who cause drought through their deviance. I take a long-term view of this waywardly queer woman who is deemed responsible for drought. I wonder at her liberatory naked walks through the ghetto and how these made her feel. What heights of freedom is a naked young woman transported to when she disrobes of her own volition? But I wonder too about how imprisoning her early family life in the village might have been. Perhaps she had found fugitive pleasures with other girls in the tall grasses of the hills. And if she did use a snake to enhance her partners' sexual pleasure, how ingenious and queer is that? How boundless is sexual pleasure among those adrift from the human, and does it fold with energy from ancestral queers? After all, a number of queer traditional healers or seers describe their gender expression as an ancestral spirit (Nyanzi 2013). Is this an ancestral return through queer reverberations in a time bind? How does queer rural pleasure explode modernity and its technologies of surveillance? How powerful might queers be if they can dry out rivers and cause drought? How do queer orientations give additional insights to *ukwakumkanya* in ways that shatter static notions of Mpondo being? Indeed, how does a multidirectional riot fragment what Stella Nyanzi (2013, 952) terms "myopic imaginings of a homogenous African-ness and pedestrian oblivion to pluralities within African sexualities"? What do this naked young woman, Ntanzi's anxiety about his queer body, Clara Germana Cele, and the possessed bodies of young people tell us about the capacity of this landscape to deal with ambiguity? Since I contend that boundlessness and ambiguity are core features of Mpondo theory, what fault lines do queer bodies point to here? As a practice, how does Mpondo theory weather neoliberal and religious orders? After her cleansing, what identifications and antagonisms with home, culture, and nation does the naked girl live with? The value of these accounts is that they point to a social heterogeneity in blackness that Roderick Ferguson (2004) terms "aberrations in black."[21] Within this vast heterogeneity is a precarious space for queer sociality in the village.

In a scholarly terrain saturated in a queer theory of unmarked whiteness and geopolitical location that occurs in settler time, Kenyan scholars Macharia (2016) and Musangi (2018) offer a useful starting place to think of queer lives from the African continent. Working with Musangi's conception of *tala*, a gender nonconforming term, Macharia (2016, 184) asks: "What would queer studies have to unlearn about its geohistories to encounter tala on shared ground? What fluencies would queer studies have to give up to enter into conversation with tala?"[22] In addition, one might ask, while tabulating the pain of African queers, how do we capture the conditions of livability enacted by differently queered Africans? With reference to the queer Atlantic, Tinsley (2008) offers that as a borderlands theory, queer moves us away from easy legibility and transparency. Eddie Ombagi (2019) similarly uses the ambivalences that underpin a queer Nairobi to open up possibilities for complicating African life in ways that "overturn and override" prevailing conceptions of livability. This resonates with my own observations of the operations of queer praxis in village life. My engagement with African queer theory is not a belated move to bring this lens to the village but a gesture invested in the new geographies and possibilities of being that emerge when one commits to reading against the grain with the knowledge that villagers do not offer easy legibility. The chapter is invested in what surfaces in the crosscurrents of the Mpondoland coastline. These emerge from the churning ocean, rivers, hills, migrancy as enacted between the village and the distant city or mining town, and the swirl of spiritual forces and ancestral ties as they rally against and rub up alongside neocolonial incursions. In order to tap into queer frequencies, Tinsley (2008, 194) urges that these explorations "would involve muddying divisions between documented and intuited, material and metaphoric, past and present." Queer intimacies in the African archive emerge from places of captivity. From Robert Morrell (2001) and T. Dunbar Moodie (1988) we learn about mining compound intimacies, and from Tinsley (2008) we discover "shipmate" intimacies as relations of care among those unmoored from their communities and families.[23] These intimacies survived the hold of the ship and traveled to the new world in the Caribbean and the Americas. Macharia (2015) and Taiwo Osinubi (2014) apprise us of prison intimacies in the 1960s. They read these from the memoirs of imprisoned anticolonial and antiapartheid African political leaders who described queer intimacies as corrupting influences that worked against freedom. A queer reading of intimacies that emerge in the hold, the schoolyard, the mining compound, the colonial mission station, the rural homestead, and the African prison would understand these bonds and feeling relations as anticapture, commitment to feeling, pleasure, and being in relation. While these relationships emerge in captivity, they exceed spaces of imprisonment by traveling across social spaces and engendering new socialities. I steer clear of the philosophical genealogy of queer studies since this project is not a response to white queer studies but fully engrossed in the lives of black indigenous villagers.[24] The people whose stories I transcribe are engulfed in a queer atmosphere of refusing subjection and grasping for the pleasure of livingness.

What Happens to Riotous Boys?

Although girls are the lightning rods of societal anxiety, boys are also riotous bodies in Mpondoland. To think about excess boys, we return to the transcriptive mode to draw out the portrait of the deathscape. It was the end of the year and I had returned home for the 2016 vacation. The grade 12 final results had been released, and I spoke to a grandmother whose orphaned grandson had been in the class of 2016. With a 2016 pass rate of approximately 63 percent in the final grade of high school, the specter of failure haunts schoolchildren in the Eastern Cape.[25] Anxiety heightens as adolescents enter high school because the reality of a high attrition rate before grade 12 confronts them. They know of countless peers who have dropped out of school over the years. Remarking on her grandson's recent successful completion of grade 12, the old woman told me that the year had been one of anxiety for him and the family. He had experienced regular headaches, was afraid, and lost weight in the course of his final year. He had ample examples of failure. A very close friend and neighbor had failed grade 11 the year before and dropped out of school. This appears to have had a chilling effect on the friendship and on his prospects of success. These conditions are ideal for anxiety attacks, suspicion and jealousy, illness from depressed immune systems, psychosomatic expression, and outbreaks of *ukukhuphuka izizwe*. Here, there are both individual psychopathology and communal forms of alienation. The problems are well known to be systemic—inadequate classrooms and facilities, poorly trained teachers, overcrowded classrooms, uneducated parents who are unable to supervise homework and school attendance, the enforcement of patriarchal norms and styles of dress (Ntombela 2011). But learners internalize these as personal inadequacies. Anxiety proliferates. "I'm not a praying woman, but I prayed for him. I prayed hard," the elder had told me with reference to her grandson. Her eyes stared apprehensively into the distance.

What happens to boys? Boys are left out on the side of the road. They generally leave school earlier than the girls (Branson, Hofmeyr, and Lam

2014). While many escape the gendered burden of childcare, when they impregnate their classmates, they live almost totally dependent lives. They have no cash. Depleted livestock means that they spend little or no time as herdsmen in the tradition of preceding generations of rural youth. And so, many hang around and wait for their futures at the side of the road. Or at the growing number of *shebeens* where beers offer cold comfort.[26]

Once upon a time in about 1999, while a group of men waited in the perpetual pause of the unemployed, a truck arrived offering employment in the sugarcane fields of KwaZulu-Natal. Whistles rang through the valley as the news spread. Mothers haphazardly packed, baked bread, strangled chickens, stuffed prayers into bags, and pushed the young men out of their nests and into their futures. Tossed bundles of clothes followed by black bodies scrambled onto the truck. The wait had ended. Hours later, the truck ambled onto a gravel road and forged its way deep into the sugarcane plantations leaving the glimmer of the Indian Ocean behind and yet tantalizingly close. The dust trail subsided minutes after the truck's shuddering engine came to a stop. Bodies were counted and money changed hands. A finder's fee. And for transportation. In the old tradition, for each body a price. The truck left and the sun fell into the sugarcane. In this account, the echoes reverberate across the centuries of trade in black bodies for labor and the enrichment of the plantation owners. Across the continent where ships arrived and set sail on multiple crossings of the oceans. One by one, the young men returned to the villages of emaMpondweni. The others before them did not return all those centuries ago. The first escaped before the initial pay cycle and the others followed after they were paid. They returned with tales of capture where they were under constant surveillance and expected to work nonstop through the penetrating heat. Hands blistered and bled, and shins cut as they hacked through the long sugarcane stalks. Echoing the Indians who had been shipped to the same coastline in 1860 to hack through the sugarcane. Trans-Indian, trans-Atlantic, trans-Mediterranean, Transkei. Always black and for sale in the service of white capital.

Cedric Nunn's photographic essay "Farm Workers" documents the abjection of workers in South Africa's rural areas. Figure 3.3, taken in 1986, captures a moment on the sugarcane plantations in KwaZulu-Natal just north of Mpondoland. The young man in the image is covered in soot and sweat from cutting down the sugarcane. But his eyes stare back at the camera and assert survivance. There is no shame in his face. The desolate and apocalyptic landscape of burned sugarcane has not extinguished the light in

3.3 A sugarcane cutter, iNyoni, 1986, by Cedric Nunn.

his eyes. He is unbowed even as he is confronted with the knowledge of the dead end that this plantation work represents. Cutting at the sugarcane stalks has to be sustained by determination and a dream. Each swing of the blade is borne by a feeling. What dreams of love and survival propel the young man to work in the humidity and soot? What desperation hounds his waking hours? Through *ukwakumkanya*, we can read the charred landscape as radiating with energy from the detritus of the earth. The young man and others like him who walk through the waste breathe in and absorb this burning queer energy and put it to multiple uses. The young man will harvest the sugarcane because he has to. Sugar from sugarcane to feed the insatiable appetites of the wealthy and addicted poor. Sugarcane for energy. For Coke. Sugarcane for molasses. Molasses for alcohol. Alcohol for spirits. Spirits for drunkenness. For numbing the pain. The young men who returned to the village resumed their wait with quizzical eyes scanning the deathscape. Some have moved to wait along the streets of the cities. Cardboard signs held close. "Carpentry, plumbing, bricklaying, tree felling." Others have remained at the village. Their hair changes color signaling the passage of time. But the story is incomplete. As the next chapters illustrate, these men resist at the rivers and on the hills.

Conclusion

If to be human can be likened to the splendor of the colonial ship that is at home in deep water, to be Mpondo is to be so many floating African fishing boats moving tenuously among the rocks, floating in the riotous spray, multiplying and adrift. In this chapter, I have sought to transcribe a series of accounts that move alongside and at times against the image of universalizing and enunciating man. These stories can be visualized as a riot of African fishing boats staying close to the shore on familiar terrain or upended on the sand, challenging universality and practicing refusal. While the preceding chapters examined the ocean, river, and hill, this chapter homed in on the spiritual dimensions of Mpondo theory with a focus on accounts of possession and worlding among adolescents. It connected the struggles of the physical, spiritual, and ancestral bodies The chapter showed that possession or *ukukhuphuka izizwe* points to alienation and simultaneous attempts to undo this through reaching for freedom in the breach. Within this Fanonian breach, which is also a queer time bind, possessed adolescents collapse temporality and enter into communion with the ancestral and erotic realms in epiphenomenal temporality. The chapter has termed this a queer zone of being for its capacity to both enable strange love and to upend constraining socialities. The context for these rioting bodies is created by multiple pressures. These include homogenizing forces of modernity, expectations to be good traditional subjects, foreclosed futures where death is writ large and unemployment rife, consumerist pressures, and the surveillance of adolescent sexuality and dreams. By excavating the story of Clara Germana Cele in order to read her alongside contemporary adolescents, I attempted to delve purposively into immolated pasts. Omise'eke Natasha Tinsley and Matt Richardson (2014, 153) contend that this assists the researcher to "unearth the skeletons of racism, misogyny, and transphobia that dominant narratives keep invisible and disconnected in our understanding of times and places." The chapter thinks of *ukukhuphuka izizwe* as worlding in ways that go beyond the constraints offered by the dissociative colonial gaze in order to attend to pleasure, feeling, and relationality (Matebeni 2013). To be attentive to feeling is to engage the bleeding-out of the deathscape but also to attend askance, beyond and through the violation, desexualization, and torture. It is to tarry with our capacities to see multiplicity and expansive queer pleasure, joy, eroticism, and play. If the chapter has been furtive and capacious in its play with queer, it is because it sought to avoid the limits of gay and lesbian categories when reading African lives.[27] African queer erotics challenge the limits of modernity to which dominant Western queer erotics aspire. School-going adolescent spirit riots are an example of a segue into illegible undisciplined desire that gives in to the body and turns its back on the superego of the disciplined mind. Adolescent *ukukhuphuka izizwe* can represent the freedom of being unmoored, adrift, corporeal, and experimental. Following Musangi (2018), an African queer erotics must recognize the vastness and experimentation that is part of the African experience. Finally, I suggested that a queer erotic is an errant drive toward the relational—an ongoing desire that is boundless even in enclosure.

4 LEVITATING GRAVES AND ANCESTRAL FREQUENCIES

The midnight hour
the midnight hour
has a special quality
a stillness of graveyards
after hours
am I the only one
alive to hear the dead
astir in their grave?

It is said

I wail of a land
hideous with open graves
waiting for the slaughtered ones

JAMES MATTHEWS, "MIDNIGHT HOUR" (1977),
"IT IS SAID" (1972)

I think of this chapter as potentially foldable into an abandoned exhibition space in a forlorn landscape showing the photographs of Santu Mofokeng and playing *Pondo Blues* performed by Eric Nomvete and his band.[1] Even though the chapter does not analyze music or photographs, I orient the reader to these media because the sensorial is an essential register for meaning-making here. The chapter focuses squarely on the ancestral arm of Mpondo theory. It attends to how Mpondo people fashion death for life. This is more riotous dying and livingness than it is total vanquishment. I am invested in portraying death with the light and shade of Mofokeng's photographic work. Because ancestors are a core feature of Mpondo theory, to think with this facet of the theory I pause to attend to their graves. I therefore think with the frequencies of blackness in what Tina Campt conceives of as different frequencies of illumination (Campt et al. 2020).[2] Since ukwakumkanya as a method of Mpondo theory is itself a frequential practice of attending, I find synergies with thinking with the register of the frequency. Because Mpondo theory displaces the human and flattens the hierarchies of the Chain of Being, frequential practice is an important register for enabling readings that are emancipated from the human. As Jonathan Sterne (2012, 5) contends, the sensorial transcends the human in ways that enable us to "talk of animals' hearing, of underwater sound, or sound on other planets." In this chapter, then, I loiter in order to attend to the graves of Mpondo villagers through a multisensorial frequency. Though my approach is similar to black queer theorists Omise'eke Natasha Tinsley and Matt Richardson's (2014) use of "graverobber methodology," I do this at the level of frequency out of reverence for the dead and because we write about different but related forms of violence.[3] I focus on the possibilities that arise from attending through keeping still, mapping, walking through, running past, and being in conversation with villagers. I come to frequency as an analytical mode by recognizing that it is a register of temporality, memory, and history. Read through ukwakumkanya, it is sonic, visual, and haptic. Since the chapter focuses on the Mpondo deathscape, I am attentive to the ways in which the dead vibrate and maintain relation and sociality with the living. This requires being attuned to the sonic vibrations that come from the narratives used to assemble the current portrait of Mpondo being. What do graves tell us about the black genocidal hauntings that stick to the deathscape? What haptic registers are stirred by attending to the vibrations that sweep the length of the deathscape? Since frequency is about attending to vibrations, it is invested in meeting places and confluences rather than in calibrations of pathways, origins, and theoretical boxes. What do we learn from attending to the quiet rumblings instead of the loud bangs? If overdetermined dyings are racialized black, what black frequential energy emits from the deathscape? In working through these questions, the chapter attempts not to capture blackness but to read it as a register of motion, opacity, relation, and as always refusing enclosure.[4] My intent is not to overlook the enclosure. On the contrary, I focus on our dying, but I am also attentive to the ways in which blackness is boundless even in death.[5]

In this chapter, I demonstrate the ways in which Mpondo theory, which is born of a deep familiarity with death and dyings, makes meaning of the repetitive frequency of black death in Mpondoland.[6] We have become so familiar with dying that our way of life is crafted to make space for death. In this way, death is a core part of our livingness. Even as we emerge on the other side of the current instantiation of the dying epoch through AIDS and COVID-19, I point to earlier tuberculosis epidemics, battles between communities, deaths of ordinary people, and the deaths of those furtively remembered in history. What do we do with all this dying? Mpondo theory is also a theory of dying. We live in relation to death. Our world making does not resist death. I surface debility, not as death, but as intersectionally bound up with black livingness and slower forms of dying.[7] If dying maims and brings us low, we are debilitated in the process. I begin with a grounded focus on village graves to highlight their everydayness but also their intimate relation to the earth and thus to Mpondo theory. By tracing my village through mapping, I paint a portrait of the losses we have borne, and the spaces left by those who died in the dying epoch. I sit with the dead and enter the graves because we must look unflinchingly into the faces of the dead. This gives us the measure of subjugation. The ancestral realm is centered in order to create space and ongoing significance for the vast numbers of us who die. What dreams are shattered by dying and what possibilities emerge beyond death? In the vein of indigenous scholarship, I recognize the dead as ancestors who possess native intelligence.[8] Dying points us to the failures of racial capitalism because it contradicts the march of neoliberalism as the optimum condition. Mpondo death undercuts capitalism and exposes the lie of its inevitability. This chapter does not offer the means to resist dying but rather suggests genres of dying. I have moments of intense longing for the dead. In my longings, I contemplate what it means to return to the dead. Like Saidiya Hartman (2008, 4), I am invested in how one revisits "the scene of subjection without replicating the grammar of violence." In this chapter, I trace the scar of the earthen grave, turn up the soil, and read the bones of the dead. I am driven by Hartman's question—how do we listen to the narratives of those who live in close proximity and in intimate relation to the dead? To make black history, I have to resurface the dead and claim them anew as historical subjects. I return to ancestors like Sarah Baartman, Nontetha Nkwenkwe, and Mangwanya, to demonstrate how they continue to permeate the lives of the living dead.

Through *ukwakumkanya* in the tradition of the black public humanities, I refract blackness and attempt to knit together a Mpondo theory of dying. As a means of attending through *ukwakumkanya*, I meet my mother on her descent from the old whitewashed mud church. We walk slowly over the uneven pathway. The sparce village lies before us as we descend the high ground. Each household has lost one or several people to death. We silently mull over this thought. It has slowed down now, this dying. My mother pauses to catch her breath and somberly says, "Remember all your age mates?" It is not really a question because she knows that I remember them. Mostly all dead now. We were in our late teens in the second half of the 1990s when it started in earnest and maintained its pace for a decade through the mid-2000s. A decade of devastation for a generation of young people beginning to live their lives as sexual beings. We resume our slow walk. Conscious of her disabling arthritis and worn cartilage, I take my mother's elbow to steady her. I look at each house. And I remember the young villagers long gone now. How we gathered on the road in the afternoons to play soccer and three tins. And I imagine that they would have been in their forties now. Some of the children they left behind as infants are past the three tins playing age. Others have children of their own. Making the dead parents and grandparents. This chapter is paced at a dawdle—a slow walk or shoaled movement through the deathscape.[9] It attends to the frequencies of black life and dying. In divining the frequential register, I reveal the dead while also respecting the opacity of burial practices and black death. For this, I look at, feel, and listen to oblique angels in the methodology of *ukwakumkanya*.

Burying Sarah Baartman

I return to Sarah Baartman because the work of violated black women is never over.[10] We are caught between retraumatizing their memories, appreciating the parameters of what cannot be known, and subjecting the dead to yet another order of violence. In relation to Baartman, Pumla D. Gqola (2010, 70) argues for "radical departures from conventional representations of her only as embodied (object), pathologized (deviant), evidence (knowable) and/or singular ('freak'/myth)." To look at a figure that has been looked at too much (Baderoon 2011), we must look sideways. Our melancholic compulsive returns say something about the anchoring effect of Venus lives and their potential to tell us about our pasts, presents, and futures. Those not buried for centuries are terribly exposed. We who honor them must rebury them. My engagement with Baartman might therefore be read as yet another reburial so that she can finally rest and do the work of an honored ancestor. However, our returns are also about our searchings in the present. Despite all that has been said about Baartman, we want to pose our own questions to her so that we can know her desires as distinct from those who sought pleasure and entertainment from her. Even though we are bound to fail in our quest, we conjecture to create a truer and fuller picture than the bare bones we are given by the archive. South Africa attempted to finally bury Baartman in 2002. My own engagement with Sarah Baartman is not to expand the already extensive scholarship but rather to provide a cylindrical echo, which is to think with epiphenomenal temporality that links ongoing black death to ancient instantiations of black capture and dying. Following Michelle Wright (2015), this is to suggest that the past is not behind us but in the here and now although in changed form—always being re-created. I use this concept to think of Baartman in the present by conceiving of time as tripartite and constituted by an ongoing past, present, and future. Baartman helps us to think about the ongoing nature of black indigenous death. Importantly, Baartman teaches an ethics of care in the meeting place between indigenous and black people. Thinking with King (2019, xv), I suggest that Baartman "interrupts the course and momentum of the flow of critical theories about genocide, slavery," and colonialism. Reiterating the claims made in chapter 1 of this text, Baartman insists that we resist the careless distinctions between black and indigenous in this context. As a person born in the meeting places between indigenous Khoekhoe and indigenous Xhosa, she instead compels us to think of indigenous and black as concepts that rub, relate, and suture.[11]

President Thabo Mbeki read the Langston Hughes poem "I Have Known Rivers" at the funeral of Sarah Baartman on the Gamtoos River, 187 years after she died in France. She was born in Hankey, in the Eastern Cape, on the banks of the Gamtoos and was buried there after being a long-time museum spectacle for the French. She epitomized the black body as spectacle in both life and death. The porous boundaries between objectification in death and life provide us with a historical view of how black death has always been a means of denigration. Baartman had known rivers. What were her longings when she bathed in the Gamtoos? What was her world like before white men entered her life? Before she came to know other rivers and travel seas. In her lonely years, marooned from her land and people, she had imagined rivers and the sound of the Gamtoos. How did she come to be a European spectacle? Sarah Baartman was a body seen as so deviant that her abductor was convinced that he had to show off the unevolved African to his people in enlightened Europe. Hendrik Cezar had discovered something more freakish than a circus animal. Gqola (2010) reminds us that Baartman was owned by an animal trainer at the time of her death. However, as I contend in earlier chapters, animalization enables a sideways move from the human. What is unearthed when we do not hasten to claim Baartman as sanctified human but as an assemblage of the ancestral, the Gamtoos river, indigenous Khoekhoe cosmology and culture, girl, woman, black, animal, African, and part of our deathscape? To knit Baartman into indigenous thought, we have to place her in kinship with entities like mountains, rivers, and animals. This requires us to remake Hendrik Cezar's animalization of Baartman by reclaiming her into her indigenous cosmology that centers "interconnectedness of plants, animals, and humans, geologic forms along with the stories that tune and shape cognition of a landscape" (Marker 2018, 454). This big-picture thinking enabled by indigenous frames demonstrates the pettiness and limitations of enlightenment thinking and positivist knowledges (Graham 2011; Wildcat 2005). A holism that embraces both visible and invisible dimensions of reality where people are inseparable from plants, animals, and geologic forms, is an important practice for reclaiming and returning Sarah Baartman to her village (Marker 2018). King (2019) informs us that to think black and indigenous studies together is to favor convergence and gathering of conceptual frames—to create a new footing of relation and to exceed metaphors that limit blackness to analytics of water and indigeneity to the analytic of land. Though King writes in a different context, the distinction between water and land analytics is particularly unhelpful in the African context. As Vincente Diaz (2015) reminds us, the sea, land, and human mutually constitute each other and are best read together.[12] Our simultaneously black and indigenous sociality requires that we bring the full force of the cosmology to conceptualizations of African life. At the risk of saturating Baartman in metaphor, she acts as a theoretical shoal that compels us to widen our conceptual cosmologies. By side-eyeing us through history, she insists on black errantry and dissidence.

Yvette Abrahams (2000) historicizes the Khoekhoe people so that we can read the abduction of Baartman in a longer temporal arc. She tells of the obsessive gaze of the colonial encounter as white men counted the testicles of Khoekhoe men and then began looking between the legs of Khoekhoe women to measure their labia and the protrusion of their backsides.[13] How many were prodded and pulled before Baartman was found as the exemplar? Zakiyyah Jackson (2020) contends that before skin color came to significance, bestial otherness was the measure of degrees of civility. She suggests that more than color, "projected sexual mores and virility were crucial determinants for measuring the being of Africans" (2020). Indeed, Cuvier (1817), the scientist who pickled Baartman's genitals, reported that it was her beastly face and the great protuberance of her buttocks that attracted people to look at her. The genital encounter with Baartman was therefore a pivotal moment for modernity. Bodies mattered in this petri dish of colonial conquest. Abrahams is squeamish about writing about the body parts of an ancestor. Like her, I worry about extending the violation that Baartman bore in the latter part of her life and in the memory of her people. But this work must be done carefully so that we are acquainted with the scale of colonial oppression in cylindrical epiphenomenal temporality. This work helps us to understand the measure of the perpetual return so that we can conceive of black mourning in ways that point to intergenerational affects. Baartman's life and death can be thought of as a generational echo in the hills of the Eastern Cape. She can be divined in the ebb and flow of the waves and the ripple of the rivers. The vibrations of the Indian Ocean, the Atlantic, and the Gamtoos.

Part of the black return to Baartman is to conceive of her as a relational being, born of parents, raised with siblings and grandparents perhaps, with hobbies and maybe a pet, foibles, illness, health, sadness, and joy too. When she was abducted and placed on a ship, we do not know of her protest and cries for freedom. We can imagine that she looked into the sea in the wake of the departure of the ship that carried her away. On the occasion of her funeral, Mbeki (2002) stitched Baartman's loss to our loss as Africans. In this conception, it is an expansive loss that chronicles the loss of an ancient freedom, dispossession of land, and the concomitant loss of independence. Abrahams introduces Baartman thus:

Sarah Baartman was a Khoekhoe woman, who was born in the southern Cape in 1788. . . . She was taken into exile in November 1809, by an Englishman named Hendrik Cezar, who first tried to sell her as a freak exhibit and later, when he could not find a willing buyer, exhibited her himself. . . . Her exhibition in London during the latter half of 1810 caused a media furor. . . . She was later exhibited in the British provinces and in 1814 was transferred to a new master in Paris. She became a sensation in Paris, as she had in London, and, amongst other things, inspired a new fashion and a play. She was also examined by three scientists in December 1814. Mrs. Baartman died shortly thereafter, in the early hours of 1815, at the age of twenty-seven. (Abrahams 2000, 3)

Baartman's premature death, which cylindrically echoes other hasty deaths in epiphenomenal temporality, perhaps caused by humiliation, respite sought in alcohol, and ultimately smallpox at the age of twenty-seven, provided the opportunity for uninterrupted dissection and measurement of her genitals and posterior by three French medical scientists. This was part of a lineage of the abusive treatment of enslaved black bodies. Dead and alive. A growing body of work maps out how enslaved Africans in the United States were subjected to unethical experiments similar to those conducted on animals. These experiments presumed that black people experienced less pain than white people. Different ethics applied to black bodies in the same way that some experiments are more acceptable on animals.[14] In this hierarchy, there are animal trials, black trials, and then, when efficacy is assured, the procedures and treatments are applied to humans—the monohuman. In seeking to understand present-day distrust of medical experiments among African Americans, Vanessa Gamble (1993, 35) provides the following illustrations of historical devaluing of black bodies: "Harriet Martineau, after an 1834 trip to Baltimore, commented that 'the bodies of coloured people exclusively are taken for dissection, because the whites do not like it, and the coloured people cannot resist.'" I connect this disregard of black death to the dying epochs that followed and that continue into the future. Elsewhere, Abrahams (1997) argues that Sarah Baartman provided the evidence of Khoekhoe primitiveness, a trope that was subsequently extended to the hinterland to justify black inferiority and white supremacy. Her exhibition was a pivotal moment in European constructions of both race and gender. This is significant as Baartman was used to scientifically justify African dehumanization and, crucially, the creation of very particular conceptions of race and gender. This is to say that the dehumanization of Sarah Baartman provided the logics for how black women were figured and by extension, the meanings of whiteness and masculinity. Baartman is therefore at the center of the creation of the hierarchy of the human that justifies black death.

4.1 Traditional herbs are burned around the coffin bearing the remains of Sarah Baartman on August 8, 2002, by Anna Zieminski.

In figure 4.1, we see the coffin bearing Baartman's ancient body, draped in the national flag and sanctified by her people's burial rights. The image beckons the onlooker. Campt tells us that "like sounds, images have frequency. . . . We calibrate our sensibility to images in the way we let them impact and contact us" (Jafa and Campt 2017, 03). I provide a reading of the image by tuning in to its frequency. In the image, Khoekhoe herbs and animal skins accompany her—giving her the send-off that she did not get 187 years earlier. The natural world is central to reconnecting Baartman to the cosmology of her people. In the image, the animal skin knits her to a kinship with the animal world but also disrupts the nationalist discursive strategy of the flag.[15] The skin supersedes the flag and obscures the design and colors of the nation. This disruption takes us to a time before the nation-state while pointing to its ongoing fragility. The smoking herbs and plant life in a large seashell reclaim Baartman from the sterile laboratories and museums and insert her into her ancestral cosmology of the oceanic. Our olfactory senses are stirred by the smoking herbs, and the onlooker registers into the frequency of the deathworld. The smoke suggests motion in the form of a temporal shift from one world to another.[16] Her reburial draws her in and fosters relation to the earth, plant, and animal life. Riffing off Lillian Siwila's (2014) formulation, Baartman's reburial allows us to claim her within the realm of African ecological foremothers.

Billy-Ray Belcourt (2015, 9) reminds us that "animals are only imagined as active agents in Indigenous mythologies but are also capable of creating kinship relations with other (human) animals." In the act of reburial, Baartman is reconnected and placed in relation to the natural world and her people from which she was taken. In an act of reclamation, Gqola (2010) recalls that Khoekhoe elders enrobed Baartman in a ceremony six days before her burial. These ancestral rights do not undo the violation, but they point to black indigenous investments in livingness and relation. Her body once a symbol of depravity and deviance, now a site for remembrance to remark on our history and to begin to make sense of how we came to be the "wretched of the earth."[17]

The simplicity demanded by customary burial practices works against the extravagance promoted by capitalist consumption. Her return to the Gamtoos resettles her spirit with the earth and the river. In this context, placeness is established in "conditions of consciousness that do not travel along positivist routes of knowledge" (Marker 2018, 457). We who walk the earth are able to visit her grave and hold her in mind as an ancestor. The memorials erected in her honor mock Hendrik Cezar, who abducted and sold her. We who claim her as an ancestor pour scorn on the scientists who thingified her. But the memorials also mock us who live today for our continued objectification of black women's bodies. She reminds us of the ongoing persecution of the Khoekhoe who now live in reserves in Botswana's Kalahari Desert enclosure.[18] She indicts postcolonial black governments whose inhumane practices of liberation and independence mimic the colonial plunderers. Baartman's spirit evokes Nongqawuse, Nontetha Nkwenkwe, Clara Germana Cele, and the girls of today and tomorrow whose bodies erupt in communion with the living dead.

If These Hills Could Talk: Cartographies of the Deathscape

In a tradition bequeathed to us by Baartman, to gather our ancestors and hold them in mind, I sat down with a young woman from across the stream and we plotted the homesteads of the village on a sheet of paper. Later, on a morning run, I stood on the highest point on top of the hill and surveyed the village. The houses were small from this vantage point. They coincided with the village map that we had drawn. From here, with my hands raised above my eyes in the posture of *ukwakumkanya*, I felt the vibrations of the dead in the hills, river, graves, and the mirage of the ocean in the distance. To attend to ancestral vibrational frequencies requires an openness to community and the natural world. Old villagers have always held me close. Since I was young, they fed me fragments of stories about their lives, those of generations before, and the natural world. Reading the village from the hilltop that morning, their wisdom and that of the cosmology of this place opened me up to experience the frequential registers of a black indigenous sociality. I recall how Leanne Betasamosake Simpson's (2017) experiences with elders enabled her to benefit from their Nishnaabeg intelligence. To be in relation with elders is to learn an unmappable ancestral cartography. When I returned home, I resumed plotting the village homesteads on a page—not to capture but to stimulate narrativity. The ridge and river map out the four arms of the sparsely populated village. The river is the center. It is the memory bank that carries culture, and indigenous and black secrets that feed Mpondo wisdom. The hills radiate outward, rising gradually from the river. In a sideways move that pauses on the putatively unimportant, I read the hills to retrieve Mpondo life worlds from the oblivion of the archive. To cast the villagers as historical subjects, I veer toward the black public humanities based on scheming hills, whispering rivers, levitating bones, and narrative traces. In this context, the black public humanities are inflected through indigenous studies which insists on place-based intellectual practices.[19] From a space of deep rootedness, we can begin to purposefully dream of freedom, speculate about what it would look like in practice, and imagine how it would renew those who have died. African indigenous philosophies understand freedom not only as a promise for our futures but as crucial for our pasts since we must also reckon with ancestral liberty.[20] This resonates with Aotearoa Maori practices of caring for the dead (Banks 2010). To affirm place and ancestors is to domesticate theorization (Simpson 2017). It is to look sideways at whiteness and capitalism and not to surrender to their violence. Transcribing this narrative and connecting it to place and ancestral wisdom counters the nothingness to which our lives have been redacted.

I sat down with my mother and we used the map to conduct a grim register of death. I began on the upper banks of the stream, a few paces from where my uncle was murdered at the bridge.[21] Four homesteads dot the hill. They are all one family, really. The children had fanned out from their parents' house and built their homes around it. The parents' house is a shell now. It is crumbling and sinking back into the earth. Their graves, which hugged the outer edge of the garden, have disappeared back into the grassy earth. The sunken graves near those of the elders hide a generational se-cret. Adult, adolescent, and infant bodies that were brought low by AIDS in the first blush of democracy of the 1990s and first decade of the 2000s. And still.[22] The landscape of Mpondoland knows black death intimately. The rolling hills contain sedimented layers of death that are reminiscent of black death's "residence time."[23] In thinking about this movement back to the earth, to look askance in the method of *ukwakumkanya*, I consider what it means for homes, people, and graves to return to the earth. What does this motion draw our attention to? I suggest that this dynamic read-ing evokes Mpondo theory since the fallibility of the human is central to the motion. The movement and motion are not necessarily about the triumph of the natural world over the animal world. Rather, this motion signals the constitutive nature of the world's ecosystem.

What does it mean to lie in death and fertilize the hills? Through tracing ancestral spirits over several generations, anthropological accounts have illustrated that ancient cosmic lineages and sense-making repertoires of *sangomas* or traditional healers traverse the worlds of the dead (Keene 2014). These accounts support the assertion that the dead are not quite dead. Their spirits enter the bodies of the living and their descendants. If we see the violent murder of the enslaved that occurred at sea off the In-dian Ocean coasts of the Western and Eastern Capes as forms of death that live on in the present, we have to consider who their spirits live with. The Khoekhoe were hunted like animals and killed. The "Hottentot" were re-moved from the census after being counted in earlier computations (Chris-topher 2002). The frontier wars or kaffir wars (Plaatje 1982; Jabavu 1962) waged between the English and Xhosa for a period of about one hundred years led to countless deaths (Mostert 1992). Where do their souls live? Are their voices in the wind that howls in the Drakensburg mountain range where the San found refuge? Do their spirits live on in the rock art that has outlasted their mortal souls? Do the ancestors live on in the ancient Xhosa songs? Are they present in the Mpondo rituals at the river? And what ener-gies waft from the graves that litter the deathscapes on which we live?

Graves are generally conceived of as sonically quiet, but the affective labor invested in them quivers with feeling. Campt's (2019, 34) reference to a frequency of quiet is instructive. She defines it as "a quietude that reso-nates in the register of the vibrato." The vibrato may be communicated in the throbbing affective inundation that often surrounds graves. Brooding with quietness. However, graves can be sites of boisterous activity and af-fects. Wailing and keening are not uncommon at funerals. The sonic tremor of heartbreak. The frequency is particularly heightened as the body is lowered into the ground and the emotional investments in the corporeal body are placed under pressure. There is movement as the earth mound settles down into its environment. In the long life of the dead beyond the funeral, while the gravesite is unmoving in the way that earth is generally stationary, when we look at the grave, we sometimes imagine the dead in motion or vibrating in place.[24] Perhaps walking alongside us, shaking with laughter, groaning with the pain of death, or quivering with rage. Or on an anniversary, the grave might emit a low-level hum that vibrates at a heightened frequency. Since the Mpondo grave is generally within the parameter of the homestead, the dead are alongside us and our rhythms and affects have moments of being in synch with the dead. To attend to the frequency of the dead requires us to be attuned to our own affects. As a young boy, I recall the hair-raising night terror that would stick to the nape of my neck when I imagined the ghostly presence of my recently deceased father. The feeling had a haptic quality—scalding yet freezing. Years later when I had made different meaning of death, I was often moved to tears of longing whenever I visited my father's grave. When I look at the graves of my peers who died in the dying epoch, I am filled with a nostalgia that conjures the dead to childhood games. They bore the brunt of what Jonny Steinberg (2008) called the three-letter plague during what Hilton Als (2019) has termed the dying epoch. To shelter from the rain in the thornbush hedge that grows alongside the graves at the foot of the garden is to feel the wind differently on one's body. It is to share space and perhaps to commune and shelter with the dead. I suggest that instead of figuring the dead as lost, in our daily lives alongside the dead, we are in constant relation. To access life on a deathscape requires attending to the dead. The frequential register allows us to surface the affects that circulate between the dead and those who live in the deathscape. An attunement to the frequential is an enactment of *ukwakumkanya*. It is an evocation of all the senses to register anew, to repeat, attend to the smell, haptic, sonic, and visual. The slowing down impulse of *ukwakumkanya* thus enables us to visualize, sonically register, and haptically attend to the ancestral dimensions of Mpondo theory.[25]

Having outlined the ways in which *Riotous Deathscapes* attends to the dead in order to give life to the bones of history, I return to the village map that I plotted on the kitchen table. Moving to the cusp of the hill, a garden separates the first cluster of homesteads from the next lot. These homesteads are made up of three families, all loosely related. The biggest of these homesteads had a huge kraal with many cattle. The man once worked in the gold mines and bought cattle almost obsessively. He returned emaciated one Christmas and never went back to his life of drilling rocks in the depths of the mines. His scrawny frame made for a sad figure sitting in the sun against the cattle kraal. He died in a coughing fit. His wife is tall, smart, and wily. She does not miss scheduled visits to the clinic and takes her medication religiously. The treatment was not always available, and her husband died just as it reached the rural outskirts. His grave is no longer visible, but the family knows that he was buried in the corner of the garden, where he looks at his cattle in their kraal. His mother died almost a decade after him, and her grave is next to his. His wife, the tall woman, is now the matriarch of this clan. His father had died in a mining accident almost thirty years earlier. The father's grave leaves no trace in the uneven earth. It is a memory. An emotional trace. What historicization can emerge from following the emotional trace? When the rhythms of life are out of synch with the ancestors, the family returns to the invisible grave and tunes into the frequency of the dead in order to reestablish connectivity to the ancestral realm. The grave is an important site for this reconnection to the frequential register.

Across the road from this family are three homesteads that all share a common surname. Here, too, the death drill has occurred, killing adults and the young. I remember the young people who died in their early twenties. I traced my finger down the map toward my home and paused in an empty plot that was a rudimentary playground when I was a child. I remembered games of soccer, and I see the traces of faces and limbs that I have not thought about in long time. The number of dead playmates turns the playground into a field of death. I contemplate what the landscape would look like if we had to undertake a cartographical project similar to *The Chinese Deathscape: Grave Reform in Modern China.*[26] Only a few of us remain from those childhood games. I think of a 2017 trip to Kigali in Rwanda. The dead of Rwanda. So many that they fill memorial fields and mass graves. An orgy of death. An entire landscape of death. Here, in my village, the deaths were frequent but gradual. This is what Teju Cole (2016) terms a cold violence. Not the hot violence of the bomb blasts of Mogadishu and Palestine. Not the mass disappearances of Argentinians. Not Rwanda. Not the antiblack earthquake that crushed Haiti. Here, in the village, the dead are buried in the homestead like ancestors have always been. Like Hartman's (1997) and Sharpe's (2016) Atlantic ocean, this too is a landscape of death.

Thinking about Selma in the North American South, Cole asks if places retain some charge of things that they have witnessed. Things they have endured. The scars on the disused maize fields along the hills of emaM-pondweni. Red and shredded by erosion. The furrows raise a haunting melody in the wind. The invisible graves at the feet of long abandoned gardens. Where does the trace of trauma hide? How does it work its way into the crevices and what does excavation mean? I was listening to the radio and the scientist Madeleine Fullard, head of the missing people's task team at the National Prosecuting Authority, was talking about how her team traced the pauper graves of people hanged by the apartheid state. They were taken from faraway places across the country to the gallows of Pretoria. Again, I think of Steve Biko's solitary journey. Huddled in the back of a vehicle and realizing that he was being driven to his death in Pretoria. The capital city that was also the capital of black death. Fullard noted that the men whose bones had now been traced had been hanged and buried in unmarked graves in various cemeteries around Pretoria. Their bare bones had just been exhumed in Mamelodi outside Pretoria. From a previous excavation, she listed the people killed in the Mpondo revolt among the bodies found. The graves perched on the slopes of Ngquza Hill are recent. The task team had discovered their bones in unmarked graves and handed them back to the community. I recalled that twenty-one of those arrested at the revolt were executed. Standing above my home village, I was struck by the irony of unmarked graves. Unmarked in the village and unmarked in the cemeteries of distant areas outside of Pretoria. Always unmarked but always there, hovering in the minds of the living. To claim that we live with death is to consider how the deathscape of black life pulsates with the ancestral energy released by death.

I looked at my sketch of the village map and was struck anew by how much places are like bodies. They are the residues of action. They bear traces of things endured. Those who exhume bodies can trace the trauma endured even after the flesh has fallen away and returned to the soil. There is a task team of about ten people who are slowly searching for over five hundred bodies reported missing in the period between 1960 and the end of apartheid. Before and after is beyond the scope of their work. Temporality truncated. Bianca van Laun (2018, 126) observes that in the Gallows Museum, which memorializes people who were hanged, only those deemed political prisoners are highlighted, while "thousands of others who were hanged on charges categorised as criminal have been excluded."[27] She notes that this creates a hierarchy of victimhood that occludes the complicated social conditions that created and decided between what counted as criminal and political. In Argentina, between 10,000 and 15,000 people were killed in a nine-year period of state-sponsored genocide. Based on her experience with divining the bones of those killed in the Argentine genocide, Claudia Bisso from the Argentine Forensic Anthropology Team joined the South African task team of the Gallows Exhumation Project to assist with the trickier cases of reading our bones. If we attend in the frequential register, what do the visual and haptic fields tell us about black death? Where does one begin to look for those who were buried furtively and concealed from their families and communities? Jacob Dlamini's *Askari* (2014) tells us that death squads operating in South Africa and the borderlands made a habit of burning people's bodies until their bones withered into ash.[28] Capital punishment was abolished over two decades ago, but black death continues apace. Next door, in 2017, Zimbabwe was looking to hire a state hangman. Nearly two hundred applications were received.[29] The rope breaks the neck. A sharp snapping sound that reverberates in the space and echoes in the mind. Bone cracking. Scientists can trace the location of the physical trauma long after the murder has occurred. Perhaps across the base of the skull. The floor below the noose gives way. The rope tightens. Screams and excrement. Feet paddling in the still air. The smell of death. And it all ends up in the ground. Unsettling the landscape. Etching it with trauma. Van Laun (2018) describes the Mamelodi cemetery outside Pretoria where the hanged were buried as resembling desolate fields. For me, these desolate fields are deathscapes. On a deathscape, shoaled by the dead, one walks with a slower step. As ancestors, our dead cannot be hidden from view. Through our indigenous practices, we theorize them into view.

I return to my map of the village. Across from the playground adjoining my home is the house of orphaned children or what we in South Africa euphemistically call a "child headed household." The woman who headed the household died and was followed shortly by her eldest son.[30] On the other side of the playground is a grave of a close childhood friend. I remember her laughter well. Loud, gurgling from the belly with a hint of mockery. She lived well and she lived hard. After her death, her estranged husband initially resisted claiming her body. She had been a free spirit who refused the prison that her marriage created. She left the relationship and embraced her freedom. It was not freedom that killed her. Against her inclination toward happiness, she succumbed to black death. Those who attended the funeral say that her body had begun to decompose. Death was in the air. Her mother and older sisters had long been buried in a tight knot at the old house where no one lives. The mudrooms have long dissolved back into the earth of the grassy slope. There is no trace that a vibrant family of women once lived here. I visited the site of the old house and, looking at the barely visible mounds where they were buried, I sat in the stillness and contemplated what it would mean to resurrect the dead women. What would they say about death that targeted free women who owned their bodies? Would they narrate the dreams that were felled with their deaths? What would they tell their children and grandchildren who are scattered beyond the village? The dead weigh heavily on the village. Everywhere we look, we are confronted by their trace.

The absence is profound when a villager dies. Each person fills a visible space. Each house and room is discernable and the spatial configuration ensures visibility. Everyone knows everyone else. We imagine each other in spacetime. The boys stand along the path and laugh. The girls play a version of netball. We know their grandmothers. We know each story because we all have a story. When someone dies, they are buried close by. As in life, the grave is visible. For a while, the dead appear to live spatially and their energy engulfs the village atmosphere. To focus on placeness as I do in *Riotous Deathscapes* is to move against dis-emplacing methodologies that, Michael Marker (2018, 457) contends, tend to "describe Indigenous community, history, and social realities without acknowledging the presence of actual sites of energy on the specific landscape." I walk the land and draw its texture in order to experience the energy of the deathscape. Following decolonial dance scholar Ojeya Cruz Banks (2010), I rely on sensual awareness to inform practices of attending. I am however conscious of the fact that what Banks describes is already encapsulated in the indigenous wisdom of *ukwakumkanya*. For Banks, this approach links "us to people, our own spiritualities, and to the landscape we live and travel through" (11). This moves us beyond the ocularcentric favored by participation-observation. Sensory intelligence is an indigenous quality that develops in tandem with a body oriented toward the natural world and the ancestral. It orients us to folds and temporalities that resist presentism.

On yet another morning run, high up on the hill, I paused, my chest heaving, and looked down on the village. I wondered what a graveyard with all the dead would look like on a heat map that illuminates where all the dead are buried. What if the bones were illuminated in a burning orange color? Would the heat map stretch all the way to the state gallows in Pretoria? Would it scald? Would the burning bones surface the biggest secret of our time and incite guilt to scorch the capitalists and politicians who dithered? There is usually no formal cemetery in the village. Because headstones are rare, with the disappearance of the grave back into the earth, to a stranger there would be no graves in the village. Our dead disappear. This is deceptive because our dead are among us. As the ancestral and spiritual arm of Mpondo theory, the dead are embedded in the memory of the hills, river, and ocean. Our grounded indigenous rituals tap into the memories retained in the hills.

The Black Dead

For John Mbiti (1990), the ancestral community can be considered as the living dead. The ancestral dead are not dead in the memories of those they leave behind or in the realm of the spirits. These continuities are a form of survivance—a profound resistance to annihilation. Like indigenous thought in Aotearoa, Oceana, Turtle Island, and elsewhere, African cosmology is self-protective; it enables a continuity of love beyond death and ruptures colonial intent.[31] Rituals such as libations and sacrificial offerings keep the dead alive within the affective realm. Those taken away from us are imbued with a power that transcends violation. When those who live recite their clan names, they begin with their ancestors and trace their lineage in ways that debunk the binary between the living and the dead. Graves vanish but the mind knows where the dead lie.

The coronavirus pandemic has recalled previous pandemics of black death like AIDS and tuberculosis. Writing about tuberculosis in Mpondoland in his capacity as god, monohuman, district surgeon, medical officer of health, and justice of the peace in Flagstaff, Mpondoland, Grant Millar (1908) wrote denigratingly about the epidemic proportions of the disease. He described the Mpondo as lazy people who were naturally susceptible to disease and whose power of resistance was very low. He contended that the overcrowding of twenty "kaffirs" in one hut made the conditions favorable to the spread of tuberculosis. The fact of migrant labor and the slave-like conditions of mine living and work and its contribution to infection in the first place is only engaged in passing. With reference to other epidemics, in 1908 Millar observed that "there is an enormous death-rate from any epidemic disease that may occur. For example, last year hundreds of Kaffir children died from measles and its subsequent results, while this year scores are dying from whooping-cough." (422). And so, the Mpondo have long been victims of deadly disease. A century ago, their deaths were evidence of Mpondo degeneracy. AIDS discourses a century later were no different. The dying epochs roll into each other and now the coronavirus rubs against these older ways of dying. We die in the epidemics and we die because there is no health care to treat even the curable illnesses. The thousands of dead nourish the rolling hills in unmarked graves.

I traced the village map, skipping over many deaths. I paused on two houses that were once large homesteads with many aunts and children. They are now empty plots with dense concentrations of black wattle trees. In summer, the trees burn with yellow blooms. I remembered the children from these houses. They were older than I was. Tall and self-assured. They wandered off to work on the mines like their fathers and grandfathers before them. They returned sick. A generation felled in the space of a few years. The elders died. The few remaining grandchildren and livestock were plucked away by relatives. At the foot of the hill at the river bend lived a large family of many girls. It was the perfect storm—the girls came of age in the mid- to late 1990s when black death was maturing and no treatment was available. Almost all the young women from the house at the river died during the dying epoch. I remember the futile trips to the hospital. I sometimes drove them there while contemplating my own death. They would wait for me on the road near the bridge, their frail bodies supported by dejected parents who watched death march through the village. I returned with them in the afternoons. The nurses would not admit them to the hospital. There were too many people with the same symptoms and not enough hospital space. The incessant cough. The gaunt bodies that were once large and supple. The whiff of tuberculosis in fading breaths. The few that survived ran off to the city and never really returned to the bitter memories of their siblings. The memories of girly laughter in concert with the gurgle of the nearby stream are too much to bear. The map of death continues up the valley on the other side of the stream. But having made the point, I will not wade in the water.

Analytically, I find the conception of black death to be more generative than the overdetermined if not quite saturated discourses of AIDS. The face of the pandemic was decidedly black, rural, and working class. The unemployed. It mostly affected women who often carried the burden of care and mourning. Many have written about AIDS as politics in the global pricing wars of pharmaceuticals and government denialism.[32] I am however making a case for the very particular manifestation of the disease in the rural countryside of emaMpondweni. I contend that it left a trace that is constitutive of the deathscape. In this deathscape, graves of young people are spatially in one's face as mounds of earth that require integration into the rural cosmology. This landscape is not exceptional, it is different. After all, death is death and, as Cathy Cohen (1999) states in relation to the death following the AIDS pandemic, death is an old phenomenon in black communities. However, if we are to see how some life forms are made bare, we must see them *in relation* to those made human. A lower form of being in the broad spread of racialized assemblages. Weheliye (2014, 27) argues that "bare life must be measured against something, otherwise it just appears as life; life stripped of its bareness, as it were." However, the riotousness of Mpondo theory works against the racial capitalist impulse to render black life bare. As I have suggested, death does not vanquish us. It does not stop our ability to see beauty everywhere. We work with death. To sit with the dead and do wake work (Sharpe 2016) is to smell the acrid stillness of death. To carry the coffin is to feel the sheer weight of the dead. A dead weight. I carried two coffins in a single week. My uncle's and my cousin's. My grandmother's dementia set in that week. I have borne many more coffins than I care to remember. While coffins are generally heavier than expected, during the dying epoch I have been surprised by the weightlessness when death has been presaged by a long illness. Sitting with the dead, washing the dead, addressing the coffin in our speech, circling the coffin in a dizzying send-off song, and looking into the open coffin. Seeing eyes and jaws forced shut. A pallor to the bluish-black and lightly powdered skin. Scents to disguise decaying flesh. These are black ways of witnessing dying and living. Remarking on the death practices of the Guam, David Atienza de Frutos and Alexandre Coello de la Rosa (2012) observe that following indigenous cosmology, death rites are passed intergenerationally in an endless practice of repetition.[33] This repetition grounds us in an ancestral inheritance and enables us to grasp and home with death. Surely, there must be something to our keening and wailing—a vitality that engenders life. Is our black wake work and regular entry into the mortuary and grave not because we recognize that we are here and that the dead are a part of us? Are our weary eyes not a protest against being rendered bare? Arthur Jafa remarks that black people have an acute sensitivity to space (Jafa and Campt 2017). This is seen in both the rhythmic ways we dance and play sports. I suggest that this sensitivity to space is born of an intimacy with living in enclosures, seeking freedom, and insisting on beauty as a means of self-authorizing. Our death dance at the numerous wakes and funerals that we attend is a part of this self-authorization and reactivation of black vitality.

There is a particular look to a mother who knows that life is escaping from her child. I saw this look often. I am haunted by the knowing look of mothers. I have wondered if the anguish etched into her eyes is a reflection of dying dreams. How do we bury dreams? Do we take on the dreams of the dead? Does their energy live on or does it shrivel and die too? When I visited a neighbor who had been my older brother's friend, he had been lowered to the floor on a mattress where people are placed in repose as they near death. Brought closer to the ancestors. The room was dark. The thin smell of death emanated from an emaciated body. His eyes loomed large in a long bony face. He had smiled at me in tired recognition. When I approached hesitantly, I saw my elongated frame dancing in his eyes. Resting his elbow on the mattress, he had reached out and we clasped hands. His hand was bony in mine. Cold already and perhaps signaling that life was scuttling away from him. For a while he had moved about on a bicycle. I remembered how he pushed at the pedals, straining up the hill before the flat between our homes. And now I watched him die and the resigned eyes of his mother observed us. And his eyes were seeing past us, perhaps watching his ancestors. This black terror unleashed on the black body. The mothers watched as death marched through the village. Sometimes mothers fell too. All this dying should not dull our senses to death. As Cohen has argued, it is we who survive who must witness the dead. We have to sit with the pain of death. "When a family is forced to lie about the cause of their son's death, when children are left alone because both parents have died of this disease . . . these things leave permanent marks in your memory" (Cohen 1999, xi). I sit with this living memory that leaves its mark in throbbing graves across the Mpondo deathscape.

There is an open plot on the northern side of my home. But a house once stood there. I remember that it was a huge but single abode. The man of the household had a long beard and was a priest of one of the multiple branches of the Zionist church. When he held church services at his house, the drums disturbed the toads' song and kept us awake late into the night. His first wife was a queer healer—always surrounded by women she was tending to. One day the healer left. I do not recall if this was before or after the priest with the big black beard obtained another wife. The second wife was younger and thinner. She quickly and regularly fell pregnant. Perhaps two of her children lived. But many others died as infants. In quick succession, she buried them below the homestead that was also next to our garden. I remember this because the soil mounds meant that we could no longer play alongside the garden. Our playground was transformed into an infant cemetery. My memory fails me. I am not sure what became of this family. Nothing remains of the sprawling house that once blocked the sun from my mother's garden. The many graves have long returned to the earth, and there is no remaining trace of their location. Except in our minds. I remember that people once lived where the grass now grows. I can hear the incessant beat of the drum when I close my eyes. A sonic vibration that collapses temporalities and keeps me awake on some nights.

We don't talk much about those who died during the black death. The dying has not quite stopped, but it has slowed dramatically and might now be characterized as slow death. Lauren Berlant (2007) defines slow death as the "physical wearing out of a population and the deterioration of people in that population that is very nearly a defining condition of their experience and historical existence" (2007, 745). As a thread that braids with other maladies, AIDS has had this effect of slowly wearing us down. Many of us are on medication now. Antiretroviral medication has eventually dropped in price, treatment has fewer side effects, and public pressure and time have convinced governments to distribute AIDS drugs widely. But when I see a tent erected on the hill, I know that the dying has not stopped. Some of us stop taking tablets when our vitality returns. We are the living dead above the earth. But the dead, those in the ancestral realm, live among us. Rituals that are conducted after a funeral demonstrate that they are for both the living and the dead. Relationality between the living and dead is demonstrated by gifts and giving that defy capitalist exchange. In the words of Simpson (2017, 77), "We have no such thing as capital. We have relatives." Traditional brews which also serve as libations to ancestors are made at all occasions that are associated with the diseased. These libations welcome the dead to the realm of ancestors. They appease ancestors and coax them to look favorably on the living. Ancestors are appealed to for good fortune and protection. When families move from the home that they lived in at the time of the death of the diseased, a ceremony to bring the spirit of the ancestors to the new home has to be conducted. Failure to practice some of the cardinal ancestral rites within Mpondo culture are said to bring misfortune to the living. An angry ancestor whose cosmological value is not affirmed or has been slighted must be appeased. For Canaan Banana (1991, 27), "Life is an endless enterprise, death is not death; it is a vehicle from the ontology of visible beings to the ontology of invisible beings. Death is part of life, it is a gateway to eternity, it's a gateway to life in the hereafter." Writing about the Karanga people of Zimbabwe, Edison Mhaka (2014) contends that death rituals and taboos provide insight into their philosophical ideas. Similarly, for amaMpondo, death illuminates life.

This relationship to the ancestral realm is an enlargement of humanity such that the lives of the living become less bare. Perhaps death is an act against dying. It is a form of resistance to what Hortense Spillers (1987) describes as the historical fixity of bare life on certain bodies. Those who are generationally excluded from the family of those considered human. The bodies to whom historical trauma is always associated are black, rural women. They are related in embodied ways to other women in rural Africa, Brazil, and India. Geographies of excess. Historically, the black women who survived the Mfecane of Southern Africa represent their condition.[34] They can be read productively in relation to the Angolan, Mozambican, and Congolese women who died and lived through the Middle Passage on their way to Brazil and the Caribbean. If one becomes a worthy ancestor, is it possible to think of death as survival—as fugitive escape, since living constitutes bare flesh? It is flesh that is brutalized by AIDS, which is itself sedimented on colonial conquest, repeated historical resistances to multiple annihilations, greed of pharmaceutical companies, tardiness of science, neoliberalism's cannibalism of labor as fodder, and the insecurities of governments. One is confronted by the corporeality of flesh when they sit with an emaciated body—black, bare, dying flesh. Close to the bone. Thinking from black flesh and its corporeality allows us to advance Spillers's aspiration to build a scholarly discourse that considers black women in conversation with the human. Following Mpondo theory, I move sideways to suggest that our death places us in relation to possibilities unleashed by the ancestral realm. Death is not foreclosure but an explosion of binaries and limitations imposed on blackness. Death is multitude and freeing. Working with Glissant's archipelagic thought, if we imagine black death as errantry, we might also see it as a claim to opacity—a demand to the end of suffering. This imbuing of black death with agency enables us to conceive of it as a practice of opting for the boundless obscurity of the ancestral realm. *Riotous Deathscapes* conceives of the ancestral as a black indigenous realm of being. It is unmappable, unreducible, unknowable, and a site where it is impossible to interdict blackness. In illuminating opacity, I align my thinking with King's (2019) contention that black and indigenous theorization should honor the nonreducibility of our life forms. Through the practice of *ukwakumkanya*, we might not see into the ancestral, but if we attend through the frequency of feeling, we may be drawn into the vibrational charge of the ancestors. For *Riotous Deathscapes*, then, the ancestral is a practical and theoretical stake in building boundless spaces for black freedom dreams. It operates in ways that cohere with the spiritual— *ukukhuphuka izizwe*, as a leap into the breach. Mpondo theory gathers these disparate unmappable spaces of black indigenous freedom.

Mpondo Theory as Parting Ways with the Human

In another reach for black freedom, in this section I attempt to dismantle the consecrated human in order to be open to all the disorderliness that constitutes our condition within an African cosmological episteme. Though black people have long been recognized as biologically human, we have largely been excess humans in the service of Wynter's formulation of the monohuman. Therefore, as Hartman (2008) reminds us, it is not so much that black humanity was denied, but to be made slaves black people had to be abjected and their humanity enslaved. Black people are therefore considered particular kinds of humans with a plasticity that simultaneously comprises being human and animal—available for both enslavement and bestial treatment. All African countries have black majority governments, but the people have a provisional humanity in the service of neoliberal global regimes, racial capitalism, debilitation, and black-elite-making characterized by stark inequality. Developing Hartman's concept of black plasticity, Jackson (2020) critiques it by claiming that "plasticity is a mode of transmogrification whereby the fleshy being of blackness is experimented with as if it were infinitely malleable lexical and biological matter, such that blackness is produced as sub/super/human at once, a form where form shall not hold: potentially 'everything and nothing' at the register of ontology."[35] In my own formulation of boundlessness as black freedom, I hold this criticism of plasticity in mind. Jackson seeks to displace animality and blackness as abjection. I too do not appeal to liberal humanism to reestablish blackness within the framework of human recognition. Instead, I pursue the potentialities of animalism for blackness. Mpondo theory does not seek recognition on the terms of the Chain of Being where Man is at the top and black people are located between Man and animals and nature at the bottom. Mpondo theory flattens the Chain of Being and calls into question the antagonism apportioned to black people and the natural world.[36] What is the value of bickering with animals for a rung above them in order to represent a kind of superior place on the hierarchy when our lived experiences are so contiguous and enmeshed with the natural world? Since my project is less about animalism, following the demands of Mpondo theory, I am invested in expanding Jackson's displacement of animalism and the human as abjection to include the natural world more broadly in order to totally distort the hierarchy of being. This is to suggest that, like animalism is not abjection, the natural world is not subordinate or ancillary to the human but central to black indigenous being (Tamale 2020).

Harry Garuba (2003) points to the innumerable ways in which African culture is a constant reenchantment of the world where animist thought is located and embodied in objects. For example, objects such as trees and rivers might come to stand in as material manifestations of animist gods and spirits. In a different context, Tiffany Lethabo King (2019, xiii) writes about the centrality of a tree for indigenous sociality between Muskogee Creek and the Cherokee. She observes: "A special pine served as a meeting place between the two nations; a place of encounter, shared breath, speaking a rhythm, flow, and exchange between two peoples at the base of the tree." Following Garuba, the special pine is enchanted and stands in for the spiritual world. It works in ways reminiscent of the hill and river in Mpondo sociality. Enchantment imbues spirits with a local habitation. In this conception, when an object such as the river represents a spiritual being, the object is elevated in significance. The mobile nature of these enchantments means that we cannot perceive animal or material life as below other life forms. The outside world is internalized, through what Garuba terms the animist unconscious, in ways that complicate the binaries of interiority and external worlds. Marker (2018), Simpson (2017), and a range of indigenous scholars similarly remind us of the place of maple syrup, turtles, trees, rivers, shoals, and rocks. These enchanted objects theorize our place in the world. Since we are so ontologically bound up with the natural world, following Jackson, the challenge may be to free the animal as a symbol with which we are in combative competition. For her, this entails rethinking and transforming the locus of possibility so that the animal does not "continue to animate anti-black discourse and institute itself biopolitically" (2016, 103). We who live in blackness know that the animal is part of us and not in competition with us. To be Mpondo, as I am, is to claim that horns are inextricably tied to my identity. There is no contradiction between the animal and the Mpondo.

The Vibrational Hum of the Mournful Congregation

I return to prophetess Nontetha Nkwenkwe, who was introduced in chapter 2. The South African History Archive tells us that the prophetess was first detained at the King William's Town magistrate's offices. In terror and resistance to the colonial administrators, her followers circled like bees around their queen. To attend to this black congregation is to hear the murmur and hum of people in rebellious protest but also in riotous fellowship and love. It is to turn up the volume and tune in to Eric Nomvete's *Pondo Blues* in a way that invokes the spirit's grasp for freedom even in enclosure.[37] Nontetha Nkwenkwe was moved to the faraway Weskoppies asylum so that her kin and followers would be deterred and cease their resistance. Out of sight was however not out of mind. The historical record demonstrates that the distance only increased the conviction of her followers (Edgar and Sapire 2000). She remained elevated in their minds. They undertook a political pilgrimage by walking thousands of miles across the country from the east to the distant north where Weskoppies is situated in Pretoria. If we attend differently through tuning in to a queer frequency, can we hear the resumption of the auditory hum of the black congregation? Building on Foucault, Lauri Siisiäinen (2013, 17) proposes that "noise/murmur is a multiplicity, which is characterised by indeterminancy." The murmur of dissent conjoins with other voices across place and time. The auditory hum of black congregation generates energy that connects with ancestral energies in the debris of the history of black explosion. I previously referred to this as a queer posture since it charts another path to freedom even in the most constrained conditions. It is a gathering underpinned by an abiding desire for freedom to alter the world. Parched from walking thousands of kilometers, the prophetess's followers rioted. This queer riot counters Katherine McKittrick's (2006, 121) observation of the tendency of drawing "ideas of black femininity, racial superiority, and difference" as spatialized to curtail "subaltern geographic desires and opportunities." Their insistent march across "demonic ground"—a space of refusing geographies of unfreedom through the distant imprisonment of Nontetha Nkwenkwe. An insistence on marching the distance from "geographic nonexistence" to a spacetime of desire for the liberation of their prophetess. McKittrick reminds us that to see black women's geographies is to recognize struggles "over the soil, the body, theory, history, and saying and expressing a sense of place." Nontetha's followers returned home disappointed because the recalcitrant state would not release her. But by homing at her church in stubborn refusal, her followers create life and a new poetics on wretched earth—on deathscapes. When her body was returned in 1998, 60 years later, it was transported along the same route that the pilgrims had taken all those years ago. North American scholar Robert Edgar found her bare bones in a pauper's grave. Her remains had not been embalmed like those of Baartman, the other ancestor. As an act of enfleshment, it was important that her spirit should be transported home.[38] Nontetha Nkwenkwe lives on in the minds of her community as a spiritual leader and a rallying cry for

African feminist aspirations and as a practice of bringing the ontological existence of black women into view.

Transcribing through the language of *ukwakumkanya* insists that I attend informed by what James Lastra (2012) terms as fidelity rather than intelligibility. Fidelity to the portrait of Mpondo theory is crucial for this undertaking. Fidelity translates as commitment to the sonic and visual airspace of *ukwakumkanya* and not to respectability. When one attends with fidelity, what are the sonic vibrations emitted and what are their affective registers? To hear, just as to see, touch, and smell depends on positionality—where one is positioned in relation to the sound and the object. As McKittrick (2006, 138) reminds us, soundscapes are "implicit technologies of the poetics of landscape"—geographic acts. Some of the events that I write about have passed by, I witnessed others, and I heard of others secondhand through protagonists. In this instance, while I recognize that what is heard or seen may be attended to differently based on one's location, I have to position myself in a posture that attends with fidelity to the occurrence and the protagonists. To tune in frequentially, I should consider how Nontetha Nkwenkwe's followers strain against this realm and remain in queer communion with her generations later. I must consider how this world rubs against that of the ancestral. The very existence of her church changes the stakes by mocking modernity and creating a continuous landscape between this world and the ancestral.

Debilitation as Slow Death in the Deathscape

To think about dying from a different vantage point, I squint in the gesture of *ukwakumkanya* and briefly turn away from events in order to pause on the quotidian in a population marked for wearing down through the vagaries of everyday life. In Foucault's (1976) conception, the move toward that which is permanent and ongoing tracks the endemic. Figured as a zone of dying, in Mpondoland, the living and dying rub against each other. Our precarity is geopolitically specific. We carry debility in bodies that die differently and more frequently. Capacity and health in some geolocations is presaged on debilitation elsewhere—through lack, extraction, no health care, hard labor, and death. Those elsewhere work to ensure the well-being of recognizable citizens. The impoverished support the rehabilitation of the wealthy. The latter are reinvigorated for and by neoliberalism (Puar 2017). Those residing in neoliberalism's deathscapes are conveniently out of sight and endure the slow death of debilitation. Lauren Berlant (2007, 756) suggests that the slow wearing down or slow death "occupies the temporalities of the endemic." Puar (2017, xiii–xiv), from whom I borrow the concept of debilitation, contends that it is "distinct from 'disablement' because the former foregrounds the slow wearing down" of people and does not signal disability as an event. Debilitation is insidious and often unrecognizable because it lacks the legibility assigned to disability. Black flesh, conceived of through Spillers as malleable and fungible, is particularly prone to debilitation. King (2019, 23) reads black fungibility through Spillers's fleshy analytic: "Black fungibility can denote and connote pure flux, process, and potential. To be rendered Black and fungible under conquest is to be rendered porous, undulating, fluttering, sensuous, and in a space and state at-the-edge and outside of normative configurations of sex, gender, sexuality, space, and time to stabilize and fix the human category." This plasticity provides verdant space for debilitation. As an antiblack practice, debilitation has featured as a brooding presence throughout this text. In a sideways move, we might consider the spiritual riots of *ukukhuphuka izizwe* as forms of resistance to being the castoffs of the processes of debilitation. In this context, disability occurs in tandem with debilitation. In Mpondoland, we are caught up in this web of sedimented maiming. Puar (2017, iv) argues that "disability is not a fixed state or attribute but exists in relation to assemblages of capacity and debility, modulated across historical time, geopolitical space, institutional mandates, and discursive regimes." Relying on both Puar and Therí Alyce Pickens, I attempt to think through some of the accounts that follow through this prism.

The following accounts about Mampinge and Mangwanya assist us to consider how disability figures and is grafted onto debilitation in the deathscape of Mpondoland. Following Therí Alyce Pickens (2019) and La Marr Jurelle Bruce (2021), in these accounts, since madness cannot procure respectability, I reckon with how black madness forces us further away from the consecrated human as a default premise of measurement of the norm. Here, I transcribe a part of Mampinge's story of death and how it features in the Mpondoland deathscape. I loved to watch Mampinge with my mother. After years of shouting at each other, my mother learned that she should just mouth her words. Mampinge was deaf. When she did not want to hear what was being said, she would look away. For the longest time, she had lived with three of her older sisters until they died at the house with black wattle trees and geese.[39] Unable to live alone as she grew older, Mampinge moved to a neighboring village where she lived with her niece.

Long after her old family home had disintegrated and caved back into the earth, Mampinge would walk to her ancestral home, cook, and leave the food for them to consume. But at this point, her family had been dead for several years. Those who observed this behavior explained that the elder woman had developed dementia. This may very well have been the case. But it begs the question that if the dead live on, do they not eat? When those who love them want to honor them, what are they to do? Are libations and sacrificial slaughters of animals not a form of eating? Mampinge was known to talk to her dead family as though they could hear her. As a deaf woman, sonic vibrations were an important frequential register for Mampinge. Struggling to live with a strange aunt who had begun to wander away, her niece took her to hospital where she was given psychotropic drugs. The medications dulled her spirit and she could no longer visit her ancestors' graves. She too has since become an ancestral spirit. In my own imagined conversations with her, I mouth my words, knowing that her spirit reads the movement of my lips.

The state disability grant plays an important role in rural livelihoods where most people are unemployed. Mampinge received a disability grant for many years before converting it to an old age pension.[40] I recall villagers who lived with biomedically legible disabilities such as deafness, blindness, deformations from childhood polio, or amputations. The recognition of these disabilities ensured that they received a disability grant. Of course, their otherness or queerness was often ridiculed, but they were also more economically secure than many of those without disability grants. The human rights struggles of disability activists had fought for legibility and concomitant, albeit limited, support from the state. I likewise recall others who had various cognitive impairments and physical wearing down that they had to exaggerate and make legible within the register of disability in order to access a disability grant. There was another category of villagers with varying debilitations that hobbled their lives but who nevertheless could not meet the limited test of biomedical definitions of disability. I return to Puar's theorization here. She observes that "while some bodies may not be recognized as or identify as disabled, they may well be debilitated, in part by being foreclosed access to legibility and resources as disabled" (2017, xv). In the deathscapes of the Global South, narrow conceptions of disability blind us to the slow death of debilitation. Puar's conception challenges us to reconsider the binaries between the disabled and the "nondisabled." Mampinge and others like her are caught in the fissures of disability and debilitation.

Douglas Baynton (2006) asks us to consider how we would retell—or with the benefit of hindsight, how we would understand—disability in history. However, following Puar, I rephrase this to consider debilitation in history. Through *ukwakumkanya*, what do I attend to if debilitation figures in the way of attending? To return to the ongoing AIDS archive in the register of debilitation is to consider those with debilitating AIDS conditions within the liminal position between dying and living. The slow death of AIDS points to death as everyday occurrence rather than catastrophe. From the prism of temporalities of the endemic, we can consider anew what state deformation did to the limbs and minds of those fighting in the Mpondo revolt. It casts a shine on how mining the bowels of the earth figures as a mass debilitation complex in the service of global capital. It refigures adolescent spirit possession riots or *ukukhuphuka izizwe* as simultaneous states of debility and freedom. Debilitation is useful in this refiguring since it avoids the suggestion that wearing down or slow death are individual abnormalities that occur through biomedical filters. Debilitation illuminates the multiple ways people are made marginal and further unhumaned. I am attuned to the ways in which some people might be assigned disabilities in order to be rendered abnormal and consequently to validate their oppression. I am interested too in how rurality and resistance to development might be seen as disability and as queer when explained through lenses of evolutionary failures and backwardness in the logics of the human in order to justify state neglect. To explain Mpondo life as backward may be used to create a hierarchy of blackness and attributions of abnormality in order to blame the victim of social oppression and systemic failures.[41] Is the political work of attributing disability a means for us unseeing debilitation?

Debilitation and violence often reside side by side. In colonial, neoliberal Africa and in global indigenous territories, the predatory nature of capitalism is closely aligned to state and corporate violence (Pereira and Tsikata 2021; Coulthard 2014). Frantz Fanon was particularly critical of state-sponsored violence in colonial Africa. The violent suppression of freedom on the continent remains a common feature of our politics. Even if we had to focus only on the massacres that mark our history, maiming and deformation are huge contributors to debilitation. While we count the dead, we are often less attentive to the slow death that trails massacres and the wearing effects of antiblack neoliberalism. In tracing the Mpondo revolt and subsequent rural upheavals, alongside my interest in the dead, I pause on the debilitating effects of the violence. In the postapartheid period, the state disguises its violence through symbolic commissions of inquiry such as the Farlam Commission that followed the 2012 Marikana massacre.[42] Glen Coulthard (2014) critiques these transitional justice mechanisms as structures that imagine violence as occurring in the past or limited to an event rather than as ongoing and lurking in the future. A constant attrition dragging us along in a trail of slow death. Commissions are less attentive to the ongoingness of violence in bodies debilitated by debasement. However, direct violence is not the only means through which dispossession and disablement are enacted in postcolonial settings. Neoliberal violence occurs through a set of relations that Fanon (1967) masterfully drew in his analysis of the recognition/freedom dialectic. To function optimally, neoliberalism requires the colonial subject to internalize values and enact behaviors that sustain domination (Musila 2020).

An important intervention by Nirmala Erevelles and Andrea Minear (2010) is that we should not see disability as a biological category that is immutable and conceived of as pathology or abnormality. In thinking of my own mother and the account provided in the introduction, I recognize that systemic pressures as well as the life stage of old age render her disabled. Her degenerative bone disease and her anxiety and panic debilitate her. Beyond his amputation, my brother and his village peers bear the marks of alcohol-induced disabilities from a debilitating environment where numbness is better than full awareness. Malawian disability scholar Ken Lipenga's (2014) reading of "nobody memoirs" demonstrates how hegemonic masculinities intersect with disability.[43] This coheres with my own investments in understanding what occurs when young men are disabled by debilitating environments and political cultures. Puar's (2017, xv) contention is generative for thinking of debilitation in the village—"capacity, debility, and disability, exist in a mutually reinforcing constellation, are often overlapping or coexistent, and that debilitation is a necessary component that both exposes and sutures the non-disabled/disabled binary." The suturing work of the lens of debilitation insists on attending to the systemic attributions. Debilitation draws us to capacity as a relation to the labor of sustaining the lives of the wealthy and the disabling consequences of this.

I heed scholars such as Lipenga (2015) and Charles Riley (2005) who warn against the lives of disabled people being drawn as symbolic gestures to make larger social commentaries about society. Instead, through the portrait of this book, I show how villagers are debilitated by despair, patriarchy, and racial capitalism. A key feature of this debilitating environment is premature aging and hobbling by illnesses that would be curable in a caring sociopolitical order. In this project, disability as a category is understood as a socially constructed, historically contingent, and context dependent feature of social life within particular economic and political conditions. Disability, gender, and race work together and have material effects for people who live in the intersections of various differences. A woman whom I call Mangwanya visited my home almost daily in my youth. She died in the course of completing this book—stooped over and prematurely aged. As a young woman, her husband called her crazy and used this as a pretext to marry a second wife. He had her committed at the regional black people's asylum in Umzimkhulu. The conditions of black women's incarceration pushed her mental faculties to the edges of madness. She returned a year later as a heavily medicated docile wife who appeared to have begrudgingly accepted the fate of being part of a polygamous marriage. However, her neighbors recall that she was at her most transgressive in the early morning. She would stand at her door at dawn and ridicule her husband and his second wife. In this case, disability worked with gender to impose a patriarchal institution of polygamy on a nonconsenting woman. However, race is crucial for understanding the institution of polygamy as well as for the class position and impoverished life that the elder woman has lived. Mangwanya's choices and options were circumscribed by a system of racial patriarchal capitalism that ensured she remained in an unhappy marriage. However, if we attend to the sonic imaginings that arise from listening to the elder woman's curses and screams carried in the early dawn, we surface the resistance enfolded in madness. Can madness be a register of radical freedom?[44] Like the death world offers liberation from oppressive life, can the vibrations from the screams of madness provide a reprieve from tyranny? Freed of her churchwoman constraints of respectability, registered at a sonic frequency, Mangwanya's volley of obscenities shouted at her husband and his younger wife made a putatively private problem a public one. All her neighbors heard and felt her disaffection. They in turn told the rest of the village. With this knowledge enabled by her madness, none of us can claim that polygamy was embraced unproblematically in the village. Here, madness can be viewed as a conscientizing force. Through her formulation of black madness and mad blackness, Pickens (2019) reminds us that there is no neat boundary between the self and the other. As black people, we are all interpolated into madness by the maddening conditions of an antiblack world. Madness and blackness are consequently figured as a complex constellation of relations. This brief vignette is illustrative of the value of incorporating debilitation as a lens through which to understand black rural life and death. What does it mean to live in the confluence of all these differences in the distant geographies of the ignored demonic village deathscape? To address this question, we must attend to the "convergence of capitalism and slow death via its enfolding into neoliberalism" (Puar 2017, 1). This reckoning compels us to see debilitation as always operating on multiple registers.

Conclusion

By focusing on the invisible features of the everyday, this chapter has sought to achieve two related aims of Mpondo theory. The first was to illustrate how the ancestral world enlarges black life. The earth that bears the dead is a space of black sociality. Indigenous theorization was important for drawing relations between space, enchanted natural objects, the death world, and this realm. The many dyings mean that Mpondoland is constituted of traumatized deathscapes—demonic ground—but that black death is not in vain. Rather than disjuncture, death is continuity. The second objective was to explode the logic of the hierarchy of the Chain of Being that sees animals and the natural world as inferior and separate from the human. By drawing on Jackson and scholars of African epistemologies, I illustrated that Mpondo theory debunks this myth by revealing how the natural world, ancestral world, and human world coconstitute each other. This requires turning away from colonial tropes of animalization and tuning in to everyday practices of people. Mpondo theory is invested in neither projects of humanization nor of dehumanization. In order to do the work of excavating everyday immolated deathscapes, I used the methodology of *ukwakumkanya*, which attends to frequential registers of the taken-for-granted. Frequential attunement allows for movement across sensorial registers in ways that stimulate the imagination and explode taken-for-granted truisms about who can speak, hear, touch, smell, feel, and see. The sensorial thus enables a way out from what Jackson (2016, 97) describes as the "near-inescapable paradoxes of liberal humanist recognition" to which the self has been conscripted. In this chapter, through *ukwakumkanya*, I have illustrated the possibilities that open up when we shift from one perspective to another. What happens when we think of death not as an end but as continuity and expanded relation? I have proposed that blackness is enlarged by tarrying on the deathscape and recognizing both the trauma of slow death and the amplification of the ancestral world. Since this imaginary pushes at the boundaries of life/death, it is equivalent to an epistemological rupture (Bourdieu, Chamboredon, and Passeron 1991). Epistemological rupture occurs through pausing or slowing down that is enabled by *ukwakumkanya* and King's concept of shoaling. This entails attending with the embodied mind, which requires us to take seriously graves' vibrational frequencies and what they may be communicating to those who are affectively receptive to poetic relations with ancestors.

In this chapter's focus on the dead, I have also attempted to think with Puar's concept of debilitation in order to trace how late capitalism debilitates those who make lives in places like emaMpondweni. I have sketched out the AIDS dying epoch in Mpondoland and the terror that the aged and debilitated live with. The slow, normalized violence allows the Mpondo to bury their dead. The dead pile high in the earth. The gravesites are all over. Some unseen. Tumors in the landscape. To enflesh the dead is to refigure ancestors as an iteration of refusal. They are remembered and centered in the lives of the living. To insist on the kinetics of black people even in death is the labor "of forging and sustaining a relationship to imperiled black bodies never physically stilled and always profoundly in motion" (Campt 2019, 43). This affective labor manifests the riotous character of the deathscape.

5 RIOTING HILLS AND OCCULT INSURRECTIONS

This is no calamity, for calamities we know. This is worse than calamity. Say, rather, it is the curse of death. For it is the doom, aye, the very annihilation of a people.

ARCHIBALD CAMPBELL JORDAN, *THE WRATH OF THE ANCESTORS* (1980)

Time does not exist for the average Kaffir. On the other hand, their memory is extraordinary.

GRANT MILLAR, "MEDICAL PRACTICE IN PONDOLAND, SOUTH AFRICA" (1908)

As a dimension of Mpondo theory, the hill is centered in this chapter. Following the previous chapter on dying, this chapter is about scratching through the debris of death as a form of resistance. The kind of resistance figured here is what Gerald Vizenor has termed native survivance and Katherine McKittrick calls black livingness. Both forms appeal to me because Mpondo theory articulates a black indigenous way of being. While the events that are catalogued in this chapter might be seen as apocalyptic collapse in the face of neoliberal consumption, I contend that a more accurate appraisal is to conceive of them as forms of survivance. Sometimes black survival entails killing or ingesting in order to live. At other times, reaching toward occult worlds and practices is a tool of survivance and livingness. I take up Tiffany Lethabo King's entreaty for us to be honest about the ways that the terms of survival are sometimes "tethered to the death of the Other" (2019, xi). This chapter explores these strategies of survivance in relation to how they entwine and give form to Mpondo theory as practices of livingness. Vizenor (2008, 1) defines survivance as "narrative resistance that creates a sense of presence over absence, nihility and victimry." Survivance refers to both survival and endurance. Elsewhere, Vizenor (1994, viii) defined survivance as "an active sense of presence, the continuance of native stories, not a mere reaction, or survivable name. Native survivance stories are renunciations of dominance, tragedy, and victimry."[1] For Mpondo people, survivance is an ability to live in the cocky posture of *ukwakumkanya*. Similarly, to think through how enslaved Africans on the *Zong* slave ship refused deadness in favor of black livingness, McKittrick (2015, 15) has called attention to how we might look for "clues to what a different form of life might look like by inscribing how freedom is worked out and worked on by those who have been unfree." In Fanonian poetics, livingness would be the ability to leap through the breach in moments where life is threatened. The ability to notice livingness when death is so pervasive necessarily requires analytical frames that attend to relational frames. Since Mpondo theory conceives of being in the cyclic relations between death and life, an attentiveness to livingness among the dead is crucial to this project. As method and form, *ukwakumkanya* enables a slowed-down form of attending to survivance and livingness.

This chapter is about market forms of violence that those excluded from capitalist accumulation and consumption engage in as they attempt to find a footing in the elusive good life of the human.[2] I linger on the violent imprint of neoliberal capital across the multiple forms of livings and dyings that I center here. I continue the work of detonating the human initiated in preceding chapters of *Riotous Deathscapes*. Following Zakiyyah Jackson (2020), I see violence as "endemic to the recognition of humanity itself—when that humanity is cast as black." This means that rather than unhumaning, terror is "the price of the ticket" for the inclusion of blackness into the nadir of the human Chain of Being.[3] Sylvia Wynter (2003, 301) describes this position as "a rung of the ladder lower than that of all humans." The price that Mpondoland has paid and continues to pay is the subject of this chapter. The chapter explores the consequences of being the dregs of the human. I demonstrate that capitalist pressure and death are related to outbreaks of vampire and cannibal activity that have proliferated in the countryside. Here, vampirism is both a material reality of ingesting the dead and a metaphor for capitalist consumption and failures. I however frame consumption practices as critical praxis of freedom—livingness. Following Xavier Livermon (2019), I conceive of this as a move that queers consumption. At one level, this conception of consumption departs from the sustained resistance to neoliberal pressures to consume that I have chronicled in preceding chapters. I however suggest that young peoples' attempts to consume are based on failed promises and that they recognize this. Instead they pervert and mock the very consumption they desire. This double register both leans into Livermon's frame of queering consumption as a praxis of freedom and it signals a queer failure to consume.

In painting this portrait of Mpondo life and death, I attend through *ukwakumkanya* to engage community narratives and news reports on cannibal and vampire activity in Mpondoland and neighboring KwaZulu-Natal. The chapter contends that these are commentaries on the commodification of the body in times of intense pressure to participate in consumptive economies. Since pervasive unemployment means that Mpondoland is omitted from the capitalist consumption that has taken root in the cities, those on the margins feed on each other in the hopes of accessing the consumer-based promises of a capitalist world order. While failure is inevitable, those who make it are models that people aspire to. I use the examples of the legendary medicine man Khotso Sethuntsa and former president Jacob Zuma to illustrate how aspirations for the good life are figured in both the village and the nation-state. In addition, I point to those who buck the trend of capitalist desires by insisting on living in relation rather than in competition. This chapter pairs violence with dying. It shows that different forms of consumption, including human flesh, and the imposition of death are a queer strategy of survivance and livingness. Here, dying is an explication of a Mpondo theory of death and life. I provide examples of community-sanctioned ways of dying as one such strategy of life. The chapter is framed by a set of questions which resonate with other themes that shoot through the entire text. How do we honor the voices of local protagonists as the heartbeat of history when the archive has excluded them? What is the counterhistory told and lived by people in the ongoing aftermath of catastrophe? How do we write about the grotesque in ways that don't exceptionalize but that provide insight on communal narratives of apocalypse? To echo Saidiya Hartman (2008), how do we sit with the open casket and face the scandal of the archive through local narratives? In order to think of the visceral pull of the past and the workings of temporality,

I begin the chapter by returning to Ngquza Hill from the vantage point of elders in my community and what it reveals about black death. Elders are important for this project since they witnessed the Mpondo revolt and they carry the wisdom and knowledge of Mpondo culture.[4] By moving across a cast of protagonists whose lives intersected with the Mpondo or Kongo revolt, I provide a living social history from different angles and refractions from the hills. While previous chapters took up different arms of Mpondo theory, this chapter extends on the work of chapter 2 by centering the hill as a place from and through which we theorize. The hill is the place of refuge, regrouping, and strategizing. Like the river, it is also the place for fortification rites.

Violence and Pathologies of Capital

Violence is the underbelly of thingification. When people are made things in contexts of brutalization, the worth of the body and its tropes of human sanctity are questioned. When black death is commonplace and consumptive economies elude the impoverished, we return to the body for making meaning and for consumption. In this chapter, we consider how the black body weathers violation. We are returned to the story of Ngquza Hill and, as in chapter 2, I suggest that it is more apt to understand Ngquza Hill as having occurred across the thousands of hills emaMpondweni. We look sideways by examining the peripheries of the revolt. In casting the shine and shade of *ukwakumkanya*, place is centered as a methodology attuned to black indigenous knowledges. Here, placeness contains the ontological meanings of local knowledges as a means to "excavate the specific effects of colonization on indigenous landscapes and communities" (Marker 2018, 454). Place is read alongside narrative accounts of village elders who narrated their recollections to me in a series of interviews framed as conversations since elders refused to engage me as a researcher and insisted in talking to me as one of their own—a neighbor, a child of their contemporary, someone they had observed grow up in their midst.

The killing and disposal of bodies during the Mpondo revolt, the Ndlavini and Nombola battles, the Marikana massacre, and, as I illustrate in this chapter, the consumption of human flesh in the current period of the Vondo are all historically connected.[5] They are however not connected as impulsive repetitive acts. They are intimately connected to memories of earlier stories in cylindrical epiphenomenal temporality. At Ngquza Hill, the bodies of eleven people murdered by apartheid police were left in the open, exposed to the elements (Fidler 2010). Black bodies have long been at the mercy of the elements. Of pigs and dogs. Fish. And occult forces. But local memorializations keep the names of the dead alive despite the silences of official archives. Mpondo people recognize fact is fiction with the endorsement of state power (Hartman 2019). In the alternative archive of the memorial at Ngquza Hill are the names of the eleven men killed on June 6, 1960. Those whose bodies lay in the sun. They are Wanna Johnson, Tshipile Dolo, Sigwebo Mfuywa, Ngqangala Caphuka, Geke Jama, Nqilitshi Nqcanda, Ntamehlo Sipika, Phothotsha Ndindwa, Khoyo Chagi, Pali No-geve, and Magxaka Khaka. Listing these names requires looking askance, queerly—beyond the apartheid canon because the names are not available in national memory and are recorded only on the local memorial at Ngquza. Marginal names that evade the archive only live on as an act of survivance and are carried from mouth to mouth through the frequential registers of black livingness. When archival administrators and state officials were unavailable and uninterested in speaking to me, local protagonists shared the stories learned from preceding generations.[6] Leanne Betasamosake Simpson (2017) reminds us that for alternative indigenous histories, one has to live in respectful relation to elders. This transcription is from such a relational practice.

In the case of the oldest woman I talked to in 2017, the events of 1960 were heightened in her memory. Her husband disappeared that year and never returned. He vanished into the Kongo. She described the turbulence that I had initially only heard associated with the areas closest to Ngquza Hill. She told me that the men did not sleep at their homes for stretches of time. She pointed into the distance, and talked of the lonely tree on the hill.[7] I intuited the vibrational frequencies that would emit from the shade cast by the lonesome tree that has outlasted generations. In the vibrational charge, I attended to the trace of affects left behind in the debris. Like the lone tree, the people with whom I spoke were filled with pride for the work of the hill committee that met in the shelter of the tree. The pride radiated from the rubble of recollection as the elder pointed across the valley. Survivance is fueled by local histories of livingness that knit our stories together and give us a mutual intelligibility even while we maintain a level of opacity from the state and its archives. "That is where the men slept. Just across from the maize fields of Mpelazwe." As though embodying *ukwakumkanya*, her eyes were at once fixed and out of focus. Age had played games with the shade of her eyes. Bluish black and milky against her jet-black skin. The folds in her skin retained haunted memories. "I was married and had had both my children. The police were wreaking havoc in the villages. It was a perpetual emergency. We kept away from the houses during daylight because the police would ask us to tell them where the men were. Children were especially dangerous because they would answer questions truthfully. So we had to teach them what to say and hide some truths from them." She was a neighbor, and I knew the story about the disappearance of her husband. I had, however, not associated his disappearance with what has come to be known as the Kongo. "He was returning to work on the mines in Gauteng. But I am not sure if he made it there. With all the troubles, perhaps something happened while he was still here. Or on his way there. Or he died under the earth at the mines. Maybe the Kongo is ongoing because he still has not returned." I calculated fifty-seven years since his disappearance. I return to this possibility that the elder has offered because it is a generative way to think of cylindrical epiphenomenal temporality. It is an example of queer temporality. For her, time had stood still. Her husband disappeared in 1960. She did not mourn him as a widow would in Mpondo culture. She has a husband who left for the mines in 1960. He has not returned. He went with the Kongo. The Kongo might not have ended. The Kongo is stuck and frozen in time. It is a haunting presence that refuses to ease. The Kongo is an affective congregation of a queer minor history with bedraggled and worn-out actors. At the Kongo's end, her husband will return. He is in his 90s now. Alternatively, he would have been in his 90s. We cannot know at this moment. For this elder, the declaration of loss had never been made. The object of her loss is uncertain (Eng and Han 2019). She is caught up in a long but tentative mourning. In 2019, two years after I conducted the initial interview with the old woman, my mother called me to report that she had gone to see the woman and that she was very ill. A few days later, the elder who had never been a widow died. She died without the declaration and validation of her loss.

And yet the old widow who was not a widow had an interior life beyond her relationship with her disappeared husband. I think about her life worlds in relation to a more abstracted Mpondo woman painted by Irma Stern in the 1929 image that appears in figure 5.1. The woman in the painting does not stand in for my dead neighbor. The two women would not have been peers although their timelines would have overlapped. My reading of this woman is meant to paint an earlier life of both my dead elder neighbor and of Mpondoland prior to the Kongo revolt. The hills that form the background of the painting are as reassuringly riotous as the hills that I

know in the present. The *Pondo Woman* of the painting, my neighbor and I,
were all raised on the hills. Despite Mpondo infamy as the red ochre people
without education and of a low social standing, the eyes in the painting
communicate a sense of rooted self-assurance.[8] They cut at the onlooker
and her mouth is pursed in contempt. Figured through *ukwakumkanya*, the
painting vibrates her livingness. The woman's clan tattoo markings on her
face label her as belonging to the hill communities of Mpondoland. The
tint of her complexion suggests that she is painted in ochre. A defiant assertion of her backwardness and refusal of modernity. An embrace of her
terribleness that is also a testimony of her livingness. She is not fungible
here. I had known our old neighbor for more than thirty years. She had
always been an elder in my eyes. Bowed and probably widowed. An inde-
terminable location. But before the troubles of the Kongo, it is not unfath-
omable that she too was the defiant Mpondo woman who stares back from
the painting. Her carriage would have been erect, her bearing certain, and
grounded in a posture of black indigenous survivance that is more than
what she has endured. Her dreams would have been in excess of how life
unfolded. Her rampant desires would be unbridled from the enclosure that

came with how the Kongo would subsequently change her life. Perhaps her death marks the end of the Kongo. Death has lifted the shroud of uncertainty that came to define her life in the decades in which I came to know her. My now dead elder neighbor teaches me to ask new questions about how to reckon with loss while simultaneously recognizing the practice of freedom as that which allows beauty to be what Hartman (2008) terms the antidote to dishonor. To recognize the vitality of the gaze and beauty radiating from the painting of the Mpondo woman is to exhume and reanimate those who have died. It is to reconvene around minor historical characters and reimagine them as worthy ancestors.

Here I move to another account of the Kongo whose occurrence changed life in the hillside villages of the Wild Coast. It was 2017 and I met with another elder woman from my village. The interview had barely begun when a sudden autumn storm crashed onto the corrugated iron rooftop. We were seated in her kitchen. She was about seventy years old and a retired teacher. The room was prematurely dark in the gloom of the storm. Through the din, I struggled to make out her words. In the fury of the storm, the Kongo was simultaneously close and far. Close because she grew up on the foothills of Ngquza Hill and far because of time and the churning rain between us. The retired teacher married a man from this village and moved here. Before that, she was raised in the shadow of Ngquza Hill. The rain ceased as suddenly as it had come, and the elder teacher's hoarse voice picked up once more, authoritative and gaining momentum like an old truck. "I was a young schoolgirl back then. You are making me remember things now. I am not the best person to speak to because I was too young." The former teacher owned this story in a conflicted way. It was her story, but she pointed to others whom she believed had more direct access to the tale. Margaret Somers (1994, 618) notes that when we locate ourselves in narrative, the "narrative location endows us with identities—however multiple, ambiguous, ephemeral or conflicting they may be." The elder simultaneously owned and distanced herself from the story. She continued the account because the story was now part of her identity.

> Oh, but I remember the police came in the largest vehicles and trucks I had ever seen. They drove all over. Across people's maize fields and the rivers. Destroying things without care for the work that goes into tending maize. This would have been November because we had begun the planting season. They turned the entire countryside upside down. Men stayed on the mountains. Those who did not go were arrested. After some time, the whites came at

night. Boers really. Big and tall. They would knock doors over and arrest the men that they found. I remember that a neighbor was arrested while he was naked. He and his wife were dragged outside stark naked. A big enclosure was built with barbed wire and that was where the men were kept. Like cattle in a makeshift prison that was patrolled by police with big weapons. Imagine! Men fenced in like animals. Women would sneak close by and throw clothes over the fence to clothe the ones that were arrested naked. To hide their shame.

I cannot imagine the open-air enclosure that is exposed to the summer elements out in the fields. A roofless enclosure on Wynter and McKittrick's demonic ground. The electric storms. But as I write, I am struck by how black people have always been treated like animals. In addition to observing the unhumaning that occurs with animalization, as I have throughout this book, I see these as occasions that allow us to revisit the boundaries of the human, and like Jayna Brown (2015), to contemplate its porousness and what occurs when we embrace our consignment to the status of the animalistic. If bodily sovereignty was never ours to begin with, what fidelity do we owe to the ethics of the human? In the misery of encampment, the men ran amok and continued the resistance that they had mounted in the hills. *A riot*: those on the outside kept the soldiers busy by throwing stones at them, women blew bugles and horns, men dressed as women, children were told not to talk to the white people. If being human was to accept their fate or to reason with the soldiers, then the people of Mpondoland elected to be riotous and their strike resounded across the hills. This general chaos against enclosure and separation from the land is how the elders remember the Mpondo revolt. Therefore, even as encampment sought to restrain, the Mpondo revolt was a breach and provided an opening out of political enclosure and alienation from ancestral land. It was a Fanonian leap out of the constraints of the human and an embrace of unbounded forms which enabled the Mpondo people to wrestle their way out of possible bondage.

If Mpondo theory relies on the river, hills, oceans, and spirits, what is the meaning of displacement from these sites that emanate our personhood? What textures of sociality emerge from enclosure and displacement?[9] What longings and dreamings for freedom enable movement in and from racialized enclosures? How do black imaginations allow us to create livingness in unlivable situations? How does memory rouse freedom with hindsight? How do those who bear wounds from the Kongo and its states of emergency divine freedom from their debilitation? Does pleasure reside in the crevices and folds between the stretches of states of emergency that characterized Mpondoland?[10] These questions crowd my mind as I meditate on my conversation with the elder. "The men who did not go up to Ngquza Hill would dress up in women's clothes to avoid arrest since women were reportedly not arrested during the revolt. Dressed in their disguises, they would work in the fields with the women. When the police came to the fields to interrogate the women, the men would not answer out of fear that their voices would give them away and reveal their gender. The police officers were horrible. Big rough men that spoke Afrikaans. Young men too." In my mind, I assumed that these young men may have been conscripted soldiers. Others like Jo Ratcliffe (2010) and Daniel Conway (2012) have documented the horrors endured by conscripted young white men who were forced into national service to maintain apartheid against their will. Very few have written about the horrors borne by communities occupied by these young men. The retired teacher told me her grounded version.

> The soldiers fed on the food of the community. They broke into houses and took livestock like fowls and sheep. They would eat our *maas* and groceries.[11] The community was simultaneously at war with itself and with the state. All grown men had to pay a fee to support the men on the hill. The funds would pay for food and other expenses associated with that revolt. Those who refused to pay were considered *impimpi*—spies. They were supposedly supplying information to the police. But to my mind, that was an intimidation tactic to raise funds and gain support for the Kongo revolt. My father was one of the men that did not pay. We were afraid for him but because he was not originally from Ngquza and he was a bit of a medicine man, the men left him alone. Those suspected of being *impimpi* would be hounded and their houses burnt down. Children would swarm about because schooling had to come to a stop in that area. I was saved because my parents took me to school this side in Lusikisiki at Palmerton.

I return to Keguro Macharia to think with the trace enabled by black queer studies. How can queerness be used to escape oppression in some situations while also inviting prejudice in others?[12] In the preceding account, the men wore women's clothing to queer gender and evade the police. This may have produced feelings of pleasure and humiliation. It may have also been read as purely performative. As a disguise and therefore as fictive. In this instance, queer behavior was an accepted and ingenious alternative to being captured and placed in the enclosure. Here queering is a beautiful embrace of the desire to evade oppression and aspire for freedom. The queer drag allowed them to momentarily break away from gendered constraints. This passing for women was an open secret—open to the women but a secret to the white soldiers. It can be read as drag time and a queer hauntology if figured in relation to traditional Mpondo dress where men did not wear trousers and gender was not strictly performed through attire. Seen as a haunting of the past, the men's drag collapses temporality and latches onto an earlier time before whiteness. Elizabeth Freeman (2010) has productively theorized drag as an obstacle to our conceptions of progress, as a backward pull that compels us to think more quizzically about the present. Drag time therefore works as *ukwakumkanya* by engaging us in the task of attending askance, thinking anew and attending to the undertow. During the Mpondo revolt, unable to think queerly or enter into drag time, the soldiers were inept at seeing the drag. The men had assumed identities to whom the state had assigned values of the benign and invisible.[13] By dragging backward, the rioters bent gendered temporalities in their favor. Women were crucial agents of duplicity as they both enabled the drag and collaborated with men. Malleability of identity and gender-bending was a fundamental strategy of the revolt. As a tactic of pulling away from the mainstream and accepted modes of being, drag enabled an interruption of hegemonic violence and gendered performances. Drag presented an obstacle to violence and its enclosures. To deceive, one has to work against accepted notions of being which modernity ties to the human, progress, and linear temporalities. Reflecting on Mpondo people in his capacity as the district surgeon in 1908, Grant Millar exasperatingly contended that "time does not exist for the average Kaffir" (422). This noncompliance with linear temporality made it almost impossible for him to compile "accurate" medical histories. As an offshoot of *ukwakumkanya*, drag has ensured Mpondo survival by enabling a subterranean undertow that pulls askance from settler time and its forms of modernity that depend on black exploitation.[14] In the context of the Kongo, then, the state's commitment to settler time blinded it to the undertows and backward queering movements of the riotous Mpondo insurgents.

In the undated image in figure 5.2 by South African painter Alfred Neville Lewis (1895–1972) is a man in earrings and bandana. He appears to take pleasure in his queer look.[15] His transgressive attire asserts a presence of living otherwise during the periods of enclosure that characterized colonialism and apartheid South Africa. Like Hartman's (2019) early

twentieth-century black girls' insistence on living exuberant lives in adversity, the people of Mpondoland showed a "proclivity for the baroque" when their lives were threatened. Queer eccentricity exceeds enclosure and leaks beyond categories. However, as I illustrated in chapter 3, adolescents who evaded gendered enclosures evoked anxiety from adults. Queer eccentricity carries risks, but it carries kernels of freedom. Moments of crises provide openings for living peculiarly. These openings may be momentary, but they produce modes of sociality that gesture to possibilities and critiques of accepted fictions. The same can be said of medicine people, wizards, and witches. They provide spaces of exception to social mores. The imagined power that they possess enables them to be overlooked, seen as odd, and provides sanctuary to survive in contexts of oppression. Here being off-center allows for decentering the human and enables Mpondo people to craft alternative ways of saying no. Disobedience and queer waywardness not only made fools of white soldiers, but they crafted new imaginaries for the living. I am a descendant of the jokers who survived the state of emergency. I marvel at how my grandfather was the most humorous person I have ever known notwithstanding the enclosure within which he lived. Black humor is freedom and a defiant hallmark of living-ness.[16] To remember the enclosure is to recall the humiliation and pain but also a moment to laugh at the soldiers and to cheer on the side of the queer deceptors.

I juxtapose the personal narrative of the elder woman with a collective one. Katherine Fidler (2010, 3) summarizes the collective narrative of the state's suppression of the revolt thus: "Within two years, the government had detained and interrogated countless numbers, arrested at least three thousand, and executed twenty-four on charges directly related to the insurgency. For the next eighteen years, until 1977 when the Transkei achieved 'independence,' the entire region remained under emergency regulations." How does it feel to live under a permanent state of emergency? Violence has been the soundtrack of Mpondo life. I know this because through repetition, violence is etched on the skin of my family and in the psychological map of emaMpondweni. I explore the idea of repetition because time has illuminated patterns that have emerged before and after 1960. Repetition is a queer gesture because it evades timetables, linearity, and the onward march of history.[17] It is mournful in its stuckness, but it also mocks progress. I think about the violence of the state and the subsequent viciousness turned inward into the community. This is a violence that Frantz Fanon (2008) and Hannah Arendt (1970) theorized as present whenever power is in jeopardy. The fragile power of the postcolonial state means that it feeds on its people. This is the methodology of producing animalized subjectivities through repetition borne from perpetual resistance to repetitive violence.

Insider Knowledge: My Village Narrates the Revolt

I continue the narrative account of the retired teacher. Her story is that of Mpondoland—a black tale. I have heard different accounts for why the revolt occurred, but the narrative in my village is consistent.[18] The retired teacher and elder tells me that the revolt was against the state's intrusion into our way of life.

> They wanted households to pay taxes. That had never happened before. They wanted to introduce all kinds of taxes. Dog taxes, radio taxes. Where were poor rural people going to find money to pay for ridiculous things? Why would dogs be taxed? This was the state attempting to entrench its authority

in the outlying areas where it held little sway over our way of life. In some areas, they wanted to move people's households to demarcate grazing land. The African National Congress [ANC] organized the people and that is how the hill committees were constituted. That is why it was called the Kongo. From Congress.

Much of the literature however contradicts the complete attribution of the revolt to the ANC. For example, Robin Kayser (2002) argues that it is more likely that the name Kongo was inspired by the resistance movement against the Belgian colonizers in the Congo. The letter K would have replaced the C because in isiMpondo these letters make different sounds. Diana Wylie (2011, 204) reports on Mr. Tshumane's account to her. "We started these things on our own. Others came with their own views and called it Congo for Congress. These people wanted to say the whole movement was derived from Congress. That is not true at all. We started it as AmaQaba."[19] Like others, Tshumane claims the revolt as a local practice of resistance rather than a grand movement orchestrated from elsewhere. Benson Dyantyi (1960, 26) reported that recently elevated subchiefs abused the money collected from villagers' tax. "No sooner had this man been elevated than he was given a farm by the government at Mahlungulu. To befit the position this man now occupied, he told the people he wanted means of transport. They bought him two horses and a car." Other accounts (e.g., Kepe and Ntsebeza 2011) have stated that the revolt was a response to communal issues and that it did not have any affiliation to the ANC. Instead, the ANC had seized on the moment that Govan Mbeki (1964) termed the peasants' revolt. In Mbeki's reckoning, the ANC's focus on urban opposition had lost sight of the ways that the peasants were revolting, and he pointed to the value of harnessing these revolts for national freedom against the apartheid state. Mbeki was queering the commonsense assumptions of the village and the city where the latter was understood as the model for the village. He was arguing that the village might in fact be the fulcrum of resistance. If we take this reversal of assumptions seriously, we enable the possibility that the Mpondo theory of resisting land dispossession radiated outward in mutually reinforcing ways between the rural and the urban. This is a queer order of events. Moreover, since Mpondo theory centers relationality and land, then the Kongo was an enactment of this theory. For indigenous communities, theory is native wisdom (Simpson 2017). The guerrilla warfare that was waged by the Mpondo for a number of years prior to the 1960 pinnacle was inspired and sustained by the wisdom that without self-determination in land use, their very way of life would be lost. The hills provided cover and space for strategic resistance. The hills were both the theory and the space for theory generation. The riotous Mpondo were guided by the ethics of Mpondo theory, which centered their survivance and livingness. Relation to the natural world is the driving force of Mpondo being.

I discovered that my aunt grew up in Hlabatini, a neighboring village of Ngquza. Before the interview with her commenced, she had handed me a large brown envelope with about ten large copies of *Drum* magazine clippings from 1960. The clippings are a seven-page write-up by Benson Dyantyi with photographs by Peter Magubane on the aftermath of the Ngquza Hill revolts.[20] My aunt presented her personal archive to me. It had sat silently in her closet waiting for this moment in 2017. The title of the long piece by Dyantyi is "symptoms of boiling Bantustan troubles are arrests, murders, burnings, illegal meetings." The newspaper reporting of the time suggests that this was a national event that received coverage from Johannesburg-based presses such as *Drum* magazine. Magubane's photographs depict blanket-clad men sitting in the dusty outdoors, gathered at the hearings that followed the revolt. White men, described as commissioners, sit on the raised dais under the protective awning of an overhanging roof. Women bear water buckets on their heads and walk from the stream. Dyantyi (1960, 23) reported that Mpondo spokesmen informed the Van Heerden Commission: "Many of the chiefs set up under the Bantu Authorities were 'Police Chiefs' or dictators. They said the people had no say in the laws that governed them, and that they no longer had any control over their destiny." The mourning created by the new laws and the repression that followed the revolt led another speaker to inform the commission that they were "living dead, and that if the Government wanted to kill them, they would lose nothing." This theme of people seeing themselves as living dead ricochets forward into the present and the future. In times of state violence and despair resulting from inequality, death is meaningless as there is nothing to be lost. Steve Biko (2004, 73) remarked, "You are either alive and proud or you are dead, and when you are dead, you can't care anyway." While Biko contends that the dead don't care, I suggest that those they leave behind do care and that the act of dying is itself an ethic of care and livingness. At the Kongo, people were prepared to die rather than lose being in relation to the land. Without land, they were living dead. In this preparedness to die, the Mpondo people were not laying individualist capitalist claims to the land. They were fighting for retaining communal access to the land.

When life is cheapened, moral codes and modes of resistance are inflected by violence and occult forms of protection and meaning-making. Magubane's photographs of men injured in battle shows them recuperating at the Henry Elliot Hospital. They single out Mr. Makoko, a man who looks like he could have been in his sixties at the time. Dyantyi's (1960, 23) account suggests that Makoko was charged with being insubordinate toward a chief. As punishment, he was "suspended by rope and chain from the rafters of a hut and used as a punch bag." He was hospitalized when he began coughing blood as a consequence of undergoing torture. According to Dyantyi, residents reported that other men had disappeared mysteriously, while the homes of others were burnt down. The rehabilitation scheme of the apartheid government consisted of culling cattle to purportedly reduce overgrazing. This meant that rural subjects were forced to rely more on a cash economy instead of the traditional subsistence farming of maize and cattle. Men were therefore compelled to be migrant laborers and leave Mpondoland to join formal employment in the mines of places far away from their families and life in Mpondoland. The chaos wrought by the rehabilitation scheme and the resistance to this program unleashed chaos that Mpondoland is still reeling from. How many people disappeared?

Sitting across from my aunt, it was apparent that she had decided to defer to the clippings contained in the envelope. She protested that she had been young and somewhat sheltered from the goings-on of the revolt. Like the retired teacher I had interviewed earlier, she deferred the authority of the account to others. But her identity is implicated in Ngquza Hill. She remembers the police trucks from the vantage point of a child. They were large and all over the place. I picture her looking up from the height of a young girl of about twelve years. It was a time of high tension. Fidler (2010) gives a *Die Burger* account of an eyewitness from Hlabatini. In this account, Elijah Lande, a former teacher, reported that the Kongo members at Ngquza Hill raised a white flag when planes dispersed tear gas on the protestors. A Mr. Johnson, a local "coloured" man, who was shot at by the police, raised the flag.[21] The Johnsons from Mpondoland are distant relations to my family. I wonder about this connection to the Johnson who led the battle against the state in Hlabatini. While my aunt was thin on details, she did, however, describe some of the aftereffects of the revolt on her family. Even though she distanced herself from the goings-on of Ngquza Hill, her sense of place and identity are in part crafted by the occurrence of the Kongo revolt. Elizabeth Bird (2002, 521) offers that "narrativity enables us to constitute our social identities and make meaning of our lives."

My aunt's family subsequently moved away from Hlabatini to the city of Durban. The Ngquza troubles led to mass migration that unsettled large parts of community life and livelihoods. Ngquza, like Marikana's aftermath, has led to cylindrical trauma. A continuous Kongo and a repetitive Marikana. Looping trauma that challenges linear temporalities and ideas of progress. The Sharpeville and Langa massacres happened the same year as the Mpondo revolt of 1960. On March 21, 1960, sixty-nine people were killed in Sharpeville in a bloodbath that lasted two minutes when police opened fire on a group of about five thousand antipass and antiapartheid protestors (SAHO 2021; Kuumba 2002; Hassim 2006). The murder of miners in Marikana fifty-two years later was an eerie repetition of this massacre. While there are generally no links drawn between the Ngquza Hill and the Sharpeville and Langa massacres, it is worth noting that they occurred at the same time.[22] Since the Mpondo revolt had been fermenting through the 1950s, I speculate that the energy of the revolts reverberated and inspired other revolts, including those against pass laws. This is to suggest that dispossessed black people had tuned into a vibrational frequency of revolt. These riots tapped into an ancestral spirit of survivance and livingness through refusal.

Later in 2017, I interviewed an elder from another village and he expanded on the details of the Kongo. He was in his garden when I arrived at his house. Pumpkin creepers climbed up maize stalks. Chickens pecked at invisible insects. His wife was bedridden with arthritis and living in the intersections of blackness, disability, and her gender. Debilitated. When he emerged from the garden, he shouted to inform her that he was meeting with me in another room. Like the retired teacher, the elder was fairly educated, and each occurrence was framed around a year and exactly what he was doing at the time. For instance, when he was in grade 7 in 1958, he recalled that armed soldiers or police came to his village. There was a hint of unrest in the run-up to what would culminate in the high point of the Kongo revolt two years later. As the tension mounted from the people's discontent with the apartheid state that was closing in on the people of Mpondoland, the communities had begun to organize. Each household was asked to pay a sum of money. These financial contributions would fund the resistance. "For weapons and food," the elder said when I asked him to elaborate. I recalled that the retired teacher had referred to these financial contributions. The elder noted that each village had to elect a small group of men to represent them at the central meeting place at Ngquza Hill. He described Ngquza Hill as the epicenter of the revolt but recalled that each village had its own hill where local men gathered in support of the revolt. His local hill committee met on the hill at Lutshaya. The elevated place of the hill allowed the villagers a vantage point from which the enemy could be seen. But as Michael Marker notes, it is also a symbolic and cosmological elevation from which communication with ancestors and the gods can occur. This is an integral part of Mpondo theory that enables relationality with those who came before. The hill or mountain occupies an important place in indigenous cosmology generally. For instance, with reference to Mount Kenya or Kirinyaga, God's mountain in Kikuyu cosmology, Wangari Maathai (2008, 5) observed that the mountain was a sacred place. "Everything good came of it: abundant rains, rivers, streams, clean drinking water. Whether they were praying, burying their dead, or performing sacrifices, Kikuyus faced Mount Kenya." In the midst of the Mpondo revolt, the local mountains and hills were sacred places of protection and fortification.

We homed in on the actual revolt, the elder and me. "It may have been on a Friday when it happened that people say men sweated buckets at Ngquza with helicopters flying low over their heads. They were fighting for freedom. That is true because I worked at the mines. And they had their boots at the backs of our heads. I worked hard to enrich the whites." The story of the helicopter is a common one. Stories abound about how sticks were thrown at police helicopters that flew over Ngquza Hill. The police opened fire with live ammunition as they would repeatedly in subsequent years and into the future. From other interviews, I had heard that part of the conflict emerged from the installation of an unpopular chief—Vukayibambe, in eastern Mpondoland. Vukayibambe was subsequently murdered. The people believed that he was colluding with the apartheid state that threatened their land. The retired teacher, whom I had interviewed in the storm, had informed me that the people encircled Vukayibambe's house, dragged him out, and killed him. They watched over his house for days and refused to let anyone enter the parameter and attempt to bury him with the rites of a king. "Instead, the dogs and pigs advanced and began to consume his remains. They tore into him in full view of the community."[23] I think about this capacity to watch over a decaying body being consumed by domesticated animals. Pigs and dogs. Based on the archival record, Fidler (2010, 124) provides a graphic account of this event:

> In the early hours of November 21, 1960, under the cover of darkness, a group of more than two hundred men arrived at Vukayibambe's kraal of ten huts and proceeded to set fire to all the structures. As the structures burned,

they pulled the Chief from the building and proceeded to kill him with an ax-strike to the back of his skull. When the chief lay dead in front of his burning kraal, his attackers mutilated his body: his right hand and left ear were chopped off and the fingers of his left hand were severed just above the knuckles.

The retired teacher's account details the intergenerational memory-making narrated by local people. In her memory, the body was left out in the open to be consumed by wandering animals under the watch of the Kongo. I am reminded of the aftermath of the increasingly regular floods in neighboring Mozambique and how villagers live with the stench of rotting family members that they find in the debris of the receding waters. I imagine that the smell comes in waves carried in the wind. The birds of prey sink their beaks and claws into exposed flesh. I register this capacity to live with death.

The Vondo: The Dead Eating the Dead

My abiding interest in the Mpondo revolt as a defining moment of recent history was piqued by recent occurrences of vampire activity in Lusiki-siki. The vampires are young men called the Vondo. *Amavondo.* I have been thinking about this name that has been especially fashioned for Mpondo or Pondo vampires.[24] The P has been substituted for the letter V in vampire. These are Pondo vampires. The Vondo. A name that is whispered in daylight and not uttered at night. I suggest that Mpondoland vampires are inspired by circulating tropes of vampires and homemade in this context. Here I am concerned with how Mpondoland has created the Vondo. I suggest that the violence of Ngquza Hill and its echoes across the hills of Mpondoland is one of the sources. Earlier echoes came with the violence of colonial conquest. There are ample examples of the grotesque in our memory and landscape. These enable us to craft our own vampire narratives. The Vondo emerge by retooling the "shrapnel of previous failed revolutions" (Freeman 2010, xxii). They reuse the energy from a traumatic history weighed down by black mourning of things lost. I ask the reader to hold the thought of the Vondo in their minds as I provide a long-time context below.

While researching the Ngquza Hill revolts, some people referred to communal battles that intensified in the years following Ngquza. They were at their peak in the 1960s and they flared again in the 1980s before petering out in the early 1990s. Many of the elder women in my village, including my mother, have a keen memory of the fights between social groupings called the Ndlavini and the Nombola.[25] These were spectacular occurrences that remain etched in the community's collective memory. The Ndlavini gathered at *etshotshweni* and the Nombola met at *eguburheni*.[26] Without oversimplifying the similarities, the two groups operated in a manner similar to that of city gangs. According to William Beinart (1991) and Keith Breckenridge (1990), migrant labor shaped these gangs as they returned to the rural areas and formed associations similar to those in the city but fashioned on the realities and customs of the countryside.[27] Their affiliations were represented through their clothing, mannerisms of walking, and linguistic codes. The Ndlavini were characterized as modern womanizers who dressed well. The Nombola were seen as traditionalists who valorized traditional masculinities and dressed simply in traditional cloth and blankets that were rubbed down with animal fat. They were queerly modeled on an earlier Mpondo identity of the "Red Kaffirs" who smeared red ochre over their bodies. Noni Jabavu (1962) called them the blanket people. An elder woman and former Nombola that I interviewed described the traditions of the Nombola with pride and nostalgia. She explained that their bodies were generally covered in red ochre—or *imbola*. The word Nombola derives from *imbola*, a marker of traditionalism and proximity to the soil. While the two gangs socialized separately, they often clashed over women. Enemy lines could be drawn between neighboring villages or within villages. The elder woman told me that the fights could be about anything. A range of older women informed me that more often than not, women were the subjects of internecine battles that raged in the countryside. An elder observed: "Men harassed us all the time. I remember walking with a Nombola friend when a man insisted on sex with my friend. She literally had to squeeze her breasts to prove that she was lactating and breastfeeding a child. It was only then that he left her." This account counters the romance of memory. The past is a terrible beauty. It reminds elders of their prime and the defiant dreams of their youth. But it also takes them back to a time of violation.

As a form of revenge, the aggrieved would kill a member of the other group and the tension would escalate, leading to mass injury, disability, and deaths. Some of the people with whom I spoke recalled the mass displacement of people who ran away from the conflict. Some went to start new lives in other villages. My mother worked at a shop in the village of Mkhata during the early 1960s and recalls that villagers would leave their homes and gather at the shop, where they slept for many nights. The shop became a temporary refugee camp. She recounts the ease with which illnesses like flu and contagious diseases like diarrhea would spread between the often hungry and afraid children whose fathers were fighting to their deaths. Gangs would enter the homes of family members from opposing camps or enemy villages and take livestock and movable possessions to replenish their food reserves on the hilltops. This echoes earlier and later hills across epiphenomenal temporality. In a forward reverberation, as I wrote this in April 2019, three hillside villages of Mpondoland were restless. People were hiding out in the forests like they did decades ago. Their homes were burned in a revenge attack and villagers lost everything.[28] Part of the contestation was a toll road that would separate the villages. Again, development has pitted villagers against each other. Those whose homes were burned were among the people resisting outside imposition in the name of development that does not actually benefit villagers but serves to divide them. Similar contestations occurred during the Mpondo revolt.

During the battles between Ndlavini and Nombola, the roles of women were communication and direction. They would warn the various camps of impending danger. Women had fulfilled a similar role during the Kongo. Fidler (2010, 122) reports that war bugles would record the enemy approach and "women standing on the ridges would sound the war cry." Using brass and cattle horn bugles, they would blow encoded bursts that told the fighters what was happening in the community and on the horizon. Here we see the foregrounding of the sonic register in times of communal conflict. In addition to communicating with warring factions, the bugle horn announced conflict and strife to communities. It sounded the alert. An elder woman described the horror of the Ndlavini and Nombola conflict as follows: "There was blood and bodies everywhere. I remember seeing the bodies of three brothers strewn along a footpath. They were all killed on the same day. Bodies would often lie there in the forest for days on end because it was too risky for families to gather and bury them. Sometimes, the families did not know about the deaths until they came out of hiding. Bodies would be eaten by wandering pigs. That's why pork is not eaten during periods of conflict." I think about this. The pigs are not wild. They might have eaten the flesh of a family member or that of a neighbor. The everydayness of death and the material remains of the dead strike me anew. The proximity of violence is old and tested. It is as calamitous as Archibald Campbell Jordan's lament that opens this chapter.

A 2017 news report that had people aghast told the story of a young man who had eaten his nephew at a seaside village on the outskirts of the

Mpondoland seaside town of Port St. Johns. He had reportedly cooked and consumed him. The boy's grandmother discovered his arm near the homestead. Upon investigation, the uncle confessed to having cut him up and eaten him. Community members report that he consumed the liver and heart as these are softer body parts that cook more easily (Feni 2017). This story has been linked to the Vondo gang that I introduced earlier. The Mpondo vampires. Months before the young boy was murdered and eaten, the Vondo had reportedly been running riot in Lusikisiki in particular. Their modus operandi were violent masculinist rituals. Their victims were mostly women who were raped, butchered, and whose blood was consumed. The blood sucking marked them as vampires. Vondo. These are young people whose lust for survival requires them to butcher living people. As abhorrent as these activities are, like Brown (2015, 337), I wonder if those perpetually consigned to the margins "are less ethically bound to honor the boundaries of a bodily sovereignty never granted" to them. Since black flesh belongs to the surplus bodies of the barely human, vampires are a part of the deathscape. A woman who had been a teacher at my primary school was allegedly killed by the Vondo. I remember her thin frame and hoarse voice well. In my recollection, I see the smoke from her cigarette form rings around her head. One of her shoes was found at the gate of the outside parameter of her house. Her brutalized lifeless body was not far away. The Vondo appear to have been most active near the technical college. The students from the college and surrounding community lived in fear. Tired of the terror and havoc wreaked by the Vondo, young people decided to look for members of this gang. Through means that remain unclear, they found two young men who were reportedly local vampires. They proceeded to set them alight in a public demonstration of revenge (Feni 2017). The fiery Vondo killing was recorded on mobile phones. The images circulated on social media and were shown by an investigative journalism program on South African television. I watched the killing from my Johannesburg home. The "Cutting Edge: Vampires—Vondos" program can be watched on YouTube.[29] As of mid-2022, it had been viewed 144,100 times. Murder on demand.

In addition to other reasons, the murders committed by the Vondo gang are also tied to robbery for financial gain. As I argue later in this chapter, the Vondo are aspiring to the good life within a context of rabid consumerism, illusive riches, and inequality. I contend that the Vondo of 2017 are an iteration of the Ndlavini and Nombola of the 1960s and the Isitshozi gang of the 1920s before them. What they share is a bond of fraternity that young dispossessed men all over the world develop as a means of self-protection and a way of queering freedom (Bastian 2001). The cult/occult behaviors are markers of belonging and differentiation from others. If we look queerly beyond the grotesque, might these behaviors be strivings of survivance in the deathscape? Following Todd Sanders, I note that as long as there is inequality on the basis of wealth—poor and rich, there is a "ready-made market for occult powers" (Sanders 2001, 162). And this market has never been larger than in present-day South Africa and her forgotten countryside. If freedom can be commodified, we must consider Natalie Oswin's (2005, 583) assertion when she argues that "commodification is therefore neither above politics nor a signification of their end. It is rather a site in which the political is played out, and in a more complex fashion than the supposition of a resistance/capitulation binary permits us to understand." This calls for a tentative analytic lens that resists the binary. It brings the pathologies of capital to view, but the consumptive failures of the Vondo also mock consumption.

What is the smell of burned human flesh? What is the residue of dead Vondo left in the street after public burning? What do public burnings represent in South Africa? How do children remember the spectacle of death? What do flames conjure for those who have witnessed the furnace of death? And when the dead were encountered in the woods, what of the smell of decay? How does the smell live on in sensorial memory? What hauntings and traces do the dead leave behind for those who touch and smell them? What does facing the open casket reveal about the trail of neoliberal failure and devastation? What mourning affects emerge from the grave and how do these live on as an energy upon which future generations draw? How does the debris of the Mpondo revolts accumulate over time, and what energy emits from these debris in the deathscapes?

Everyday Death, the State, and the Occult

To explicate the death dimensions of Mpondo theory, I look at several kinds of death in this section. In each case, I point to where the state comes in as executioner, as absentee landlord, and as institutional killer. I also highlight the hand of capitalism as operating in concert with the state. David McNally (2011) is an important source for thinking through the operation of capitalism in producing "the monsters of the market." The logic of the market has perverse effects on the subjugated. As a desolate place whose indigenous economies have been decimated, rural people are turned into monsters who will feed on each other to access the impossible promise of consumer capitalism.

I introduced my brother in the introduction of this book. A renowned vascular surgeon and professor at one of the universities where I trained performed my brother's amputation. A few years later, the professor was tried for performing live organ harvesting in what turned out to be a global cartel of live human organ harvesting. The sellers were mostly impoverished South Americans. The organ buyers were predominantly wealthy northerners. South Africa provided a world-class and yet cheap venue to perform the harvesting. Here we see a global trade of body parts for cash where the state is an absentee landlord. McNally contends that the revulsion we may feel at this exchange masks another everyday enterprise in the form of cash for labor within a normalized capitalist system. For him, the irony is that we assign monstrous status to organ harvesting, but we do not see the system of capitalism as monstrous. Survival requires trading our life energy in the marketplace. Like organ harvesting, blood sucking and flesh eating, this debilitating practice feeds off flesh and blood. The people of Mpondoland know this. All too often, they have buried miners whose blood has been drained in mine falls. The state and the global system of capitalist extraction are culpable for these deaths. If we look closely, the quotidian horrors are everywhere. But my gaze is informed by the rural context, among those at the famished end of the capitalist trickle.

The story of the Vondo is at once mundane and spectacular. But there are quieter ways of sanctioned dying. These include deaths with the tacit acquiesce of family and the wider community. Local shops sell what we call *iyeza letanki* or tank medicine. A harmless name for a deadly pesticide for eradicating weevils and mold. The tablets are placed in cast iron tanks used to store maize grain after it has been harvested and shelled. The pill is a well-known way of dying. A few years ago we heard that the tablets might have been given to a boy with a history of a mental illness who had been assaulting people in the community. The boy died and he was buried. The assault problem ended. Community members reportedly had a meeting and resolved an end to the assaults and the shame. The family had to acquiesce. The line between animal and human pests is unclear, and they share cognate ways of dying. Therí Alyce Pickens's (2019) conception of black madness and mad blackness demonstrates that those at the intersections of blackness and madness are pushed further from the human as the default premise of measurement of the norm. They are a more expendable form of blackness. The elders tell me about villages with beautiful gorges where the terrain suddenly gives way to sheer drops that plunge into the yawning earth. I have stood over some of these gorges and shouted to hear my voice echoed in the plummeting depths. In these villages, aberrant villagers who have committed acts of murder or rape are instructed to walk over the edge of the gorge and plunge to their death. Their screams may momentarily quiet the sonic chorus of the cicadas. In an age-old practice, the community resolves its issues without the intervention of an intransigent, nonresponsive state and absentee landlord. Rural communities have had prolonged ambivalence about the involvement of the state in their lives. If the hills are a place of refuge, the gorges show that the hills are also a place of death where amaMpondo dispense their own justice. The Vondo do not have a monopoly on killing. Death hides the ambivalence and unpredictability of the state.

In the account of the 2016 robbery and assault on my mother that is detailed in the introduction, I omitted the legal case that followed the capture and arrest of some of the men. My aged and debilitated mother and brother had to sit through the legal proceedings and testify by recounting a trauma that they live with daily. This accounting had to be performed in front of their assailants. The people who looked at my mother as she spoke with her voice quivering on the verge of a panic attack included the man who stomped on her rib cage. The assault and subsequent court case incurred a trauma that shakes my mother from a fitful sleep. She awakens to sit and listen at the window until dawn fires the horizon. The court case was an exercise in repetition. Repetitive trauma in cylindrical epiphenomenal temporality. A year after the violent assault that fractured my mother's ribs, bruised her head, and shattered her peace of mind, the men were all released from prison. The testimony of the police against the men had shown up inconsistencies. It was easier to release them. Now my mother and her community fear a reprisal. Anxiety rattles my brother's remaining limbs. They live in fear that the robbers may return. Here, debilitating paranoia is a form of black madness. It functions as a black episteme that Pickens (2019, 83) defines as an orientation of mad blackness "developed towards a sanist anti-black world." While I borrow from Pickens's formulation of mad blackness, I do not attribute biopsychiatric designations onto the people about whom I write. Rather, I point to the maddening conditions in which they live. Had the community been at liberty to deal with the criminals in their own way, they might have been taken for a walk over the gorges of the rolling hills to ensure communal survivance.

As a child in the 1980s, I had seen other killings and burnings on the evening news. Vehicle tires slung around people's necks and set alight. The practice was called necklacing. A fiery necklace. A special kind of death reserved for spies, people who reportedly shared information about local resistances and activists with apartheid police. In addition to suspected spies, elder women alleged to be witches were necklaced. According to Isak Niehaus (2001), in the period between 1985 and 1995, an estimated 389 witch-related murders occurred. In the early 1990s, my grandmother's sister was killed in this way. In the same way that the two Vondo men were killed in 2016. Doused in petrol and set alight. She died to the sound of the chant of antiapartheid freedom songs and the singeing and charring of her flesh. By inserting the narrative of my own family into this text, I illustrate that violence is ever close and grotesque in its ugliness. It is routine and familiar. I sit with my mother's and grandmother's mourning. But this is also a community's shroud of endless mourning. The personal narrative indexes the community narrative of repeated assaults on life and repeated forms of death. Violence has been etched into the landscape of the rolling hills. In cylindrical epiphenomenal temporality, to shore up livingness, the Mpondo resist violence with violence. Through their queer sensibilities that rub up against the grotesque, how do the Vondo and other killers of Mpondoland take up the provocation of embracing their inhumanness?[30] How do the Vondo, Kongo revolutionaries, Ndlavini and Nombola, possessed adolescents, and witches "mine the present for signs of undetonated energy from past revolutions" (Freeman 2010, xv)? How does time move and jam between these moments in ways that disrupt and disorient linear temporalities? In writing about the violence of Mpondoland, I do not seek to naturalize violence in this landscape and people. I own up to the violence by saying that it is part of us, and it flows through our lineage. The nation was forged in a violent birth. It was created on the combustible factory floor of colonial frontier wars, apartheid subjugation, violence, and resistance.[31] Sol Plaatje (1982) and Aimé Césaire (1972) tell us so. But sitting at the end of history as I do, I see the repetition.[32] Violence adapts to the times and is influenced by mobility, contemporary forms of marginality, and social media. It is tied to and feeds off the undetonated energy of historical memories of extraction and devastation.

How does adopting a queer lens assist us to read the failure of capitalism and orders of modernity? How can we think of villagers who fail at being proper citizens of the nation-state? Following the earlier definition of queerness in this text as inclusive of those with nonnormative sexualities and those figured as strangely out of synch with the human and as illegible subjects, I ruminate on black villagers who fail at being gainfully employed and live on the dredges of capitalist abjection. Tina Takemoto (2016, 86) contends that "queer failure can engage the psychic and emotional dimensions of loss, failure, disappointment, and shame that accompany LGBTQI existence as well as the utopian potentialities of failure as a mode of resistance, intervention, speculation, and queer world making." With my more inclusive characterization of the queerly oriented, I attempt to read the lives of villagers who have been failed by capital in relation to both registers outlined by Takemoto—the affective dimensions of failure and failure as resistance to abjection, and therefore as invention, suture, and survivance. What happens to young people who have no prospects of employment in an economy that has no place for unskilled labor? The mining boom and its demand for migrant labor meant that besides young boys and old men, there were almost no adult men in the hillside villages during the 1970s and 1980s. Adult men toiled in the mines and sent remittances to Mpondoland. This led to a decline in the Ndlavini and Nombola social clubs. A certain kind of peace prevailed without men in the villages. But now, with a mortally wounded education system in the rural areas, the failed promise of education, declining mining activity, and ready access to AIDS treatment, young men are in abundance again (Canham 2017). They are disenchanted, wearied, and angry. Hard drugs made of deathly and addictive cocktails containing AIDS medication, rodent poison, powder from flat screen television sets, and marijuana, among other ingredients, enhance the desperation. Drugs called Woonga or Nyaope.[33] Addiction fuels theft because without money to sustain the expensive habit, addicts must steal. However, if we queer the consumption of drugs and flesh as complex maneuvers toward freedom, new pathways appear. Substances aid in momentary forgetting. AIDS medications have been a dominant discourse and the product of activism for prolonging life—freedom from certain death. A commodity and perhaps a fetish too. I can see the attraction of tasting the fruits of this long forbidden and out of reach life-giving drug. Television screens stand in for modernity and the good life. They are placeholders for traveling to distant lands. And since the young know that they will never travel, surely, televisions too can be eaten. To be high is to travel. And the old flirtation with death and invisibility enabled by poisonous mixtures has always had an allure for queerly aligned youth. Conceived as invention, speculation, and queer world making, these ways of being positioned in the debris of the neoliberal apocalypse signal a black and indigenous commitment to fugitivity. But as Xavier Livermon suggests, consumption is a dynamic practice in South Africa. It has always been critically tied to ideas of freedom. He contends that excess might be understood as a queering of consumption. In his assessment, it is a way for "bodies to navigate both their marginal material realities and the forms of social censure and moral panic that surround their consumptive practices. Consumption is revealed as a practice that is deeply connected to individual and communal processes of self-creation" (Livermon 2020, 25–26). However, for rural protagonists, excess is a misnomer—a queer impossibility that we can only approximate. While Livermon theorizes excessive material consumption, I extend this to consider occult and enchanted forms of consumption.

Young men with no employment prospects enter into pacts and target vulnerable people. While I do not discount satanism in the Vondo gang, I suspect that the familiar and the occult fuel the perversity of their tactics.[34] The reader will recall that queer deviance, as in the cases of Thanduxolo and Clara Germana Cele, is always associated with satanic influences.[35] I concur with Nicky Falkof (2012), who observes that satanic readings of the occult have increased with the rising popularity of Pentecostal churches. Satanic readings operate in tandem with the powerful relationship to the demands of capitalist consumption and its muddled intersections with the occult.[36] I contend that occult consumption symbolically represents the multiple dyings that occur in the wake of the capitalist apocalypse in the countryside. In addition to the everydayness of dying and the dead, addict gangs develop their own codes. Can human blood not be part of a drug cocktail—particularly one already made from other deadly mixtures such as battery acid and rodent killer concoctions? What if the ultimate high is capped by blood spurting out of a warm body and into a waiting mouth? In the city, mounting reports indicate that the cremated remains of people are being excavated from graveyards and mixed into opiates to help the young to forget and to perhaps imagine futures queerly unhinged from the devastating realities of the terrible present. Inhaling human ash.[37] As I have proposed, the Vondo are a recurrence constituted by all that has preceded this moment and more. Perhaps signaling a future time that is always upon us but is too ugly to contemplate.

Adeline Masquelier (2000) suggests that occult practices such as cannibalism and headhunting are aspects of rural Nigerian experiences. To this, we might add the advent of kidnapping young girls by Boko Haram. These practices emerge as part of a way of life characterized by migration and smuggling. In turn, these are imbricated in capitalism, international relations, and globalization. As McNally (2011, 208) notes, the fetishes that torment sub-Saharan Africa are a consequence of continued plunder for natural products, including diamonds, gold, cotton, cocoa, ivory, and rubber. He contends that "with each manic effort to seize their continent's wealth, Africans have been captured, whipped, beaten, worked to death, structurally adjusted—all so that . . . people might be downtrodden, and capital might accumulate." In causing mass debilitation, forcing people off their land, grabbing their resources, and stifling self-sufficiency, primitive accumulation occurs. People become dependent on paid work, but with soaring unemployment, desperation grips the countryside. Global, national, and local capital circulates and is accumulated illicitly. Wealth is a magical force characterized by unfair competition, historical inequalities that privilege some and marginalize others nationally and within the local community. But capital accumulation is always elusive for the local communities. Those who want good fortune and wealth must consider occult means.

I linger on the community's relationship to different modes of death and forms of dying. I suggest that death and dying are integral parts of people rendered irrelevant to high capitalism. The community has incorporated dying into the Mpondo way of life. In the practice of Mpondo theory, dying is a relational practice. It is embedded in communal decision making, ancestral relations and rituals, and has become a ready script in the absence of the state. Alongside the dyings are seeming overlaps between different forms of mental and sociopathic deviance, and the community's modes of addressing them. Death has become a solution to sociopathic deviance. If we glance back at the errant chief who was killed and then eaten by dogs and pigs, bodies strewn about in the Mpondo revolt, the deaths in the battles between the Ndlavini and Nombola social clubs, and forward to the people the Marikana miners killed before they themselves were killed by the state, as well as the predominance of necklacing during apartheid and in the postapartheid period, the echoes of death ricochet through history.[38] Time is queerly bent.

Cannibalism and Power in Cylindrical Epiphenomenal Temporality

Consumer commodities such as guns and beauty products which now circulate within Mpondoland create ambiguities in rural subjectivities that occult and spiritual forces assist in resolving.[39] The occult are perceived as possible means to facilitate access to the good life of consumerism (Parish 2001). A few months after the cases of cannibalism and Vondo activities, the news erupted with reports of rampant cannibalism in the rural hinterlands of Escort in the neighboring province of KwaZulu-Natal. The story broke because a self-confessed cannibal handed himself over at the local police station claiming that he was exhausted from living the life of a cannibal. He presented a human hand and a limb to assure the police that he was not making up the story (Wicks 2017b). At his residence, they discovered eight ears in a pot. Rosalind Shaw (2001) contends that cannibal confessions are not new, and they are particularly common in times of turbulence.[40] Following the cannibal confessions, investigations revealed more human remains in the village of Rensburgdrift, and suspects were also arrested in the Amangwe area. Accusations circulated of heart eating, raping, murder, cutting women open and eating their flesh. Claims that human remains may have been dug up from graves.[41] The *Ladysmith Gazette* reported that at least three hundred people confessed to knowingly eating human remains served to them by a traditional healer in the Amangwe area (*Northern Natal News* 2017). The sheer number of people knowingly participating in cannibalism further links the inequalities wrought by consumer capitalism to aspirations to livingness and invention through the occult. The logic of cannibalism is both seamless with that of the inequalities of capital accumulation and parodies the failures of capitalism (McNally 2011). It is the logic of the postcolony and a mockery of the corrupt state (Shaw 2001). Everyone is trying to eat themselves out of their abjected position. The rural poor eat to counter the violence of abstraction and poverty (Comaroff and Comaroff 1999).

Shaw's (2001) conception of time in her historicization of cannibalism appeals to me as it coheres with my own attempt to think about the present within a cylindrical epiphenomenal temporal conceptual frame. She argues that the postcolonial state retains many features of colonial plunder, and in countries like Sierra Leone, the trace of the Atlantic slave trade is a heavy transregional psychic memory. For her, as it is for me, the postcolonial period of rupture is another iteration of earlier ruptures that enable the commodification of freedom through the occult of which cannibalism is but one instance. According to Shaw (2001, 50), images of cannibalism are "continuously refashioned, creating accounts that are both 'new' and 'old.'" Therefore, while cannibalism may flare in the moment of the Vondo of emaMpondweni, in the time of the vampires of Malawi, or the cannibals and gravediggers of rural KwaZulu-Natal, it is not new, but neither is it a signal of regression to an earlier "primitive" moment. McNally's (2011) global cartography of a monstrous market demonstrates the ways in which this is a global phenomenon.[42] Césaire (1972, 5) reminds us that in the European quest to civilize the barbarism of Africa, colonial adventurers diced African bodies. He quotes one of the conquerors of Algeria: "It is true that we are bringing back a whole barrelful of ears collected, pair by pair, from prisoners, friendly or enemy." Césaire describes villages as hideous butcheries, and colonizers as collectors of heads and ears who found sadistic pleasure in warm blood. This was particularly marked in the Congo. Césaire's reminder of colonial cannibalism is important for disassociating this violent practice from African origin. Instead, we see cannibalism as colonial violence and as a pathology of capitalism. This is to suggest that it is not inherently African. However, even as we know this to be true, the stain of cannibalism has a historically African visage. As Frantz Fanon (1967, 115) reminds us, even the despised Jew "belongs to the race of those who since the beginning of time have never known cannibalism. What an idea, to eat one's father! Simple enough, one has only not to be a nigger."

What do cannibalism and vampirism signal beyond pathology? What do they tell us about the decentered human, survivance, and black livingness? Vampire and cannibal activities and their cyclical emergence question the sanctity of the body as beyond consumption. Animals eat human flesh. Since black people are animalized and made junior humans in the Chain of Being—a feature of modernity—the boundaries of human ethics are tested in conditions of abjection. When the social contract fails, its moors are loosened. When the deaths of the black and poor are everyday events and the smell of decaying flesh is normalized, the sanctity of the body is called into question. But there is something else afoot in the consumption of flesh. If we hold the idea that the body is also constituted of spirits that do not die, the consumption of the body can also signal the literal swallowing of the spirit. To offset ill fortune, eating the body of a young child might be seen as a cleansing force. Here the child is perceived as innocent and spiritually clean.[43] To take over the spirit of a wealthy person, their body might be consumed. According to Maureen Mswela and Melodie Nöthling-Slabbert (2013), in Tanzania, people with albinism are believed to be immortal, and *sangomas* value their genitals as these are perceived to attract wealth.[44] Gloria Anzaldúa (2004, 1020) captures the paradox of disability: "But there is a magic aspect in abnormality and so-called deformity. Maimed, mad, and sexually different people were believed to possess supernatural powers by primal cultures' magico-religious thinking. For them, abnormality was the price a person had to pay for her or his inborn extraordinary gift." People with albinism often pay the price of life. Throughout Southern Africa, those living with albinism are simultaneously feared as cursed and valued for the fortune that their body parts might have.[45] There are therefore both economic and spiritual possibilities invested in the body. Cultures of consumption encourage those of us who live famished lives to desire and aspire to eat those whose bodies are imbued with possibility—children, the wealthy, and those with albinism. This too is an aspiration to freedom. But as I have also suggested, occult practices operate at multiple registers. They are queer failures that serve as grotesque parodies of consumption. If we attend closely, we might detect the dark humor at play.

In Lusikisiki and neighboring Kokstad, Khotso Sethuntsa and his legend about wealth accumulation is a historical touchstone for occult means to wealth and power. His legend was particularly important in the middle of the twentieth century when it was impossible for black people to acquire wealth in the countryside. On the occasion of Khotso Sethuntsa's ninetieth birthday in 1970—when he also married three more women—*Drum* magazine published a comprehensive account of Khotso's riches. The article by Jack Blades (1970, 28) begins as follows: "Khotso Sethuntsa came down from the mysterious depths of the Lesotho mountains decades ago with a secret formula for long life and virility. Today he is one of South Africa's wealthiest men, living in self-satisfying happiness that few people achieve." Among the possessions that Blades accounts for Khotso's happiness are his diamonds, gold, cash, long life, twenty-three wives, and more than two hundred children. Among the attributes of the good life ascribed to Khotso were his excellent health, great eyesight, and sense of hearing at the age of ninety. At the time of his death at ninety-two in 1972, the *Mercury* newspaper reported that a whirlwind led to his change in fortunes when he was much younger. He is reputed to have summoned the whirlwind to his rescue when a white farmer, for whom he was a herd boy, was beating him up. The farmer's barn was blown away by the whirlwind. The attribution of magical powers and his thriving work as an herbalist purportedly led to his wealth. The point of this accounting is that many Mpondo people and others believed in his power and sought his remedies for which they paid, thus leading to his fabled wealth. Khotso had queerly cheated apartheid, revenged whiteness, and achieved the good life when it was impossible for black people to be wealthy and respected. Others aspired to the good life and, through Khotso's example, tried to access it through engaging in occult practices.

As an adolescent, a chance meeting with his granddaughter led me to Khotso's house in Lusikisiki. The house was said to have remained unchanged from the time of his death. My visit to the house marked my first time seeing a Cadillac. The black Cadillac is reputed to have remained stationary since the death of its owner. The house had a spooky aura created by low lighting and was decorated with items that brought to mind body organs, such as eyes floating in jars of liquid. Khotso was supposedly buried in the house. In 1972, the *Mercury* reported that parts of the floor had been lifted and a tomb built where Khotso's body would be buried. On arrival at the house, I had to cleanse myself of evil, take my shoes off, and remove my hat. A bald elder wiped my feet with medicated water. In 1958, *Drum* had reported that no smoking or drinking was allowed on Khotso's properties. The magazine stated that spirits and snakes often visited him. Khotso claimed that snakes were the spirits of the dead. Felicity Wood and Michael Lewis (2007) write that during the Mpondo revolt, unpopular paramount chief Botha Sigcau was alleged to have been shielded from the anger of the people by charms administered by Khotso. These potions would turn chief Sigcau into a dog or a chicken when Mpondo villagers confronted him. This resonates with the account of the schoolchildren who said that Thanduxolo had turned into a snake, pig, and a fat cake, as described in chapter 3. The prohibitions and decorative allusions that I witnessed in Khotso's house were no doubt meant to retain the performative allure and power of an influential ancestor or even to cast doubt on the fact that he had indeed died. In 1958, Khotso told *Drum*, "I twice died and came back. The first time was in 1924, two years after I began my practice. The second was in 1956. On the first occasion I was dead for three days, on the second for two days" (Ngcobo 1958). Who knows how long he has been dead this time or if he has returned from the dead for the third time. The *Mercury* (1972, 1–2) billed the funeral as a farewell and not an interment, and it noted that this was the biggest social event seen in the "primitive" area for many years. This is a moral order we live in. Everyone in Lusikisiki knows the main parts of the Khotso legend. We keep it as a point of reference for our own lives. Khotso's story is a shared narrative. His story of triumph when black material success was not possible means that magical powers retain an intoxicating allure for a people for whom the good life remains impossible in the present. But we also laugh at how Khotso was able to parody consumption and state power in ways that queered the order of things. Khotso's laughter in figure 5.3 below continues to queer relations to consumption.

5.3 Khotso Sethuntsa, Lusikisiki, 1962. Courtesy of the *Daily Dispatch*.

Former president Jacob Zuma, who rose to power against the odds as a barely literate man of rural origin, is presumed to be reliant on traditional potions for his power both in the party-state and in his bed. The latter is to enhance sexual potency for his relations with his younger wives and his girlfriends. Like Khotso, the former president married more wives at an advanced age. He is estranged from one of his young wives because he believes that she tried to poison him (News24 2021). Reports indicate that "although a direct link between Ntuli-Zuma and the poison plot could not be established, it is understood that the president believes she was involved due to her unhappiness at having been side-lined as a wife following reports of her extramarital affair a few years ago" (News24 2015). Ruling masculinities that combine wealth and sexual prowess are allegedly propped up by magical potions (Ratele 2013). To add to enchanted wealth and to retain power and sexual prowess, further rituals, prohibitions, and potions are required. These are said to ward off jealousy. The more shocking the ingredients, the more powerful the remedy. The ingredients might include animal and human organs. This may shed light on why as many as three hundred villagers claimed to have knowingly used potions consisting of human materials such as ears and hearts. Shaw (2001) contends that following their preparation, potions can be consumed. One can wash with them as people do in cleansing rituals after exposure to violence, they can be rubbed into incisions in the skin as my family did in the wake of violent terror, they can be sewn inside a belt or tied around the waist, one can wear undergarments that have been soaked in the medicine, or the potion can be placed inside an amulet and hung around the neck. These are practices of black livingness in the deathscapes.

Conclusion

"Poverty can cause you to do all sorts of bad things, from witchcraft, pilfering and sleeping with other women's husbands. Most of us have secret boyfriends [*amaqabane*] who give us money to buy food for *iintsapho* [family]. If there is no work, no food in the house—what would you do?" (Ngonini 2007, 178). This excerpt is an account by a woman from the northeast of Mpondoland. Daily poverty often drives people to unwanted decisions that nevertheless ensure survivance. When communities such as those of Mpondoland live under conditions of constant anxiety, the occult becomes a more or less permanent feature of our existence. The incisions on my body in the wake of the terror experienced by my family and the prohibitions under which we live are efforts to control ambiguity and bring order to our lives. The charms and spells are our efforts to claim a personhood not designated for black subjects. In this conception, occult practices that furtively turn us into pigs and dogs serve to profoundly decenter the consecrated human. They are a part of Mpondo theory that authorizes resistance and survivance in the face of certain annihilation. Out of the wasteland of torture and death, we harvest affective energies for our survival. Leaning on Livermon's queering of consumption as political, this chapter has sought to think of vampire, cannibal, and magical activity as practices of queer consumption—critical reaches for freedom in the wreckage of capitalist failure. Since *ukwakumkanya* positions amaMpondo queerly in relation to modernity, the nation, and respectability, the concept enables us to work with the abhorrent and enchanted as practices of self-authorization. Through a queer orientation, we can thus locate fugitivity in fungibility.[46] While this chapter has stayed with the grotesque, it has also painted a portrait of agential bodies that make demands of the world—to parody and mock capitalist consumerism, to fail while attempting to consume their way to freedom, and to claim a place in the world.

FITFUL DREAMSCAPES: AN AFTERWORD

I wanted to write *Riotous Deathscapes* in a tense untethered from the present, speculative and open.[1] This collapse of tenses would signal the capaciousness of time, the sedimented and interlocking nature of the past, present, and future. Time always now. Which is to say, the collapse of neoliberalism, the precolonial, colonialism, slavery, the postcolonial, apartheid—is now. This book is not in the past. It pokes in the debris of a perpetual now. Linguistic conventions and frames of legibility however required a grounding in tense. But I hope you attended to the moments that time failed and that you perceived the reverberations of things that push against the surface of temporality and rest in its folds. In this afterword, I ask that you indulge an untethered tense that leans into the wind of *ukwakumkanya*.

My grandmother sometimes gets lost in her nineties. Villagers occasionally bring her home. At other times, we look for her and find her at the graves, which is also where the sheep graze. To prevent her from straying, my aunt locks the gate. My grandmother sometimes slips into her childhood to seek a home she has not known for more than seventy years. At other times, she crawls under the fence and goes in search of sheep in the fields. But to prevent her from getting lost, her son sold the sheep a number of years earlier. On some days, she dresses up in her church clothes and walks to church. She finds nobody there because it is not Sunday. When my mother spends time with her, they pray before bed. But just as my mother falls asleep, her mother wakes her to remind her to pray. Her mother sings until her voice grows faint. The same song. They pray several times until exhaustion overtakes them. Sometimes, my grandmother greets you as though seeing you for the first time. She never forgets our names, though. She laughs aloud when we express surprise that she remembers. In those last years, she lives across timescapes. Her mind is vast and uncontainable. Home straddles place—she longs for home from home. The dementia sets in the day we bring news of her son's death. She is eighty-six years old. Her son was shot and killed the night before. We set out to tell her in the morning. She crumbles in front of us. In the shade of the whispering gum tree, a veil falls across her mind. It blunts the sharp edges of loss. If losing two children before had made her mad, this loss drives her to lose her mind. Time collapses and opens her up to multiple temporalities. There she is with a ninety-year temporal frame and perhaps time untethered—spreading out to incorporate ancestral plains and forward toward horizons we cannot fathom. My grandmother dies at ninety-three years in 2012. She is now an ancestor to whom we look. She is everywhere.

It is August 2021. I am home with my mother. The television flickers between us. COVID-19 figures hover amidst enlarged green viral spikes on the screen. Explosions. Quick bursts that are out of sync with the news. I am disoriented. But my mother knows the sounds of this place. Her panicked voice simultaneously asks and tells me, "A gun, shooting." Debilitated, she can't stand on her own. I surge forward to pull her up from her seat. We should be crouching and keep away from the windows, but she cannot crouch. She suddenly needs to pee and makes for the bathroom while repeating my brother's name like an incantation. "Where is your brother?" she keeps asking. A volley of shots rings out again. It is outside. From the kitchen window, I see that the building where my brother should be is totally still and its open double doors spill out incandescent lighting like an illustration of an open box bursting with shards of light. I am a coward and do not leave the house to check on my brother until the sound of wailing breaks the deathly silence. A chorus of voices keens into the night. The sound chills the air and cuts holes into the dark. My mother groans, and I ask her to join me in breathing. In. We inhale. Out. We exhale. Repeat. Sonic triggers. The traumas roll into each other and her breathing races. To slow it down, we breathe in unison and enter into drag time. Voices ring out and intermingle with the keening night. Whatever is happening, we are now in the immediate aftermath. I leave the house to investigate. There has been a shooting. The neighbor has been shot. A vehicle is arriving, and

I make out a form, a body carried, legs hanging, bundled into a bakkie. It speeds off. The young man had been talking to my brother. His niece had come to call him. She explained that there were two men asking to talk to him on the road. As he approached the middle ground between my home and his, he was met with a hail of bullets. Just across from him was his home. He ran headlong into the fence and then burst into the room where his mother was. The shooters followed him and fired the last shots against the sound of the mother's pleas. Then, like a pair of bats, they dashed into the night. Months later, this scene will be repeated when his young wife is executed in the same room with her son in her arms.

But it is August now and the night is cold with fear. My brother has blood on his face. He finds his missing crutch in the garden where he'd crawled under the guava trees when the guns went off. I return to my mother and update her. She wants to go to her neighbor's house. It is dark and the uneven ground is difficult to navigate. Her hip is on fire today. A persistent throbbing pain where the cartilage is worn. She is insistent. Her neighbors have rallied on nights when the shooting happened at her house. "At least wear your mask," I say. We walk slowly and join throngs of women already gathered to pray and hold the weeping mother. The women have spoken hope into the room. "The boy will survive," they say with a queer certainty. My mother has already lowered her mask because everyone else's masks sit slackly under their chins. In my city voice, I mutter that she should raise it. We know the conditions under which the coronavirus is spread. She does not refuse but she cannot raise it. The black sociality of gathering, mourning, hope, and comfort refuses the logic of viral contagion. To be present in the traditions of this place, we must come together fully. Masks disrupt sociality, impose hierarchies, and blunt relation.

I join the men outside. There is rage here. It spreads thick and wide. The men feel violated. One of their own was shot at in their presence and they'd been unable to stop it. A man from the fold in the hills phones the driver of the vehicle that had spirited the young man away to hospital. On the fifth attempt, the driver answers: "He has died." I am next to the man; I hear the conversation. We sit with the news and swallow our tongues because we cannot tell the family. We watched the boy grow up. From our kitchen doorway, we see into his home. The men go off and form a circle. The rage moves and then gathers and hovers in the black circle. Like other times, the days ahead will be difficult. Grief will claw at my brother. Anxiety attacks and sleeplessness. For now, we rage. The house next door will be home to wailing and prayer. The little girl who'd called her uncle to the road—to his

execution—has been shot through her thigh by a stray bullet. It is too serious for the local hospital. Like my brother when he lost his leg years before,
she is sent on to Nelson Mandela Academic Hospital in Mthatha. Hours
pass before the police arrive at the house. Blue lights cutting into the solid
darkness. They shush everyone out. They break the news to the family. Grief
punctuates the night. I return home with my mother. We meet other old
women slowly emerging from the valleys into which they had run to hide.
The police will not find the killers. I know this like I know that other killers have not been apprehended. Those who killed my uncle and ushered
in my grandmother's dementia are still at large. The men who stamped
on my mother's ribs while shooting into the air. They haunt the shadows.
Unemployment has spiraled and desperate men are for hire. The stakes are
low and black death is cheap. We squabble over the spoils of capital. We sift
through the rubble of devastation. The death of some supports the survival
of others. We bury our dead. Like our ancestors, we gather for ritual, solidarity, and fortification.

Now it is past midnight. The wind volleys around the awnings and
shakes the early spring flowers off the fruit trees. In the morning there will
be a carpet of white blossoms from the orange trees and pink flowers from
the peaches. I imagine my mother's fitful sleep in the room next to me. And
in my mind's eye, next door a mother pleads with men who kill her son. But
they shoot at him. He falls, over and over again. Tonight, she will not sleep.
Grief will wrack her body, pinning her to the floor. Accompanied by the
wind's Mpondo blues, I lay awake and before me spreads a vast deathscape
of ancestors who demand witnessing.

Introduction

1   Nguni people primarily lived in the Eastern Cape, KwaZulu-Natal, and Mpumalanga provinces. While they previously lived as diverse clans and did not share an overarching identity, some kings attempted to consolidate their power and influence by creating homogeneity across their subjects. Though the Mpondo share commonalities with the broader Xhosa group and the Zulu people, they have distinct chieftaincies, overlapping cultures, and language. For more on Mpondo people, see Timothy J. Stapleton (2006) and Abner Nyanende (1996).

2   For more on *ihahamuka*, see Athanase Hagengimana and Devon E. Hinton (2009). While my mother has not lived through violence as extreme as that of the Rwandan genocide, she has experienced repeated violence over many years.

3   Although the term *kaffir* was initially reserved for people living between the Cape and Natal, in what is modern-day Eastern Cape, it was used to describe black South Africans in both colonial and apartheid South Africa (Theal 1886). All references to the term are in scare quotes. I however insist on its use in recognition of its continued salience. I see it as an apt representation of the sedimented trauma of black people and Mpondo people in particular. Historically, the name was so entrenched in the making of blackness that it appeared in the titles of several books. See, for example, Theal (1886), *Kaffir Folk-Lore*; Drayson (1858), *Sporting Scenes*; Angas (1974), *The Kafirs Illustrated*; and Mathabane (1986), *Kaffir Boy*. Gabeba Baderoon (2004a) has written an important paper titled "The Provenance of the Term 'Kafir' in South Africa and the Notion of Beginning."

4   I find synergies with Cornel West's conception of niggerization in the US context. In a 2007 article in the *Atlantic*, he observed: "Niggerization is neither simply the dishonoring and devaluing of black people nor solely the economic exploitation and political disenfranchisement of them. It is also the wholesale attempt to impede democratization—to turn potential citizens into intimidated, fearful, and helpless subjects" (West 2007).

5   Failure indexes refusal and resistance.

6   Here, I refer to *Man* to signal Sylvia Wynter's (2001) critique of the universal representation of the human as masculine, Western, and white—monohuman.

7   I alternate between Mpondoland and emaMpondweni. I similarly use both descriptors of Mpondo people and amaMpondo.

8   For more on indigenous inscriptive practices, see Rumsey (1994).

9   I note Gayatri Spivak's (1999) contentions on the native informant. One who writes from a position of alterity is always caught in a foreclosing double bind—damned if they do, damned if they don't.

10 This is not a widely used word, and its meaning is slippery and unsettled. Like isiMpondo, *ukwakumkanya* is unwritten and exists as a colloquial word among older villagers.

11 Tiffany Lethabo King (2019) uses the concept of black shoals to think of black and indigenous studies together. She imagines the shallow part of the water in the shore as the meeting place of land and water for theorizing black studies and staging an ethical engagement with native studies.

12 In this respect, I am in conversation with Deborah A. Thomas (2019), whose work on Jamaica theorizes from inside in order to claim sovereignty, witnessing, and repair in the wake of colonialism and in this epoch of neoliberal exploitation and state violence.

13 Jill Bradbury (2019) productively theorizes narrative timescapes and how they work with history.

14 I expand on King's (2019) conception of black shoals in the discussion on indigenous studies.

15 By dyings, I signal the deathbound position of black life in contexts where dying is overrepresented and a constant feature and preoccupation of the living.

16 This as an attribute that resonates with indigenous values of honoring the natural world as sacred and as essential for living.

17 For more on this, see Mignolo (2009).

18 I follow Hartman's (2019) intervention when she endows the enslaved and wayward woman with a critical voice with authorial gravity.

19 For more on this African philosophy, see Nonceba Nolundi Mabovula (2011) and Julius Gathogo (2008).

20 Unlike the extractive tradition of anthropology, this work sees local villagers as theorists and as coprotagonists. The village is a crucial place from which to think.

21 Katherine McKittrick (2006) has usefully framed blackness beyond violation with the question, "What else happened?"

22 For an excellent critical engagement with the limits and possibilities of posthumanism and animalism, see Zakiyyah Iman Jackson (2013).

23 Alexander Weheliye (2014) provides a useful analysis of the genres of the human.

24   Indigenous mapping seeks to render legible community rights, resource uses, sacred places, and other important spatial features to outside entities (Caballero Arias 2007; Mansutti Rodríguez 2006; Offen 2003; Sletto 2009). Indigenous mapping has the potential for an alternative means of storytelling and place-making, a radical change in the ways landscapes and places are documented, represented, and vested with meaning. For thinking from low spaces, see Charne Lavery's (2020) sea-level theorization.

While countermapping enables a defense of local territory, it is caught in the politics of legibility, which are counterintuitive to indigenous space making. For more on countermapping, see Bjørn Sletto (2012).

25   Dionne Brand (2012) has evocatively drawn the limits of mapping and the failures of grafting belonging onto maps.

26   However, as I watch the standoff between the state in partnership with mining corporations and the villagers of Mgungundlovu, I can see the value of an indigenous map that would visually claim the land earmarked for development. Joel Wainwright and Joe Bryan (2009) have termed this the cartographic-legal strategy. This contestation between villagers and the state is explicated in chapter two.

27   To name the territory of interest Mpondoland is to return to nativism, which might be read as making essential claims to land on the basis of ethnic origins. However, not to do so falls foul of purportedly neutral naming such as the now defunct Transkei or the current designator, Eastern Cape. The Kei River after which the Transkei territory was named is quite a distance from Mpondoland and in some ways discounts the specificities (and rivers) of the place. The Eastern Cape on the other hand is a return to the colonial name that reads the land from the Cape whose center is Cape Town. Both the Eastern Cape and Transkei might therefore be considered as misrecognitions of people and place.

28   The Mpondo people, like the Xhosa, Thembu, Mpondomise, Mfengu, Phuthi, Ntlangwini, Qwathi, Xesibe, Hlubi, Bhaca, and Bomvana people of the Eastern Cape, have occupied this part of the continent long before 1700.[1] Oral sources and shipwreck records attest to this existence (Hendricks and Peires 2011). Theal (1886) observed that the first white explorers found four major chieftaincies, the AmaMpondomise, the AmaMpondo, the AbaThembu, and the AmaXhosa, occupying the land between the Cape and Natal in 1688. Even as I side-eye colonial records, Theal suggests that the land has a long association with the people who currently reside on it.

29   The apartheid Bantustan system created ethnicized homelands for the different major ethnic groups of South Africa. These segregated homeland spaces were seen as surplus to South Africa. For more on this system, see William Beinart (2012).

30   Achille Mbembé and Sarah Nuttall's (2004) "Writing the World from an African Metropolis" is a seminal example of this. An earlier (1973) version

of this location of blackness in the city is N. Chabani Manganyi's *Being-Black-in-the-World*, republished in 2019.

31   Counterpoised to Collis-Buthelezi are works that argue against race in South Africa. These include Zimitri Erasmus (2017) and Njabulo Ndebele (2016).

32   For examples of work in South Africa and beyond, see African contributors such as N. Chabani Manganyi (2019), Keguro Macharia (2019), Gabeba Baderoon (2014), Yvette Abrahams (2000), Bhekizizwe Peterson (2000), Harry Garuba (2003), Neo Musangi (2018), Grace A. Musila (2020), and Sylvia Tamale (2020), among others.

33   See, for example, Grace A. Musila (2019) and Amanuel Isak Tewolde (2019).

34   Frantz Fanon (1967) has argued that instead of postcolonialism, neocolonialism more accurately follows colonialism.

35   My invocation of Mpondo music, later in this introduction, is to highlight the aural means through which we attend, witness, respond, and remain in step with each other.

36   Indigenous storytelling and scholarly discourse are both forms of knowledge. The former is nurtured intergenerationally and taught by elders and indigenous cosmologies, while the latter is taught within formal institutions like universities.

37   In posing this question, I engage the works of Mohamed Adhikari (2010), Yvette Abrahams (2000), Jauquelyne Kosgei (2021), Naomi Kipuri (2017), and Riswan Laher and Korir Sing'Oei (2014).

38   Kerugo Macharia (2020) has argued that it is not politically and conceptually useful to say that Africans are always queer because this framing does not address endemic nationalist homophobia and structural misogyny in Africa. Billy-Ray Belcourt (2016a) has similarly described indigenous reserves as queerphobic. While I find resonance in Macharia's and Belcourt's contentions, a return to earlier meanings of queer enables us to repurpose the concept to engage our supposed oddness and the ways in which we are always negated and primitivized. It is also to recognize the possibilities enabled by being queerly positioned.

39   Similarly, Macharia's (2020) evocation of African belatedness to critique the ways in which Africans are indexed as delayed, not "yet" ready, or primitive is a commentary on African failure to be proper.

40   Xavier Livermon (2020) takes up urban queer making in Johannesburg by centering cultural labor for queer visibility. I gesture to something different in the rural context—a freedom to live freely in all its possibilities even if it means being unmoored from the nation and aspirations of modernity. Here, queering does not center legibility.

41   T. J. Tallie signals the double possibilities of queer by considering how practices can be simultaneously normative and queer. Through *ukuphazama iNatali*, Tallie disturbs and queers colonial historiography.

42 To extend Paul Gilroy's (1993) observation that sex is another means of talking about race, I add that queer is a language of race.

43 Musangi (2018) provides a seminal lesson on the intellectual contribution of black women who live in community beyond kinship, thus embodying black theory and a logic of care.

44 In Nira Yuval-Davis's (2006) formulation, our multiple identities are constitutive of the experience of life.

45 For Alistair Hunter (2015), deathscapes can encompass durable markings of the landscape (e.g., cemeteries) as well as more ephemeral manifestations and artifacts such as the scattering of ashes.

46 The dying epoch was Hilton Als's (2019) formulation to make sense of queer death from AIDS in 1980s United States.

47 Coulthard (2014, 24) terms this a resurgent politics of recognition that is "premised on self-actualization, direct action, and the resurgence of cultural practices that are attentive to the subjective and structural composition of settler-colonial power."

48 Walcott (2015) similarly observed that Caribbean writing insists on exploding distinctions between the creative and theoretical.

49 Édouard Glissant (1997) has defined this as the energy of preserving poetics and the refutation of order and established norms. Even though it has a hidden logic, this order does not presuppose hierarchies of all forms, including languages or peoples.

50 Referring to *Pondo Blues* by Eric Nomvete, performed in 1962, Dlamini (2010, 169) writes that the song had a triple consciousness: "The horns, like human voices, intoned wordlessly a well-known melody of symbolic performance significance, to the accompaniment of traditional drum rhythms and piano reconstruction of the voices of the absent choir."

51 For a comprehensive account of *ukugwaba*, see Deirdre Hansen (1981), whose work I think with here.

52 Among unofficial languages are isiMpondo, isiBhaca, and languages that fall between the cracks of seSotho and seTswana. Descendants of enslaved people such as those of Malaysian and Indonesian descent are truncated into the "coloured" category in ways that obscure their histories and complex identifications. Zimitri Erasmus (2001) uncovers some of this complexity.

53 See Yvette Abrahams (2000) for an explication of cylindrical time and Michelle Wright (2015) for more on epiphenomenal temporality. I work with these terms throughout the text.

54 Ngquza Hill marks the highpoint of the Mpondo revolt, an occurrence that is central to this text.

55 For more on this massacre, see Peter Alexander et al. (2012) and Greg Marinovich (2016). On mining on Amadiba land and resistance, see Andrew Bennie (2011).

Chapter 1: Watchful Ocean, Observant Mountain

1   I refer only obliquely to Asian and African castaways who were on some ships as passengers or enslaved captives. They appear to have been relatively limited in number and their origins are uncertain.

2   Hazel Crampton (2004) provides a comprehensive outline of Minna's lineage among the amaMolo clan.

3   Aboriginal ancestors in Australia similarly left sacred engravings for subsequent generations to retain an unbreakable relation that has spanned across the centuries of dispossession. For more, see Lynn Hume (2000).

4   The Khoekhoe of neighboring Botswana who refuse the trappings of modernity have been corralled into camps or reserves.

5   The stuckness of black and native peoples is framed against terms of incommensurability (lack of commonality/relationality, solidarities, and antagonism).

6   The "Hamitic myth" that attributes the origins of Bantu people to West and Central Africa has been challenged by scholars such as Samwiri Lwanga-Lunyiigo (1976) who have questioned linguists' assumptions of common Bantu linguistic roots. However, more recent genetics studies reassert the origins story of western Bantu migrations from West Africa (Beleza et al. 2005).

7   Similarly, East Africa has not been able to fully reconcile how minoritized indigenous people fit into the postcolonial project. These include groups like the Benet, Batwa, Ik, Karamojong, and the Basongora of Uganda; the Hadzabe and Akiye of Tanzania; the Ogiek, Yaaku, Sengwer, Elmolo, Waata, and Aweer of Kenya; the Batwa of Rwanda and Burundi; and the Toposa and Murle of South Sudan (Kipuri 2017). In the broader East African region, other indigenous groups include seasonal pastoralist people such as the Barbaig (and the wider Datoga), Baraguyu, Maasai, Samburu, Turkana, Rendille, Pokot, Borana, and Endorois (Kipuri 2017).

8   Dorothy Hodgson (2009) provides a compelling outline of the controversies related to becoming indigenous in Africa.

9   There are of course many other African scholars who have contributed to continental understandings of Africans. In South Africa, these include Sol Plaatje in the early twentieth century, N. Chabani Manganyi in the 1960s and 1970s, and continentally, Obioma Nnaemeka, Amina Mama, Catherine Obianuju, Grace Musila, and Sylvia Tamale in the early twenty-first century.

10   Michael Marker (2003) cautions against reducing indigenous people to exotic artifacts of the past. They have a stake in the present and the future—political and economic conditions matter to them.

11   The pejorative name for San people is Bushmen. This descriptor is still widely used.

12 By kaffirization, I point to the process of black dehumanization and traumatization. This is a localized version of Aimé Césaire's (1972) thingification. In Uri McMillan's words, thingification indexes "the forceful disciplining of black subjects into different types of humanity, a lesser-than-human" (2015, 225).

13 For the fiction of race, see Aníbal Quijano (2000).

14 My great-grandfather was known as Reme in the village.

15 Tracing the history of the shipwrecks, Henderson Soga (1927) outlines various lineages that have Mpondo and Xhosa names.

16 For instance, Zimitri Erasmus (2017) tells of her own lineage in St. Helena off the Atlantic Ocean.

17 The book *The Sunburnt Queen* (Crampton 2004) details some stories of Europeans who were shipwrecked on the Transkei coastline.

18 For an account of the *Grosvenor* shipwreck, Ian Glenn (1995) and Nigel Penn (2004) provide an authoritative overview.

19 Saidiya Hartman (2008) and Amira Baraka (1967) have written of the frequency of sexual assault and rape on board the slave and trade ships. These children could have been the consequence of these violent intimacies. We must however always leave room for the possibilities of consent and pleasure alongside the violence.

20 For enslavement in the Cape, see Mohamed Adhikari (1992).

21 For more on this shipwreck, see Chris Auret and Tim Maggs (1982).

22 The term Hottentot is a pejorative name for Khoekhoe and the San.

23 Alexander Dalrymple's 1785 account was reproduced by Percival R. Kirby (1953, 31).

24 The Amadiba Crisis Committee was established to resist mining on the ancestral land of Mpondoland villagers of the Mgungundlovu community. The community has also resisted government attempts to build a toll highway across their land.

25 I refer to the Khoekhoe rock paintings in the Drakensburg mountain range. For more on this, see Frans E. Prins (2009).

26 Nongqawuse was orphaned when her parents were killed in the battles of Waterkloof. For more on Nongqawuse, see A. Yolisa Kenqu (2019) and Jennifer Wenzel (2009).

27 Here, her prophecy is seen as manipulation, a frontier tactic that would lead to black dependence on the colonial authorities who would then enlist them into poorly paid migrant labor. See Jeffery B. Peires (1989) for more on this.

28 See Saidiya Hartman (2019), Toni Morrison (1987), Bessie Head (2013), and Donald Burness (1977).

29 I return to conceptions of fortified bodies being impervious to bullets in coming chapters.

30 For more on Robben Island as a leper colony, see Harriet Jane Deacon (1996).

31　Here and throughout this text, my use of the word *deviant* points to the expulsion of those who opposed normative expectations of docility in the face of colonial, apartheid, patriarchal, and neoliberal subjugation.

32　Peterson made this provocation at the NEST conference at the University of the Witwatersrand in 2017.

Chapter 2: Fortifying Rivers

1　See Jayna Brown (2015) for an exposition on decentering the human from a cellular level.

2　Leanne Betasamosake Simpson (2017) points to how indigenous wisdom is passed down through ritual practice. Mpondo rituals are enactments of indigenous wisdom.

3　Pieter Jolly (1986) details the practice of medicated cuts in the body of San and other indigenous groups in South Africa.

4　The Mpondo revolt climaxed at Ngquza Hill.

5　Fenwick's report can be found in Katherine Fidler's (2010, 85) account of the Mpondo revolt.

6　The Marikana massacre occurred on August 12, 2012, when 112 were shot down and thirty-four men killed by police officers. I take particular interest in this massacre because twenty-six of the men killed were from Mpondoland in the northeastern parts of the Eastern Cape.

7　Useful work in this direction includes Saba Mahmood (2001), Grace Eseosa Idahosa (2020), and Sylvia Tamale (2020).

8　We know that savagery exists only in the mirror of colonial modernity.

9　My use of *queer* here is more aligned to strange than it is to sexually nonnormative. I however include sexually nonnormative practices—differently queered people—because Mpondo sexual mores include colonial sensibilities, but they are not loyal to colonial discipline and dimensions of desire and pleasure.

10　These young men were lured into boarding trucks with the promise of jobs on sugarcane plantations, but the slave-like conditions on the plantations shattered their dreams for the good life and its liberatory promise.

11　Having almost drowned in the Indian Ocean on two occasions, and as a person who cannot swim, I have my own embodied response to the ocean.

12　Sarah Baartman was a black woman born in the Southern Cape of South Africa in 1788. She was taken into captivity and showcased like a circus animal in Europe before her death. She is discussed comprehensively in chapter 4.

13　See Bibi Burger's (2020) analysis of the ocean.

14　Albert Grundlingh (2011) presents a compelling argument for being skeptical of the likelihood that Wauchope's death drill would have occurred given the speed with which the ship sank and the inexperience of many of those on board. It is however the very need to create and hold on to myth that is important for me. The poet Mqhayi is credited with memorializing the event through a heroic lens. Without the myth making, we have black men who not only died in vain but who had nothing to show for it.

15 See John Gribble and Jonathan Sharfman (2015) for this account.

16 For S. E. K. Mqhayi's poems, see Mqhayi (2017).

17 Macharia (2019) suggests that black and queer do not play well together. I return to this provocation in chapter 3.

18 I refuse to surrender the term *queer* to Euro-American whiteness.

19 I occasionally refer to Nontetha Nkwenkwe by her first name, not to disrespect an honored ancestor but in the tradition of spiritual leaders often being called by their first names. Nongqawuse and Khotso are similarly named.

20 South African History Online provides an account of her life; see SAHO (2019b).

21 Robert Edgar and Hilary Sapire (2000) observe that she was diagnosed with "dementia praecox of the hebephrenic type," which preceded the current category of schizophrenia.

22 For white fear of black assembly, see Nirmal Puwar (2004).

23 For more on these differences, see William Beinart and Colin Bundy (1987).

24 The Eastern Cape has a number of prophetesses, including maRadebe or Umthandazeli of Cancele and Elizabeth Paul Spalding of Tsolo. For more, see Janet Hodgson (1983).

25 Jayna Brown's (2021) work on black utopias extends these arguments.

26 The Bulhoek massacre of May 24, 1921, in what is today the Eastern Cape, where the police killed 163 civilians, is one example.

27 This act enabled the white officials to systematically steal the land from black people.

28 Max Mamase as cited in Leslie Bank and Gary Minkley (2005, 6).

29 I pursue these queer lines of thought more fully in chapter 3 where I pause on the lives of the differently queered.

30 On the continent, Garveyism was seen as a triumphant return of enslaved African Americans.

31 For more on the Soviets and the African National Congress, see Tom Lodge (1987), and Irina Filatova and Appollon Davidson (2013).

32 See Lazarus Lebeloane and Madise Mokhele (2006), and Willem Berends (1993).

33 Some of those executed in Pretoria are Masipalati Nkomani, Wilson Ngobhe Nomqwazi, Mcezulwa Ngwevu, Madusu Sandlobe, Gavu Zadunge, Nwayi Singxesa Baka, Khwahla Majayinethi, Motha, Khekani Gudluwayo, Mfuywa Mtholeni, Samani Mpambaniso, Shadrack Joji Dlamini, Rhawuzela Mdlungu Mtshudela, and Voxwana Maphamela Sheleni.

34 For more on Mahlangu, see Judy Froman (2011), Sabine Marschall (2008), and Pethu Serote (1992).

35 See Karel Anthonie Bakker and Liana Müller (2010).

36 For more on these removals, see Tom Lodge (1981).

37 A *koppie* is a small hill in an area that is mostly flat.

38 A *sangoma* is a traditional healer who can mediate between the ancestral world and that of the living.

39 See Grace Musila (2020) and Wangari Maathai (2008) for more on the symbolic value of the natural world.

40 For this series of rebellions, see Leonard Guelke and Robert Shell (1992), and Susan Newton-King and V. C. Malherbe (1981).

41 For more on the state of inequality in South Africa and the role of global capital in extractivism, see Charmaine Pereira and Dzodzi Tsikata (2021), and Patrick Bond (2013).

42 The 100-year period in which Xhosa people along the eastern coastline resisted British forces who sought to colonize the area. For more on this, see Clifton C. Crais (1992).

43 For more on the Gum Tree Rebellion, see Jacques De Wet (2011).

44 For melancholic relations to land, see Bhekizizwe Peterson (2019).

45 Katherine McKittrick (2006, 123) defines demonic grounds as "the space of Otherness, the grounds of being human, poverty archipelagos, archipelagos of human Otherness, les damnés de la terre/the wretched of the earth, the color-line, terra nullius/lands of no one."

Chapter 3: Riotous Spirits—*Ukukhuphuka izizwe*

Epigraph: Nontsizi Mgqwetho's "The Stream of Despair" (2007) was translated by Jeff Opland.

1 While I use the word *possession* for its legibility for most readers, I hope to convey a located deeper meaning that suggests the emergence of worlds in the Mpondo conceptual frame of *ukukhuphuka izizwe*.

2 *Worlding* is my intervention to displace the linear temporality of dissociation.

3 See Hugo Canham (2017) for rage as self-love.

4 Macharia (2019) productively draws out Lorde's commitment to the erotic and its world making possibilities.

5 E. P. Johnson's grandmother used the word *quare* to signal the strangeness of her grandson's orientation to sexuality.

6 On the US archive and black girlhood, see Corinne T. Field et al. (2016).

7 Nigel Thrift (2008) theorizes this contagion by asserting that affect is not reducible to perceptions and affections of a single subject.

8   Michelle Wright's epiphenomenal temporality is useful for thinking through blackness, while Elizabeth Freeman's (2010) queer binds is a productive lens of thinking queer temporalities. Together, these conceptions of time assist in advancing the current project of queer manifestations of blackness. The boundlessness of queer registers of blackness is essential for the current work.

9   People older than sixty are eligible for an old age pension.

10   In 2016, only 63 percent of learners passed their final examinations compared to 93 percent in the best-performing province (Wicks 2017a). But even the 63 percent pass rate does not withstand close scrutiny since it is unevenly spread in the Eastern Cape Province. City schools and middle-class neighborhoods inflate the percentage pass that is sometimes as low as 10 percent in Mpondoland.

11   Ukhozi FM is the largest radio station in South Africa and broadcasts in isiZulu.

12   Here, we may read horror as evil and allusions to the devil that purportedly takes control of the possessed.

13   For a fuller account of the possession at Mdizimba High School, see Greg Newkirk (2011) and Musa Nhleko (2011).

14   The full Twitter thread can be accessed here: https://twitter.com/ikentanzi _/status/1016720308361887744.

15   Ntazi's consent required that I acknowledge him as the creator of the thread.

16   For more on virginity testing, see Suzanne Leclerc-Madlala (2003).

17   Michelle Wright (2015) conceives of *spacetime* to think of temporality as always located in context. This departs from Newtonian time, which conceives of time as objective and independent.

18   For more about Clara Germana Cele, see Francis Young (2016).

19   See Elizabeth Freeman (2010) on time binds.

20   *Intelezi* is a plant that is ground and added to bathing water in order to remove *isicito* or jealousy-induced maladies. For more on the cultural and medicinal use of plant life in Mpondoland, see Thembela Kepe (2007).

21   Here Roderick Ferguson underscores forms of blackness that are omitted by black respectability politics and black nationalism.

22   Neo Musangi (2014) observes that they belong to the Akamba people of Kenya who refer to them as *tala*. A description that marks their sexual identity.

23   Through Tinsley's (2008) English translation, Gloria Wekker (1994, 145) explains the endurance and pervasiveness of these relations of queer care by tracing the names used to describe these bonds across the Caribbean. "The Brazilian 'malungo,' the Trinidadian 'malongue,' the Haitian 'batiment'

and the Surinamese 'sippi' and 'mati' are all examples of this special, non-biological bond between two people of the same sex."

24 Keguro Macharia (2019) has similarly cautioned against the debilitating effects of a black queer studies that sees itself as constantly responding to white queer studies.

25 In 2016, the Mpondoland failure rate in grade 12 was 37 percent (Wicks 2017a).

26 A *shebeen* is an informal tavern or bar serving alcoholic beverages in working-class communities.

27 In order for my coprotagonists to recognize themselves, I have to avoid reductive theorizing that flattens their experience and instead portray them as committed to desire as a praxis of resistance.

Chapter 4: Levitating Graves and Ancestral Frequencies

1 Santu Mofokeng was a South African photographer whose later work was invested in the spiritual. His work titled *Graves* is particularly evocative for me. A selection of his work can be seen here: https://aperture.org/editorial/santu-mofokengs-sean-otoole/. To attend to Eric Nomvete's performance of *Pondo Blues* at the Cold Castle National Jazz 1962 Festival in Moroka, Jabavu, see https://www.youtube.com/watch?v=z6jetAovKbQ.

2 Tina Campt's conversation with Zara Julius, Jenn Nkiru, and Alexander Weheliye (2020) as part of *The Sojourner Project* was influential in shaping my thoughts on the frequencies of blackness. For this conversation and other resources on *The Sojourner Project*, see https://www.thesojournerproject.org.

3 Tinsley and Richardson (2014, 153) define "graverobber methodology" as an approach "to delve into the purposely and accidentally immolated pasts of a variety of times and sites, in order to unearth the skeletons of racism, misogyny, and transphobia that dominant narratives keep invisible and disconnected in our understanding."

4 This view of blackness as motion has fidelity to Édouard Glissant and Fred Moten's conceptions of errantry and movement. For these, see Glissant (1997) and Moten (2017).

5 Jenn Nkiru's (2017) *Black Star: Rebirth Is Necessary* is useful in attending to boundless blackness. For the short film, see https://www.youtube.com/watch?v=vemJFbayDrM.

6 I use the term *dyings* to point to the multiplicity, regularity, and ongoingness of death.

7 As I will explain, Jasbir K. Puar's (2017) concept of debility as slow death in the service of neoliberal life is better aligned to this project than disability.

8 Leanne Betasamosake Simpson (2017) provides an excellent engagement with the praxis of native intelligence.

9   King (2019) refers to acts of slowed movement or pausing as shoaling.

10   This compulsive writing is remarked upon by Saidiya Hartman (2008) in her returns to the Venus figure.

11   I borrow from Keguro Macharia's (2019) formulation of frottage to complicate relation as a space of friction, touchings, and entanglements.

12   I however displace Diaz's human since the African does not figure in this calculus. The black/indigenous/queer being of *Riotous Deathscapes* is boundless and constituted by animal, plant life, water, land, spirit, and the ancestral realm.

13   Yvette Abrahams (2000) calls this the genital encounter.

14   For an example of these critiques, see Jayna Brown (2015).

15   The eland and blue antelope are totems that are central to Khoekhoe cosmologies.

16   This conception of motion is drawn from Tina Campt's definition of motion as a change in the position of an object in relation to time; see Arthur Jafa and Tina Campt (2017).

17   This is a reference to Frantz Fanon's (2007) account of how blacks were made wretched.

18   See Maitseo Bolaane (2004).

19   Simpson (2017) insists that indigenous thought systems are generated in relationship to place.

20   The work of feminist activists and the first black government in fighting for and returning Sarah Baartman is an example of how we are entrusted with the responsibility of ancestral freedom.

21   My mother's brother was murdered during the Christmas holidays of 2005. His killers have never been apprehended. South African Police Service (SAPS 2021) crime statistics for the fourth quarter of 2020 indicate that Lusikisiki has the highest incidence of sexual offences and ranks in the top thirty places for murder in South Africa.

22   Kylie Thomas (2013) warns that AIDS deaths continue as one of the leading causes of death.

23   Christina Sharpe (2016) conceives of the bones of black people killed at sea in the Middle Passage as doing residence time.

24   Of course those of us who have attended to the earth know that it is never really stationary. The weather, people, and the natural world are always actively engaged with the earth. The earth hums with activity of ants and other insects.

25   This works in ways that are similar to King's (2019) concept of shoaling—the slowing down of movement.

26   For this project and its interactive mapping, see Thomas S. Mullaney et al. (2019).

27   Bianca van Laun notes that 4,003 names appear on the memorial of those hanged between 1912 and 1989.

28 For more on this, see Jacob Dlamini (2014) and Pumla Gobodo-Madikizela (2013).

29 For more on the Zimbabwean hangman, see Tawanda Karombo (2017).

30 I innumerate these deaths in a general way for purposes of preserving some aspects of anonymity.

31 For example, see C. V. M. Mutwa (1996).

32 See, for example, Nicoli Nattrass (2007), and Christopher J. Colvin and Steven Robins (2009).

33 Guam is in the Mariana Islands territory.

34 The Mfecane was a nationalist war to expand the Zulu empire of King Shaka. He sought to vanquish smaller tribes and incorporate them into the Zulu nation. The Mfecane destabilized Southern Africa, and some tribes ran away as far north as modern-day Zimbabwe. See Carolyn Hamilton (1995).

35 Jackson attributes the descriptor of plasticity as "everything and nothing" to Patrice Douglass (2016, 116).

36 Sylvia Tamale (2020) and Wangari Maathai (2008) both engage the modernist wedge placed between the human and the natural world.

37 Sazi S. Dlamini (2010, 160) cites Ndikho Xaba, who described the scene of Eric Nomvete and his band playing *Pondo Blues* as spiritually riotous. He writes that Nomvete's arrangement "resulted in the crowd rioting and throwing beer bottles."

38 When one dies outside of the home, a ceremony is conducted to collect the spirit of the dead and bring it home so that the person might not be a restless spirit but occupy the place of a worthy ancestor.

39 These women may have been her older sisters, but having read Neo Musangi's account of queer kinship patterns among the women in their family, I remain open to the multiple potentialities of the homing arrangements among these women. For more, see Musangi (2018).

40 Disability grants are more tenuous than old age grants because beneficiaries of the former have to routinely prove the persistence of their disability.

41 In the 1920s, the surgeon general of a district in Pondoland described the Mpondo as less magnificent than their Zulu neighbors. I provide an account of this in chapter 1.

42 The Farlam Commission was chaired by retired Judge Ian Gordon Farlam to probe the deaths that resulted from the standoff between protesting mine workers and the police sponsored by Lonmin and the government. The event is commonly known as the Marikana massacre.

43 Lorraine Adams (2001) defines "nobody memoirs" as life stories by ordinary people.

44 La Marr Jurelle Bruce (2021) suggests that madness can advance a radical politics.

Chapter 5: Rioting Hills and Occult Insurrections

1   With *ukwakumkanya*, and to echo Tiffany Lethabo King (2019), black and indigenous people implicate each other in a mutual form of survival. As described in chapter 1, through the poetics of relation, they refused to be wiped out.

2   Market forms of violence refer to the destruction of local forms of communal livelihood that are tied to the land, turning Mpondoland into an unskilled labor reserve, and promoting individualist consumer-based capitalist lifestyles that are out of reach for local communities. In an environment where neoliberal forms of production and accumulation are not possible, the local means of wealth acquisition appeal to occult economies that are perceived as alternative routes to the good life.

3   James Baldwin (1985) wrote despairingly about the price of inclusion of black people into American democracy.

4   Indigenous communities understand elders as carriers of wisdom. Throughout most of this book and particularly in this chapter, I rely on indigenous wisdom from elders. For more on elders as conveyors of wisdom, see Michael Marker (2003).

5   For more on Ndlavini and Nombola, see William Beinart (2014), and T. Dunbar Moodie and Vivienne Ndatshe (1994).

6   Constructed as minor history, the Mpondo revolt elicited blank stares from archival officers.

7   King (2019) similarly points to the place of the tree as a site of relation for various indigenous groups.

8   Uneducated people of the Eastern Cape were sometimes derisively referred to as red people to mark their low social standing as unrefined. The smearing of red ochre over one's body is meant to protect against the sun's ultraviolet radiation and against insects such as mosquitoes. However, these reasons are overlooked in favor of denigration.

9   Listening to the story of the Mpondo camp at Ngquza Hill evokes Giorgio Agamben's (1998) concept of encampment.

10 The apartheid state often instituted states of emergency in order to suppress civil unrest. A state of emergency suspended the law and expanded the powers of the security apparatus to implement any measures to quell resistance.

11 *Maas* is fermented milk commonly consumed in South Africa.

12 Here I use *queer* as introduced in chapters 2 and 3 with a fidelity to both sexual orientation and the unsanctioned, uncanny, strange, and off-center.

13 In the state's reckoning, women did not feature as a serious threat during the Mpondo revolt.

14 Billy-Ray Belcourt (2015) outlines how indigenous communities operate in timescapes that defy settler time.

15 Current owner of the painting Robert Jackson points to the homophobic attitude in Lewis's biography. I take pleasure in queering his work.

16 For more on black humor, see Glenda Carpio (2008) and Thomas LeClair (1975).

17 For more on queer repetition, see Jerry Thomas (2017) and Margaret E. Johnson (2013).

18 Chapter 2 deals with the revolt from the perspective of the historical unfoldings and its devastation.

19 AmaQaba are self-identified uneducated people who align themselves to local tradition and customs. While they are similar to the Nombola, unlike the latter they have a cultural alignment and are not an affinity group.

20 Peter Magubane is a renowned photographer whose work came into prominence in the mid-1950s. He was there to record the events of the Kongo.

21 In South Africa, "coloured" refers to people of mixed race heritage but also Malaysian and Indonesian descendants of enslaved people, Khoekhoe, and other indigenous groups. The category is not without contestation and for this reason is often used in scare quotes. For more, see Zimitri Erasmus (2001).

22 The Langa massacre occurred at Cape Town's Caledon Square police headquarters following the mass march of between 30,000 to 50,000 people from Langa and Nyanga townships who were protesting against apartheid's pass laws. Close on to 100 people were killed, about 400 injured, and thousands arrested. For more on the Langa and Sharpeville massacres, see Saul Dubow (2015).

23 This recollection aligns with Diana Wylie's (2011) observation that people commonly recollected the consumption of bodies by dogs.

24 Mpondo is also commonly written as Pondo.

25 For more, see William Beinart (2014).

26 *Etshotshweni* and *eguburheni* are the names of places where the respective groups met.

27 Keith Breckenridge (1990) reported that in the 1920s the Isitshozi gang began as an organization of Mpondo migrant workers around the mining compounds of the Witwatersrand.

28 For more on the violent displacement, see Lubabalo Ngcukana (2019).

29 For an account of the Vondo, see SABC1 (2017).

30 Jayna Brown (2015, 337) asks what it might look like if we took up the provocation to embrace the prevailing enlightenment notion that we are inhuman.

31 See Michael Legassick (1972) and Colin Bundy (1972).

32 Francis Fukuyama (1989) famously wrote about the end of history.

33 For more on this drug, see Kebogile Mokwena and Neo Morojele (2014).

34 People that I spoke to about Vondo activity ascribed it to satanic behavior.

35   Thanduxolo and Cele are discussed in chapter 3.

36   Birgit Meyer (1995) has pointed to the intersecting relationship between satanic awareness in Pentecostal Christian Ghana and capital accumulation. Also see Jean Comaroff and John Comaroff (2000).

37   Drug addiction has often been associated with vampire behavior. Those who make this claim argue that the altered state of mind explains why people would engage in the shocking practice of blood sucking.

38   In the days leading up to the August 12 Marikana massacre, there were acts of intimidation, including shootings, and at least five people were hacked to death for refusing to participate in the mining strike. For more, see SAHO (2017).

39   For more on the ambiguities introduced by modern hygiene practices and cosmetics, see chapter 3.

40   The occult activities in the Afrikaans community of Krugersdorp suggest that these activities mark precarity beyond race.

41   For more on this story, see eNCA (2017).

42   For David McNally (2011), monstrous market refers to the cannibalistic nature of capitalist accumulation. High capitalism preys on the poor.

43   The phenomenon of child rapes in the 1990s was seen as a possible cure and cleansing of HIV/AIDS. For more on this, see Banwari Lal Meel (2003), and Rachel Jewkes, Lorna Martin, and Loveday Penn-Kekana (2002).

44   Sangomas are traditional healers.

45   For some of the myths about people with albinism, see Charlotte Baker et al. (2010).

46   King (2019) usefully points to the ways that we might think of "fungible fugitivity" as an expansive concept to suture blackness and indigeneity.

Fitful Dreamscapes: An Afterword

1   Dionne Brand (2021) makes a case for an untethered tense that frees us from the tyrannies of time.

Abrahams, Peter. 1953. *Return to Goli*. 2nd ed. London: Faber & Faber.

Abrahams, Yvette. 1996. "Was Eva Raped? An Exercise in Speculative History." *Kronos* 23 (November): 3–21.

Abrahams, Yvette. 1997. "The Great Long National Insult: 'Science', Sexuality and the Khoisan in the 18th and Early 19th Century." *Agenda* 13, no. 32: 34–48.

Abrahams, Yvette. 2000. "Colonialism, Disjuncture and Dysfunction: Sarah Baartman's Resistance." PhD diss., University of Cape Town.

Adams, Lorraine. 2001. "Almost Famous: The Rise of the 'Nobody' Memoir." *Washington Monthly*, April 1, 2001. https://washingtonmonthly.com/2001/04/01/almost-famous/.

Adhikari, Mohamed. 1992. "The Sons of Ham: Slavery and the Making of Coloured Identity." *South African Historical Journal* 27, no. 1: 95–112.

Adhikari, Mohamed. 2010. "A Total Extinction Confidently Hoped For: The Destruction of Cape San Society under Dutch Colonial Rule, 1700–1795." *Journal of Genocide Research* 12, no. 1–2: 19–44.

Agamben, Giorgio. 1998. *Homo Sacer: Sovereign Power and Bare Life*. Redwood City: Stanford University Press.

Ahmed, Sara. 2006. "Orientations: Toward a Queer Phenomenology." GLQ 12, no. 4: 543–74.

Ahmed, Sara. 2010. *Happy Objects*. Durham, NC: Duke University Press.

Aidoo, Ama Ata. 1997. *Our Sister Killjoy*. Harlow, UK: Longman.

Alexander, M. Jacqui. 2005. "Pedagogies of Crossing: Meditations on Feminism." *Sexual Politics, Memory, and the Sacred*. Durham, NC: Duke University Press.

Alexander, Peter, Thapelo Lekgowa, Botsang Mmope, Luke Sinwell, and Bongani Xeswi. 2012. *Marikana: A View from the Mountain and a Case to Answer*. Auckland Park, SA: Jacana Media.

Ali, Ashna. 2020. "Ugly Affects: Migritude and Black Mediterranean Counternarratives of Migrant Subjectivity." *Journal of Narrative Theory* 50, no. 3: 376–404.

Allen, Victor Leonard. 1992. *The History of Black Mineworkers in South Africa*. Vol. 2. Shipley, West Yorkshire, UK: Moor Press.

Als, Hilton. 2019. *White Girls*. New York: Penguin.

Angas, George. 1974. *The Kafirs Illustrated: A Facsimile Reprint of the Original 1849 Edition of Hand-Coloured Lithographs, with a New Introduction by F. R. Bradlow*. Cape Town: A. A. Balkema.

Anzaldúa, Gloria. (1987) 2004. "Borderlands/La Frontera." In *Literary Theory: An Anthology*, edited by Julie Rivkin and Michael Ryan, 1117–30. Malden, MA: Blackwell.

Arendt, Hannah. 1970. *On Violence*. New York: Houghton Mifflin Harcourt.

Arendt, Hannah. 1975. *The Origins of Totalitarianism*. New York: Harcourt Brace.

Arondekar, Anjali. 2005. "Border/Line Sex: Queer Postcolonialities, or How Race Matters outside the United States." *Interventions* 7, no. 2: 236–50.

Atienza, David, and Alexandre Coello. 2012. "Death Rituals and Identity in Contemporary Guam (Mariana Islands)." *Journal of Pacific History* 47, no. 4: 459–73.

Auret, Chris, and Tim Maggs. 1982. "The Great Ship São Bento: Remains from a Mid-sixteenth Century Portuguese Wreck on the Pondoland Coast." *Annals of the Natal Museum* 25, no. 1: 1–39.

Baderoon, Gabeba. 2004a. "The Provenance of the Term 'Kafir' in South Africa and the Notion of Beginning." *Annual Review of Islam in South Africa* 7.

Baderoon, Gabeba. 2004b. "The Underside of the Picturesque Landscape: Meanings of Muslim Burial in Cape Town, South Africa." *Arab World Geographer* 7, no. 4: 261–75.

Baderoon, Gabeba. 2009. "The African Oceans—Tracing the Sea as Memory of Slavery in South African Literature and Culture." *Research in African Literatures* 40, no. 4: 89–107.

Baderoon, Gabeba. 2011. "Baartman and the Private: How Can We Look at a Figure that Has Been Looked at Too Much?" In *Representation and Black Womanhood*, edited by Natasha Gordon-Chipembere, 65–83. New York: Palgrave Macmillan.

Baderoon, Gabeba. 2014. *Regarding Muslims: From Slavery to Post-Apartheid*. New York: New York University Press.

Bakare-Yusuf, Bibi. 1999. "The Economy of Violence: Black Bodies and the Unspeakable Terror." In *Feminist Theory and the Body: A Reader*, edited by Janet Price and Margrit Shildrick, 311–23. Edinburgh: Edinburgh University Press.

Baker, Charlotte, Patricia Lund, Richard Nyathi, and Julie Taylor. 2010. "The Myths Surrounding People with Albinism in South Africa and Zimbabwe." *Journal of African Cultural Studies* 22, no. 2: 169–81.

Bakker, Karel Anthonie, and Liana Müller. 2010. "Intangible Heritage and Community Identity in Post-apartheid South Africa." *Museum International* 62, no. 1–2: 48–54.

Baldwin, James. 1984. *Notes of a Native Son*. Vol. 39. Boston: Beacon.

Baldwin, James. 1985. *The Price of the Ticket: Collected Nonfiction, 1948–1985*. New York: Macmillan.

Banana, Canaan. 1991. *Come and Share: An Introduction to Christian Theology*. Gweru, ZW: Mambo Press.

Bank, Leslie. 2004. "Review: *The Politics of Evil: Magic, State Power and the Political Imagination in South Africa*." In "Writing in Transition in South Africa: Fiction, History, Biography," special issue, *Journal of Southern African Studies* 30, no. 4: 912–15.

Bank, Leslie, and Gary Minkley. 2005. "Going Nowhere Slowly? Land, Livelihoods and Rural Development in the Eastern Cape." *Social Dynamics* 31, no. 1: 1–38.

Banks, Ojeya Cruz. 2010. "Of Water and Spirit: Locating Dance Epistemologies in Aotearoa/New Zealand and Senegal." *Anthropological Notebooks* 16, no. 3: 9–22.

Baraka, Amira. 1967. *Slave Ship: A Historical Pageant*. Newark, NJ: Jihad Productions.

Barthes, Roland. 2005. *The Neutral: Lecture Course at the Collège de France (1977–1978)*. Translated by Rosalind Krauss and Denis Hollier. New York: Columbia University Press.

Bastian, Misty L. 2001. "'The Demon Superstition': Abominable Twins and Mission Culture in Onitsha History." *Ethnology* 40, no. 1: 13–27.

Baynton, Douglas C. 2006. "'The Undesirability of Admitting Deaf Mutes': US Immigration Policy and Deaf Immigrants, 1882–1924." *Sign Language Studies* 6, no. 4: 391–415.

Becken, H. J. 1968. "On the Holy Mountain: A Visit to the New Year's Festival of the Nazaretha Church on Mount Nhlangakazi, 14 January, 1967." *Journal of Religion in Africa* 1, no. 2: 138–49.

Behrend, Heike. 1999. *Alice Lakwena and the Holy Spirits: War in Northern Uganda, 1985–97*. Oxford: James Currey.

Beinart, William. 1979. "Joyini Inkomo: Cattle Advances and the Origins of Migrancy from Pondoland." *Journal of Southern African Studies* 5, no. 2: 199–219.

Beinart, William. 1991. "The Origins of the Indlavini: Male Associations and Migrant Labour in the Transkei." *African Studies* 50, no. 1: 103–28.

Beinart, William. 2001. *Twentieth-Century South Africa*. New York: Oxford University Press.

Beinart, William. 2012. "Beyond 'Homelands': Some Ideas about the History of African Rural Areas in South Africa." *South African Historical Journal* 64, no. 1: 5–21.

Beinart, William. 2014. "A Century of Migrancy from Mpondoland." *African Studies* 73, no. 3: 387–409.

Beinart, William, and Colin Bundy. 1987. *Hidden Struggles in Rural South Africa: Politics and Popular Movements in the Transkei and Eastern Cape, 1890–1930 (No. 40)*. Oakland: University of California Press.

Belcourt, Billy-Ray. 2015. "Animal Bodies, Colonial Subjects: (Re)locating Animality in Decolonial Thought." *Societies* 5, no. 1: 1–11.

Belcourt, Billy-Ray. 2016a. "Can the Other of Native Studies Speak?" *Decolonization: Indigeneity, Education and Society* 1 (February 1). https://decolonization.wordpress.com/2016/02/01/can-the-other-of-native-studies-speak/.

Belcourt, Billy-Ray. 2016b. "A Poltergeist Manifesto." *Feral Feminisms* 6: 22–32.

Beleza, Sandra, Leonor Gusmao, Antonio Amorim, Angel Carracedo, and Antonio Salas. 2005. "The Genetic Legacy of Western Bantu Migrations." *Human Genetics* 117, no. 4: 366–75.

Bennie, Andrew. 2010. "The Relation between Environmental Protection and 'Development': A Case Study of the Social Dynamics Involved in the Proposed Mining at Xolobeni, Wild Coast." PhD diss., University of the Witwatersrand.

Bennie, Andrew. 2011. "Questions for Labour on Land, Livelihoods and Jobs: A Case Study of the Proposed Mining at Xolobeni, Wild Coast." *South African Review of Sociology* 42, no. 3: 41–59.

Berends, Willem. 1993. "African Traditional Healing Practices and the Christian Community." *Missiology* 21, no. 3: 275–88.

Berlant, Lauren. 2007. "Slow Death (Sovereignty, Obesity, Lateral Agency)." *Critical Inquiry* 33, no. 4: 754–80.

Best, Stephen, and Sharon Marcus. 2009. "Surface Reading: An Introduction." *Representations* 108, no. 1: 1–21.

Biko, Steve. (1978) 2004. *I Write What I Like*. Cape Town: Raven.

Bird, S. Elizabeth. 2002. "It Makes Sense to Us: Cultural Identity in Local Legends of Place." *Journal of Contemporary Ethnography* 31, no. 5: 519–47.

Blades, Jack. 1970. "Khotso's Treasures." *Drum*, March 1970.

Boddy, Janice. 1989. *Wombs and Alien Spirits: Women, Men, and the Zar Cult in Northern Sudan*. Madison: University of Wisconsin Press.

Boddy, Janice. 1994. "Spirit Possession Revisited: Beyond Instrumentality." *Annual Review of Anthropology* 23, no. 1: 407–34.

Bolaane, Maitseo. 2004. "The Impact of Game Reserve Policy on the River BaSarwa/Bushmen of Botswana." *Social Policy and Administration* 38, no. 4: 399–417.

Bond, Patrick. 2013. "Debt, Uneven Development and Capitalist Crisis in South Africa: From Moody's Macroeconomic Monitoring to Marikana Microfinance Mashonisas." *Third World Quarterly* 34, no. 4: 569–92.

Bongela, Knobel Sakhiwo. 2001. "Isihlonipho among amaXhosa." PhD diss., University of South Africa.

Bourdieu, Pierre, Jean-Claude Chamboredon, and Jean Claude Passeron. 1991. *The Craft of Sociology: Epistemological Preliminaries*. Berlin: Walter de Gruyter.

Bradbury, Jill. 2019. *Narrative Psychology and Vygotsky in Dialogue: Changing Subjects*. London: Routledge.

Brand, Dionne. 2012. *A Map to the Door of No Return: Notes to Belonging*. Toronto: Vintage Canada.

Brand, Dionne. 2020. "On Narrative, Reckoning and the Calculus of Living and Dying." *Toronto Star*, July 4, 2020. https://www.thestar.com/entertainment/books/2020/07/04/dionne-brand-on-narrative-reckoning-and-the-calculus-of-living-and-dying.html.

Branson, Nicola, Clare Hofmeyr, and David Lam. 2014. "Progress through School and the Determinants of School Dropout in South Africa." *Development Southern Africa* 31, no. 1: 106–26.

Braun, Lindsay Frederick. 2008. "The Colonial Archive and Maps of the Transkei, 1857–1898." In *Proceedings of the Symposium of the Commission on the History of Cartography in the 19th and 20th Centuries*, International Cartography Association, edited by Elrie C. Liebenberg, Imre Josef Demhardt, and Peter Collier, 2–17. Pretoria: ICA.

Breckenridge, Keith. 1990. "Migrancy, Crime and Faction Fighting: The Role of the Isitshozi in the Development of Ethnic Organisations in the Compounds." *Journal of Southern African Studies* 16, no. 1: 55–78.

Brown, Jayna. 2015. "Being Cellular: Race, the Inhuman, and the Plasticity of Life." *GLQ* 21, no. 2–3: 321–41.

Brown, Jayna. 2021. *Black Utopias: Speculative Life and the Music of Other Worlds*. Durham, NC: Duke University Press.

Bruce, La Marr Jurelle. 2012. "'The People inside My Head, Too': Madness, Black Womanhood, and the Radical Performance of Lauryn Hill." *African American Review* 45, no. 3: 371–89.

Bruce, La Marr Jurelle. 2021. *How to Go Mad without Losing Your Mind: Madness and Black Radical Creativity*. Durham, NC: Duke University Press.

Bundy, Colin. 1972. "The Emergence and Decline of a South African Peasantry." *African Affairs* 71, no. 285: 369–88.

Burger, Bibi. 2020. "'Our Respect for Water Is What You Have Termed Fear': The Ocean in the Poetry of Ronelda S. Kamfer and Koleka Putuma." *Journal of Southern African Studies* 46, no. 1: 23–38.

Burness, Donald. 1977. "'Nzinga Mbandi' and Angolan Independence." *Luso-Brazilian Review* 14, no. 2: 225–29.

Butler, Judith. 2004. "Bodies and Power Revisited." In *Feminism and the Final Foucault*, edited by Dianna Taylor and Karen Vingtes, 183–94. Chicago: University of Illinois Press.

Caballero Arias, Hortensia. 2007. "The Demarcation of Indigenous Lands in Venezuela." *Venezuelan Journal of Economics and Social Sciences* 13, no. 3: 189–208.

Callaway, Godfrey. 1919. *Mxalmi, the Feaster*. New York: Macmillan.

Campbell, David. 2009. "'Black Skin and Blood': Documentary Photography and Santu Mofokeng's Critique of the Visualization of Apartheid South Africa." *History and Theory* 48: 52–58.

Campt, Tina, Zara Julius, Jenn Nkiru, and Alexander Weheliye. 2020. "Frequencies of Blackness. A Listening Session." The Sojourner Project, November 20, 2020. https://www.thesojournerproject.org/sessions/frequencies-of-blackness-a-listening-session/.

Campt, Tina Marie. 2019. "Black Visuality and the Practice of Refusal." *Women and Performance* 29, no. 1: 79–87.

Canham, Hugo. 2017. "Embodied Black Rage." *Du Bois Review* 14, no. 2: 427–45.

Canham, Hugo. 2021. "Black Death and Mourning as Pandemic." *Journal of Black Studies* 52, no. 3: 296–309.

Carpio, Glenda. 2008. *Laughing Fit to Kill: Black Humor in the Fictions of Slavery*. New York: Oxford University Press.

Carson, James. T. 2006. "When Is an Ocean Not an Ocean? Geographies of the Atlantic World." *Southern Quarterly* 43, no. 4: 16–45.

Carter, George. (1791) 1927. *The Wreck of the Grosvenor, Containing a Narrative of the Loss of the Grosvenor, East Indiaman, Wrecked on the Coast of Caffraria, 1782.* Vol. 8. Cape Town: Van Riebeeck Society.

Césaire, Aimé. (1955) 1972. *Discourse on Colonialism.* Translated by Joan Pinkham. New York: Monthly Review Press.

Chami, Felix A. 1999. "Graeco-Roman Trade Link and the Bantu Migration Theory." *Anthropos* 1, no. 3: 205–15.

Cheng, Anne Anlin. 2000. *The Melancholy of Race: Psychoanalysis, Assimilation, and Hidden Grief.* New York: Oxford University Press.

Christopher, Anthony J. 2002. "'To Define the Indefinable': Population Classification and the Census in South Africa." *Area* 34, no. 4: 401–8.

Clothier, Norman. 1987. *Black Valour: The South African Native Labour Contingent, 1916–1918, and the Sinking of the Mendi.* Pietermaritzburg: University of Natal Press.

Cock, Jacklyn. 2018. *Writing the Ancestral River: A Biography of the Kowie.* Johannesburg: Wits University Press.

Cocks, Michelle Linda, and K. Freerks Wiersum. 2003. "The Significance of Plant Diversity to Rural Households in Eastern Cape Province of South Africa." *Forests, Trees and Livelihoods* 13, no. 1: 39–58.

Cohen, Cathy J. 1999. *The Boundaries of Blackness: AIDS and the Breakdown of Black Politics.* Chicago: University of Chicago Press.

Cole, Ernest. 1968. *House of Bondage.* London: Penguin.

Cole, Teju. 2016. *Known and Strange Things: Essays.* New York: Random House.

Collis-Buthelezi, Victoria J. 2017. "The Case for Black Studies in South Africa." *Black Scholar* 47, no. 2: 7–21.

Colvin, Christopher J., and Steven Robins. 2009. "Social Movements and HIV/AIDS in South Africa." In *HIV/AIDS in South Africa 25 Years On*, edited by Poul Rohleder, Leslie Swartz, Seth C. Kalichman, and Leickness Chisamu Simbayi, 155–64. New York: Springer.

Comaroff, Jean, and John L. Comaroff. 1999. "Occult Economies and the Violence of Abstraction: Notes from the South African Postcolony." *American Ethnologist* 26, no. 2: 279–303.

Comaroff, Jean, and John L. Comaroff. 2000. "Privatizing the Millennium, New Protestant Ethics and the Spirits of Capitalism in Africa, and Elsewhere." *Africa Spectrum* 35, no. 3: 293–312.

Conway, Daniel. 2012. *Masculinities, Militarisation and the End Conscription Campaign: War Resistance in Apartheid South Africa.* Manchester: Manchester University Press.

Coulthard, Glen Sean. 2014. *Red Skin, White Masks: Rejecting the Colonial Politics of Recognition.* Minneapolis: University of Minnesota Press.

Crais, Clifton. C. 1992. *White Supremacy and Black Resistance in Pre-Industrial South Africa: The Making of the Colonial Order in the Eastern Cape, 1770–1865 (Vol. 72).* New York: Cambridge University Press.

Crampton, Hazel. 2004. *The Sunburnt Queen*. Johannesburg: Jacana.

Crush, Jonathan. 1994. "Scripting the Compound: Power and Space in the South African Mining Industry." *Environment and Planning D: Society and Space* 12, no. 3: 301–24.

Cuvier, Georges. *Extrait d'observations faites sur le cadavre d'une femme connue à Paris et à Lodres sous le nom de Vénus Hottentotte.* Muséum national d'histoire naturelle, 1817. Translated by Mara Vena.

Das, Veena. 2007. *Life and Words: Violence and the Descent into the Ordinary.* Berkeley: University of California Press.

Davies, Nick. 2015a. "Marikana Massacre: The Untold Story of the Strike Leader Who Died for Workers' Rights." *Guardian*, May 19, 2015. https://www.theguardian.com/world/2015/may/19/marikana-massacre-untold-story-strike-leader-died-workers-rights.

Davies, Nick. 2015b. "The Savage Truth behind the Marikana Massacre." *Mail and Guardian*, May 21, 2015. https://mg.co.za/article/2015-05-21-the-savage-truth-behind-the-marikana-massacre/.

Davis, Angela. 2000. "Masked Racism: Reflections on the Prison Industrial Complex. [Article reprinted from Colorlines]." *Indigenous Law Bulletin* 4, no. 27: 4–7.

Davison, Patricia. 1998. "Museums and the Reshaping of Memory." In *Negotiating the Past: The Making of Memory in South Africa*, edited by Sarah Nuttall and Carli Coetzee, 143–59. Cape Town: Oxford University Press.

Deacon, Harriet Jane. 1996. "Madness, Race and Moral Treatment: Robben Island Lunatic Asylum, Cape Colony, 1846–1890." *History of Psychiatry* 7, no. 26: 287–97.

Deleuze, Gilles. 1991. "The Fold." *Yale French Studies* 80: 227–47.

Deloria, Vine. 2003. *God Is Red*. Golden, CO: Fulcrum.

De Veredicis, David. 2016. "Tracing the Ancestors of Mpondo Clans along the Wild Coast of the Eastern Cape." PhD diss., University of the Witwatersrand.

De Wet, Jacques. 2011. "We Don't Want Your Development: Resistance to Imposed Development in Northeastern Pondoland." In *Rural Resistance in South Africa*, edited by Thembela Kepe and Lungisile Ntsebeza, 259–78. Leiden, NL: Brill.

De Wet, Jacques. 2013. "Collective Agency and Resistance to Imposed Development in Rural South Africa." *Working Papers Development Sociology and Social Anthropology No. 373*. Bielefeld, DE: Universität Bielefeld, Fakultät für Soziologie, AG Sozialanthropologie.

Diaz, Vincente. 2015. "No Island Is an Island." In *Native Studies Keywords*, edited by Stephanie Teves, Andrea Smith, and Michelle Raheja, 90–108. Tucson: University of Arizona Press.

Diaz, Vincente M. 2011. "Voyaging for Anti-colonial Recovery: Austronesian Seafaring, Archipelagic Rethinking, and the Re-mapping of Indigeneity." *Pacific Asia Inquiry* 2, no. 1: 21–32.

Dlamini, Jacob. 2014. *Askari: A Story of Collaboration and Betrayal in the Anti-apartheid Struggle*. Johannesburg: Jacana.

Dlamini, Sazi Stephen. 2010. "The South African Blue Notes: Bebop, Mbaqanga, Apartheid and the Exiling of a Musical Imagination." PhD diss., University of KwaZulu-Natal.

Douglass, Patrice. 2016. "At the Intersections of Assemblage: Fanon, Capécia, and the Unmaking of the Genre Subject." In *Conceptual Aphasia in Black: Displacing Racial Formation*, edited by P. Khalil Saucier and Tryon P. Woods, 103–26. Lanham, MD: Lexington Books.

Drayson, Alfred Wilks. 1858. *Sporting Scenes amongst the Kaffirs of South Africa*. London: Routledge.

Drew, Allison. 2011. "Govan Mbeki's *The Peasants' Revolt*: A Critical Examination." In *Rural Resistance in South Africa: The Mpondo Revolts after Fifty Years*, edited by Thembela Kepe and Lungisile Ntsebeza, 67–90. Leiden, NL: Brill.

Dubow, Saul. 2015. "Were There Political Alternatives in the Wake of the Sharpeville-Langa Violence in South Africa, 1960?" *Journal of African History* 56, no. 1: 119–42.

Dyantyi, Benson. 1960. "Trouble in the Bantustans." *Drum*, September 1960.

Edgar, Robert R., and Hilary Sapire. 2000. *African Apocalypse: The Story of Nontetha Nkwenkwe, a Twentieth-Century South African Prophet*. Athens: Ohio University Center for International Studies.

Edwards, Brent Hayes. 2009. *The Practice of Diaspora: Literature, Translation, and the Rise of Black Internationalism*. Cambridge, MA: Harvard University Press.

eNCA. 2017. "Four in Court for 'Eating Human Flesh.'" eNCA, August 21, 2017. https://www.enca.com/south-africa/four-in-court-for-eating-human-flesh -in-estcourt.

Eng, David L., and Shinhee Han. 2019. *Racial Melancholia, Racial Dissociation: On the Social and Psychic Lives of Asian Americans*. Durham, NC: Duke University Press.

Erasmus, Zimitri, ed. 2001. *Coloured by History, Shaped by Place: New Perspectives on Coloured Identities in Cape Town*. Cape Town: Kwela Books.

Erasmus, Zimitri. 2017. *Race Otherwise: Forging a New Humanism for South Africa*. New York: New York University Press.

Erevelles, Nirmala, and Andrea Minear. 2010. "Unspeakable Offenses: Untangling Race and Disability in Discourses of Intersectionality." *Journal of Literary and Cultural Disability Studies* 4, no. 2: 127–46.

Fabian, Johannes. 2014. *Time and the Other: How Anthropology Makes Its Object*. New York: Columbia University Press.

Fabricius, Peter. 2012. "Digging Up the Dirt." *Sunday Tribune*, February 9, 2012. https://www.iol.co.za/sunday-tribune/digging-up-the-dirt-1230973.

Falkof, Nicky. 2012. "'Satan Has Come to Rietfontein': Race in South Africa's Satanic Panic." *Journal of Southern African Studies* 38, no. 4: 753–67.

Fanon, Frantz. 1967. *Black Skin, White Masks*. Translated by Charles Lam Markmann. New York: Grove.

Fanon, Frantz. 2007. *The Wretched of the Earth*. New York: Grove.

Fanon, Frantz. 2008. *Concerning Violence*. London: Penguin.

Feni, Lulamile. 2017. "Slaughterhouse: Boys Lured by Family Members and Muti-lated." *DispatchLive*, April 20, 2017. https://www.dispatchlive.co.za/news/2017 -04-20-slaughterhouse-boys-lured-by-family-members-and-mutilated/.

Ferguson, Roderick A. 2004. *Aberrations in Black: Toward a Queer of Color Critique.* Minneapolis: University of Minnesota Press.

Fidler, Katherine. 2010. "Rural Cosmopolitanism and Peasant Insurgency: The Pondoland Revolt, South Africa (1958–1963)." PhD diss., Emory University.

Field, Corinne T., Tammy-Charelle Owens, Marcia Chatelain, Lakisha Simmons, Abosede George, and Rhian Keyse. 2016. "The History of Black Girlhood: Recent Innovations and Future Directions." *Journal of the History of Childhood and Youth* 9, no. 3: 383–401.

Filatova, Irina, and Appollon Davidson. 2013. *The Hidden Thread: Russia and South Africa in the Soviet Era*. Jeppestown, SA: Jonathan Ball.

Forbes, Curdella. 2014. "Caribbean Women Writing: Social Media, Spirituality and the Arts of Solitude in Edwidge Danticat's Haiti." *Caribbean Quarterly* 60, no. 1: 1–22.

Foucault, Michel. 2003. "17 March 1976." In *"Society Must Be Defended": Lectures at the Collége de France, 1975–76*, translated by David Macey, edited by Mauro Bertani and Alessandro Fontana, 240–41. New York: Picador.

Fraser, Miriam, and Monica Greco. 2005. "Bodies and Social (Dis)order." In *The Body. A Reader*, edited by Miriam Fraser, and Monica Greco, 67–71. Abingdon, UK: Routledge.

Freeman, Elizabeth. 2010. *Time Binds: Queer Temporalities, Queer Histories*. Durham, NC: Duke University Press.

Freud, Sigmund. 1917. "Mourning and Melancholia." In *The Standard Edition of the Complete Psychological Works of Sigmund Freud*. Vol. 14, edited by Sigmund Freud, 237–60. London: Hogarth.

Freud, Sigmund. 1921. "Group Psychology and the Analysis of the Ego." In *The Standard Edition of the Complete Psychological Works of Sigmund Freud*. Vol. 18, edited by J. Strachey, 65–143. London: Hogarth.

Froman, Judy. 2011. *Solomon's Story*. Northlands: Pan Macmillan South Africa.

Fugard, Sheila. (1972) 2002. *The Castaways*. Johannesburg: Donker.

Fukuyama, Francis. 1989. "The End of History?" *National Interest* 16: 3–18.

Gamble, Vanessa Northington. 1993. "A Legacy of Distrust: African Americans and Medical Research." *American Journal of Preventive Medicine* 9, no. 6: 35–38.

Garuba, Harry. 2003. "Explorations in Animist Materialism: Notes on Reading/ Writing African Literature, Culture, and Society." *Public Culture* 15, no. 2: 261–85.

Gathogo, Julius. 2008. "African Philosophy as Expressed in the Concepts of Hospi-tality and Ubuntu." *Journal of Theology for Southern Africa* 130: 39–53.

Gilroy, Paul. 1993. *The Black Atlantic: Modernity and Double Consciousness*. London: Verso.

Gilroy, Paul. 2005. *Postcolonial Melancholia*. New York: Columbia University Press.

Glasson, Barbara. 2009. *A Spirituality of Survival: Enabling a Response to Trauma and Abuse*. London: A&C Black.

Glenn, Ian E. 1995. "The Wreck of the *Grosvenor* and the Making of South Africa Literature." *English in Africa* 2, no. 2:1–18.

Glissant, Édouard. 1997. *Poetics of Relation*. Ann Arbor: University of Michigan Press.

Glover, Kaiama L. 2021. *A Regarded Self: Caribbean Womanhood and the Ethics of Disorderly Being*. Durham, NC: Duke University Press.

Gobodo-Madikizela, Pumla. 2013. "Acting Out and Working through Traumatic Memory: Confronting the Past in the South African Context." In *Hurting Memories and Beneficial Forgetting: Posttraumatic Stress Disorders, Biographical Developments, and Social Conflicts*, edited by Michael Linden and Krzysztof Rutkowski, 217–25. Amsterdam: Elsevier.

Goffe, Tao Leigh. 2020. "Unmapping the Caribbean: Toward a Digital Praxis of Archipelagic Sounding." *Archipelagos* 5:1–23.

Gordon, Avery. 1997. *Ghostly Matters: Haunting and the Sociological Imagination*. Minneapolis: University of Minnesota Press.

Gordon, Lewis R. 2015. *What Fanon Said: A Philosophical Introduction to His Life and Thought*. New York: Fordham University Press.

Gqola, Pumla Dineo. 2010. *What Is Slavery to Me? Postcolonial/Slave Memory in Post-apartheid South Africa*. Johannesburg: Wits University Press.

Graham, Mekada. 2011. "Expanding the Philosophical Base of Social Work." In *Social Work: A Reader*, edited by Viviene Cree, 142–48. London: Routledge.

Green, E. C. 1996. "Purity, Pollution and the Invisible Snake in Southern Africa." *Medical Anthropology* 17, no. 1: 83–100.

Gribble, John, and Jonathan Sharfman. 2015. "The Wreck of ss *Mendi* (1917) as an Example of the Potential Transnational Significance of World War I Underwater Cultural Heritage." In *Underwater Cultural Heritage from World War I: Proceedings of the Scientific Conference on the Occasion of the Centenary of World War I, Bruges, Belgium, 26 and 27 June 2014*, edited by Ulrike Guérin, Arturo Rey da Silva, and Lucas Simonds, 78–85. Paris: Unesco.

Grosz, Elizabeth A. 1994. *Volatile Bodies: Toward a Corporeal Feminism*. Bloomington: Indiana University Press.

Grundlingh, Albert. 2011. "Mutating Memories and the Making of a Myth: Remembering the ss *Mendi* Disaster, 1917–2007." *South African Historical Journal* 63, no. 1: 20–37.

Guelke, Leonard, and Robert Shell. 1992. "Landscape of Conquest: Frontier Water Alienation and Khoikhoi Strategies of Survival, 1652–1780." *Journal of Southern African Studies* 18, no. 4: 803–24.

Hagengimana, Athanase, and Devon E. Hinton. 2009. "'Ihahamuka,' a Rwandan Syndrome of Response to the Genocide." In *Culture and Panic Disorder*, edited by Devon E. Hinton and Byron J. Good, 205–29. Stanford, CA: Stanford University Press.

Hamilton, Carolyn, ed. 1995. *The Mfecane Aftermath: Reconstructive Debates in Southern African History*. Johannesburg: Wits University Press.

Hammond-Tooke, W. D. 1960. "Some Bhaca Religious Categories." *African Studies* 19, no. 1: 1–13.

Hansen, Deirdre. 1981. "The Music of the Xhosa-Speaking People." PhD diss., University of the Witwatersrand.

Harney, Stefano, and Fred Moten. 2013. *The Undercommons: Fugitive Planning and Black Study*. New York: Autonomedia.

Hartman, Saidiya V. 1997. *Scenes of Subjection: Terror, Slavery, and Self-Making in Nineteenth-Century America*. New York: Oxford University Press.

Hartman, Saidiya V. 2008. *Lose Your Mother: A Journey along the Atlantic Slave Route*. New York: Macmillan.

Hartman, Saidiya V. 2019. *Wayward Lives, Beautiful Experiments: Intimate Histories of Social Upheaval*. New York: Norton.

Harvey, David. 2018. *The Limits to Capital*. London: Verso.

Hassim, Shireen. 2006. *Women's Organizations and Democracy in South Africa: Contesting Authority*. Madison: University of Wisconsin Press.

Head, Bessie. 2013. *When Rain Clouds Gather*. Long Grove, IL: Waveland.

Hendricks, Fred, and Jeff Peires. 2011. "All Quiet on the Western Front: Nyandeni Acquiescence in the Mpondoland Revolt." In *Rural Resistance in South Africa*, edited by Thembela Kepe and Lungisile Ntsebeza, 115–40. Leiden, NL: Brill.

Heng, Terence. 2018. "Photographing Absence in Deathscapes." *Area* 53, no. 2: 219–28.

Hill, Dominique C. 2019. "Blackgirl, One Word: Necessary Transgressions in the Name of Imagining Black Girlhood." *Cultural Studies* ↔ *Critical Methodologies* 19, no. 4: 275–83.

Hodgson, Dorothy, L. 2009. "'Becoming Indigenous in Africa.' Toward an Endarkened Epistemology." *African Studies Review* 52, no. 3: 1–32.

Hodgson, Janet. 1983. "The Faith-Healer of Cancele: Some Problems in Analysing Religious Experience among Black People." *Religion in Southern Africa* 4, no. 1: 13–29.

Hollan, Douglas. 2000. "Culture and Dissociation in Toraja." *Transcultural Psychiatry* 37, no. 4: 545–59.

Hountondji, Paulin J. 2009. "Knowledge of Africa, Knowledge by Africans: Two Perspectives on African Studies." *RCCS Annual Review: A Selection from the Portuguese Journal Revista Crítica de Ciências Sociais*: 121–31.

Hunter, Alistair. 2015. "Deathscapes in Diaspora: Contesting Space and Negotiating Home in Contexts of Post-migration Diversity." *Social and Cultural Geography* 17, no. 2: 247–61.

Hurtado, Aida. 2003. "Theory in the Flesh: Toward an Endarkened Epistemology." *International Journal of Qualitative Studies in Education* 16, no. 2: 215–25.

Idahosa, Grace Ese-osa. 2020. "Dirty Body Politics: Habitus, Gendered Embodiment, and the Resistance to Women's Agency in Transforming South African Higher Education." *Gender, Work and Organization* 27, no. 6: 988–1003.

Ingquza Hill Municipality. 2020. *Integrated Development Plan 2019/2020 Financial Year*. https://www.cogta.gov.za/cgta_2016/wp-content/uploads/2020/11 /INGQUZA-Hill-FINAL-IDP-2019-2020.pdf.

Jabavu, Davidson Don Tengo. 1920. *The Black Problem: Papers and Addresses on Various Native Problems*. Alice, SA: Book Department, Lovedale.

Jabavu, Nontando Noni Helen. 1962. *Drawn in Color: African Contrasts*. New York: St. Martin's.

Jackson, Zakiyyah Iman. 2013. "Animal: New Directions in the Theorization of Race and Posthumanism." *Feminist Studies* 39, no. 3: 669–85.

Jackson, Zakiyyah Iman. 2016. "Losing Manhood: Animality and Plasticity in the (Neo) Slave Narrative." *Qui Parle: Critical Humanities and Social Sciences* 25, no. 1–2: 95–136.

Jackson, Zakiyyah Iman. 2020. *Becoming Human: Matter and Meaning in an Antiblack World*. Vol. 53. New York: New York University Press.

Jafa, Arthur, and Tina Campt. 2017. "Love Is the Message, the Plan Is Death." *E-flux Journal* 81: 1–10.

Jewkes, Rachel K., and Katherine Wood. 1999. "Problematizing Pollution: Dirty Wombs, Ritual Pollution, and Pathological Processes." *Medical Anthropology* 18, no. 2: 163–86.

Jewkes, Rachel, Lorna Martin, and Loveday Penn-Kekana. 2002. "The Virgin Cleansing Myth: Cases of Child Rape Are Not Exotic." *Lancet* 359, no. 9307: 711.

Johnson, E. Patrick. 2001. "'Quare' Studies, or (Almost) Everything I Know about Queer Studies I Learned from My Grandmother." *Text and Performance Quarterly* 21, no. 1: 1–25.

Johnson, Margaret E. 2013. "'Never the Same One Twice': Melodrama and Repetition in *Queer as Folk*." *Genre: Forms of Discourse and Culture* 46, no. 3: 419–42.

Jolly, Pieter. 1986. "A First Generation Descendant of the Transkei San." *South African Archaeological Bulletin* 41, no. 143: 6–9.

Jordan, Archibald Campbell. 1980. *The Wrath of the Ancestors*. Alice, SA: Lovedale Press.

Kanu, Ikechukwu Anthony. 2013. "The Dimensions of African Cosmology." *Filosofia Theoretica* 2, no. 1: 533–55.

Karombo, Tawanda. 2017. "Avoiding the Noose: The Job Crisis in Zimbabwe Means Dozens of People Are Keen to Take a Long-Vacant Hangman Job." *Quartz-Africa*, October 18, 2017. https://qz.com/africa/1105133/zimbabwes-hangman -post-has-been-overwhelmed-with-applicants/.

Kayser, Robin. 2002. *Land and Liberty: The Non-European Unity Movement and the Land Question, 1933–1976*. Master's diss., University of Cape Town.

Keegan, Tim. 1997. *Colonial South Africa: Origins Racial Order*. London: A&C Black.

Keene, Liam. 2014. "Invoking Heterogeneous Cultural Identities through Thokoza Sangoma Spirit Possession." Master's diss., University of Cape Town.

Kelley, Robin. 2017. "What Did Cedric Robinson Mean by Racial Capitalism?" *Boston Review*, January 12, 2017. https://bostonreview.net/articles/robin-d-g -kelley-introduction-race-capitalism-justice/.

Kenqu, A. Yolisa. 2019. "Splitting and Becoming Double in Zakes Mda's *The Heart of Redness.*" *Safundi* 20, no. 1: 58–81.

Kepe, Thembela. 2007. "Medicinal Plants and Rural Livelihoods in Mpondoland, South Africa: Towards an Understanding of Resource Value." *International Journal of Biodiversity Science and Management* 3, no. 3: 170–83.

Kepe, Thembela, and Lungisile Ntsebeza, eds. 2011. *Rural Resistance in South Africa: The Mpondo Revolts after Fifty Years.* Leiden, NL: Brill.

King, Tiffany Lethabo. 2019. *The Black Shoals: Offshore Formations of Black and Native Studies.* Durham, NC: Duke University Press.

King, Tiffany Lethabo, Jenell Navarro, and Andrea Smith, eds. 2020. *Otherwise Worlds: Against Settler Colonialism and Anti-Blackness.* Durham, NC: Duke University Press.

Kipuri, Naomi. 2017. "Indigenous Peoples' Rights, Conflict and Peace Building: Experiences from East Africa." In *Indigenous Peoples' Rights and Unreported Struggles: Conflict and Peace,* edited by Elsa Stamatopoulou, 68–79. New York: Institute for the Study of Human Rights, Columbia University.

Kirby, Percival R. 1953. *A Source Book on the Wreck of the Grosvenor East Indiaman.* Cape Town: Van Riebeeck Society.

Kirby, Percival R. 1954. "Gquma, Mdepa and the Amatshomane Clan: A By-Way of Miscegenation in South Africa." *African Studies* 13, no. 1: 1–24.

Kosgei, Jauquelyne. 2021. "Swahili Seafarers' Musings and Sensuous Seascapes in Yvonne Owuor's *The Dragonfly Sea.*" *Eastern African Literary and Cultural Studies* 8, no. 1–2: 6–19.

Kros, Cynthia. 2017. "'We Do Not Want the Commission to Allow the Families to Disappear into Thin Air': A Consideration of Widows' Testimonies at the Truth and Reconciliation Commission and the Fariam (Marikana) Commission of Inquiry." *Psychology in Society* 55: 38–60.

Kuumba, M. Bahati. 2002. "'You've Struck a Rock' Comparing Gender, Social Movements, and Transformation in the United States and South Africa." *Gender and Society* 16, no. 4: 504–23.

Laher, Ridwan, and Korir Sing'Oei. 2014. "Introduction." In *Indigenous People in Africa: Contestations, Empowerment and Group Rights,* edited by Ridwan Laher and Korir Sing'Oei, x–xxi. Pretoria: Africa Institute of South Africa.

Lakoff, George, and Mark Johnson. 2008. *Metaphors We Live By.* Chicago: University of Chicago Press.

Lastra, James. 2012. *Film and Culture Series: Sound Technology and the American Cinema: Perception, Representation, Modernity.* New York: Columbia University Press.

Lavery, Charne. 2020. "Thinking from the Southern Ocean." In *Sustaining Seas: Oceanic Space and the Politics of Care,* edited by Elspeth Probyn, Kate Johnston, and Nancy Lee, 307–15. New York: Rowman & Littlefield.

Lebeloane, Lazarus, and Madise Mokhele. 2006. "The Use of Different Types of Water in the Zion Christian Church." *Studia Historiae Ecclesiasticae* 32, no. 2: 143–52.

LeClair, Thomas. 1975. "Death and Black Humor." *Critique: Studies in Contemporary Fiction* 17, no. 1: 5–40.

Leclerc-Madlala, Suzanne. 2003. "Protecting Girlhood? Virginity Revivals in the Era of AIDS." *Agenda* 17, no. 56: 16–25.

Legassick, Martin. 1972. "The Frontier Tradition in South African Historiography." In *Collected Seminar Papers, Vol. 12*, 1–33. London: Institute of Commonwealth Studies.

Lemarchand, René. 2002. "A History of Genocide in Rwanda." *Journal of African History* 43: 307–11.

Levack, Brian P. 2013. "Possession: Past and Present." In Levack, *The Devil Within*, 240–53. New Haven, CT: Yale University Press.

Lipenga, Ken J. 2014. "Disability and Masculinity in South African Autosomatography." *African Journal of Disability* 3, no. 1. https://doi.org/10.4102/ajod.v3i1.85.

Lipenga, Ken J. 2015. "Weaving a Path from the Past: Gender, Disability and Narrative Enablement in *Zulu Love Letter.*" *Agenda* 29, no. 2: 112–21.

Livermon, Xavier. 2020. *Kwaito Bodies*. Durham, NC: Duke University Press.

Lodge, Tom. 1981. "The Destruction of Sophiatown." *Journal of Modern African Studies* 19, no. 1: 107–32.

Lodge, Tom. 1987. "State of Exile: The African National Congress of South Africa, 1976–86." *Third World Quarterly* 9, no. 1: 1–27.

Lorde, Audre. 1979. "The Great American Disease." *Black Scholar* 10, no. 8–9: 17–20.

Lugones, María. 2007. "Heterosexualism and the Colonial/Modern Gender System." *Hypatia* 22, no. 1: 187–219.

Lwanga-Lunyiigo, Samwiri. 1976. "The Bantu Problem Reconsidered." *Current Anthropology* 17, no. 2: 282–86.

Maathai, Wangari. 2008. *Unbowed: A Memoir*. London: Arrow.

Mabovula, Nonceba Nolundi. 2011. "The Erosion of African Communal Values: A Reappraisal of the African Ubuntu Philosophy." *Inkanyiso* 3, no. 1: 38–47.

Macharia, Keguro. 2015. "Mbiti and Glissant." *New Inquiry*, March 9, 2015. https://thenewinquiry.com/blog/mbiti-glissant/.

Macharia, Keguro. 2016. "On Being Area-Studied: A Litany of Complaint." GLQ 22, no. 2: 183–90.

Macharia, Keguro. 2019. *Frottage: Frictions of Intimacy across the Black Diaspora*. Vol. 11. New York: New York University Press.

Macharia, Keguro. 2020. "Belated: Interruption." GLQ 26, no. 3: 561–73.

Mahmood, Saba. 2001. "Feminist Theory, Embodiment, and the Docile Agent: Some Reflections on the Egyptian Islamic Revival." *Cultural Anthropology* 16, no. 2: 202–36.

Mahone, Sloan. 2006. "The Psychology of Rebellion: Colonial Medical Responses to Dissent in British East Africa." *Journal of African History* 47, no. 2: 241–58.

Mama, Amina. 2017. "The Power of Feminist Pan-African Intellect." *Feminist Africa* 22, "Feminists Organising—Strategy, Voice, Power": 1–15.

Mamdani, Mahmood. 2003. "Making Sense of Political Violence in Postcolonial Africa." In *War and Peace in the 20th Century and Beyond*, Proceedings of the Nobel Centennial Symposium, edited by Geir Lundestad and Olav Njølstad, 71–99. Singapore: World Scientific.

Manganyi, N. Chabani. (1973) 2019. *Being-Black-in-the-World*. Johannesburg: Wits University Press.

Mansutti Rodríguez, Alexander. 2006. "The Demarcation of Indigenous Territories in Venezuela: Some Operating Conditions and the Role of Anthropologists." *Antropológica* 105–106: 13–39.

Marinovich, Greg. 2016. *Murder at Small Koppie: The Real Story of the Marikana Massacre*. Cape Town: Penguin Random House South Africa.

Marker, Michael. 2003. "Indigenous Voice, Community, and Epistemic Violence: The Ethnographer's 'Interests' and What 'Interests' the Ethnographer." *International Journal of Qualitative Studies in Education* 16, no. 3: 361–75.

Marker, Michael. 2018. "There Is No Place of Nature; There Is Only the Nature of Place: Animate Landscapes as Methodology for Inquiry in the Coast Salish Territory." *International Journal of Qualitative Studies in Education* 31, no. 6: 453–64.

Marriott, David. 2011. "Inventions of Existence: Sylvia Wynter, Frantz Fanon, Sociogeny, and 'the Damned.'" *CR: The New Centennial Review* 11, no. 3: 45–89.

Marschall, Sabine. 2008. "Pointing to the Dead: Victims, Martyrs and Public Memory in South Africa." *South African Historical Journal* 60, no. 1: 103–23.

Martin, Robert Montgomery. 1837. *The British Colonial Library: In 12 Volumes*. Vol. 7. London: Mortimer.

Masilela, Ntongela, Frederik van Zyl Slabbert, and Martin Bernal. 2011. *Becoming Worthy Ancestors: Archive, Public Deliberation and Identity in South Africa*. New York: New York University Press.

Masquelier, Adeline. 2000. "Of Headhunters and Cannibals: Migrancy, Labor, and Consumption in the Mawri Imagination." *Cultural Anthropology* 15, no. 1: 84–126.

Matebeni, Zethu. 2013. "Intimacy, Queerness, Race." *Cultural Studies* 27, no. 3: 404–17.

Mathabane, Mark. 1986, *Kaffir Boy: The True Story of a Black Youth's Coming of Age in Apartheid South Africa*. New York: Macmillan.

Matthews, James David. 1972. "It Is Said." In *Cry Rage!*, edited by James Mathews and Gladys Thomas, 1. Johannesburg: Spro-cas.

Matthews, James David. 1977. "The Midnight Hour." *Pass Me a Meatball, Jones*. Athlone, Cape Town: BLAC.

Mbambo, Wiseman Lulama. 2000. "The Construction of Ngquza Site Memories in the Eastern Pondoland." PhD diss., University of the Western Cape.

Mbeki, Govan. 1964. *The Peasants' Revolt*. Johannesburg: Penguin African Library.

Mbeki, Thabo. 2002. "Speech at the Funeral of Sarah Bartmann, 9 August 2002." http://www.dirco.gov.za/docs/speeches/2002/mbek0809.htm.

Mbembe, Achille. 2001. *On the Postcolony*. Vol. 41. Oakland: University of California Press.

Mbembe, Achille, and Sarah Nuttall. 2004. "Writing the World from an African Metropolis." *Public Culture* 16, no. 3: 347–72.

Mbiti, John S. 1990. *African Religions and Philosophy*. Oxford: Heinemann.

McKittrick, Katherine. 2006. *Demonic Grounds: Black Women and the Cartographies of Struggle*. Minneapolis: University of Minnesota Press.

McKittrick, Katherine. 2015. "Yours in Intellectual Struggle: Sylvia Wynter and the Realization of the Living." In *Sylvia Wynter: On Being Human as Praxis*, edited by Katherine McKittrick, 1–8. Durham, NC: Duke University Press.

McKittrick, Katherine. 2016. "Diachronic Loops/Deadweight Tonnage/Bad Made Measure." *Cultural Geographies* 23, no. 1: 3–18.

McMillan, Uri. 2015. "Objecthood, Avatars, and the Limits of the Human." *GLQ: A Journal of Lesbian and Gay Studies* 21, no. 2–3: 224–27.

McMillan, Uri. 2018. "Introduction: Skin, Surface, Sensorium." *Women and Performance* 28: 1–15.

McNally, David. 2011. *Monsters of the Market: Zombies, Vampires and Global Capitalism*. Vol. 30. Leiden, NL: Brill.

Mda, Zakes. 2000. *Heart of Redness*. Cape Town: Oxford University Press South Africa.

Meel, Banwari Lal. 2003. "The Myth of Child Rape as a Cure for HIV/AIDS in Transkei." *Medicine, Science and the Law* 43, no. 1: 85–88.

Mercury. 1972. "Air of Festivity for Khotso Burial." *Mercury*, August 2, 1972. Durban, SA: Independent Media.

Meyer, Birgit. 1995. "'Delivered from the Powers of Darkness': Confessions of Satanic Riches in Christian Ghana." *Africa* 65, no. 2: 236–55.

Mgqwetho, Nontsizi. 2007. *The Nation's Bounty: The Xhosa Poetry of Nontsizi Mgqwetho*. Edited by Jeff Opland. Johannesburg: Wits University Press.

Mhaka, Edison. 2014. "Rituals and Taboos Related to Death as Repositories of Traditional African Philosophical Ideas: Evidence from the Karanga of Zimbabwe." *Academic Research International* 5, no. 4: 371–85.

Mignolo, Walter D. 2009. "Epistemic Disobedience, Independent Thought and Decolonial Freedom." *Theory, Culture and Society* 26, no. 7–8: 159–81.

Millar, J. Grant. 1908a. "Medical Practice in Pondoland, South Africa." *Glasgow Medical Journal* 70, no. 6: 409–25.

Millar, J. Grant. 1908b. "On the Spread and Prevention of Tuberculous Disease in Pondoland, South Africa." *British Medical Journal* 1, no. 2459: 380.

Mokwena, Kebogile, and Neo Morojele. 2014. "Unemployment and Unfavourable Social Environment as Contributory Factors to Nyaope Use in Three Provinces of South Africa: Substance Abuse." *African Journal for Physical Health Education, Recreation and Dance* 20 (Supplement 1): 374–84.

Moletsane, Relebohile. 2007. "South African Girlhood in the Age of AIDS: Towards Girlhood Studies?" *Agenda* 21, no. 72: 155–65.

Monyane, Chelete. 2013. "Is Ukuthwala Another Form of 'Forced Marriage'?" *South African Review of Sociology* 44, no. 3: 64–82.

Moodie, T. Dunbar. 1988. "Migrancy and Male Sexuality on the South African Gold Mines." *Journal of Southern African Studies* 14, no. 2: 228–56.

Moodie, T. Dunbar. 2011. "Hoyce Phundulu, the Mpondo Revolt, and the Rise of the National Union of Mineworkers." In *Rural Resistance in South Africa*, edited by Thembela Kepe and Lungisile Ntsebeza, 141–64. Leiden, NL: Brill.

Moodie, T. Dunbar, and Vivienne Ndatshe. 1994. *Going for Gold: Men, Mines, and Migration*. Vol. 51. Berkeley: University of California Press.

Moore, Henrietta L., and Todd Sanders, eds. 2001. *Magical Interpretations, Material Realities: Modernity, Witchcraft, and the Occult in Postcolonial Africa*. London: Routledge.

Morrell, Robert. 2001. *From Boys to Gentlemen: Settler Masculinity in Colonial Natal, 1880–1920*. Pretoria: University of South Africa.

Morrison, Toni. 1987. *Beloved*. New York: Knopf.

Mostert, Noël. 1992. *Frontiers: The Epic of South Africa's Creation and the Tragedy of the Xhosa People*. New York: Knopf.

Moten, Fred. 2003. *In the Break: The Aesthetics of the Black Radical Tradition*. Minneapolis: University of Minnesota Press.

Moten, Fred. 2017. *Black and Blur*. Durham, NC: Duke University Press.

Moten, Fred. 2018. *Stolen Life*. Vol. 2. Durham, NC: Duke University Press.

Mqhayi, S. E. K. 2017. *Iziganeko Zesizwe: Occasional Poems (1900–1943)*. Edited by Jeff Opland and Peter T. Mtuze. Pietermaritzburg: University of KwaZulu-Natal Press.

Mswela, Maureen, and Melodie Nöthling-Slabbert. 2013. "Colour Discrimination against Persons with Albinism in South Africa." *South African Journal of Bioethics and Law* 6, no. 1: 25–27.

Mtshemla, Sinazo, Gary Minkley, and Helena Pohlandt-McCormick. 2016. "Listening to Red." *Kronos* 42, no. 1: 121–42.

Mudavanhu, Selina. 2019. "'Girl, You Are a New Species of Krazy': An Analysis of Criticisms on YouTube to Dr. Stella Nyanzi's Nude Protest in April 2016." *Communicare* 38, no. 2: 74–92.

Muholi, Zanele. 2018. *Somnyama Ngonyama, Hail the Dark Lioness*. New York: Aperture.

Mujila, Fiston Mwanza. 2014. *Tram 83*. Paris: Métailié.

Mukamana, Donatilla, and Petra Brysiewicz. 2008. "The Lived Experience of Genocide Rape Survivors in Rwanda." *Journal of Nursing Scholarship* 40, no. 4: 379–84.

Mullaney, Thomas Shawn, Christian Henriot, Jeffrey Snyder-Reinke, David William McClure, and Glen Worthey. 2019. *The Chinese Deathscape: Grave Reform in Modern China*. Stanford, CA: Stanford University Press.

Musangi, Neo Sinoxolo. 2014. "In Time and Space." In *Reclaiming Afrikan: Queer Perspectives on Sexual and Gender Identities*, curated by Zethu Matabeni, 53–58. Cape Town: Modjaji Books.

Musangi, Neo Sinoxolo. 2018. "Homing with My Mother/How Women in My Family Married Women." *Meridians* 17, no. 2: 401–14.

Musila, Grace A. 2015. *A Death Retold in Truth and Rumour: Kenya, Britain and the Julie Ward Murder*. Vol. 2. Suffolk: Boydell & Brewer.

Musila, Grace A. 2019. "Thinking While Black." In *Black Academic Voices—the South African Experience*, edited by Grace Khunou, Edith Phaswana, Katijah Khoza-Shangase, and Hugo Canham, 65–80. Cape Town: HSRC Press.

Musila, Grace A., ed. 2020. *Wangari Maathai's Registers of Freedom*. Cape Town: HSRC Press.

Mutwa, C. V. M. 1996. *Song of the Stars: The Lore of a Zulu Shaman*. Barrytown, NY: Station Hill.

Mwambene, Lea, and Julia Sloth-Nielsen. 2011. "Benign Accommodation? Ukuthwala, 'Forced Marriage' and the South African Children's Act." *African Human Rights Law Journal* 11, no. 1: 1–22.

Nattrass, Nicoli. 2007. "AIDS Denialism vs. Science." *Skeptical Inquirer* 31, no. 5: 31–37.

Ndebele, Njabulo. 2016. "To Be or Not to Be, No Longer at Ease." *Arts and Humanities in Higher Education* 15, no. 1: 15–28.

Ndebele, Njabulo. 2019. "Afterword: Being Black-in-the-World and the Future of 'Blackness.'" In N. Chabani Manganyi, *Being-Black-in-the-World*, 115–41. Johannesburg: Wits University Press.

Newkirk, Greg. 2011. "Demons Invade South African High School, Shut Down Operations." *Week in Weird*, May 20, 2011. http://weekinweird.com/2011/05/20/demons-invade-south-african-high-school/.

News24. 2015. "Zuma's Wife Ousted over Plot to Poison Him—Report." News24, February 22, 2015. https://www.news24.com/News24/Zumas-wife-ousted-over-plot-to-poison-him-report-20150222.

News24. 2017. "Vigilantes Kill Six Suspected 'Vampires' in Malawi." News24, October 3, 2017. https://www.news24.com/news24/Africa/News/vigilantes-kill-six-suspected-vampires-in-malawi-20171003.

News24. 2021. "Zuma's Estranged Wife MaNtuli Allegedly Detained Unlawfully by SSA after Poison Plot." News24, January 26, 2021. https://www.news24.com/news24/southafrica/news/zumas-estranged-wife-nompumelelo-allegedly-detained-unlawfully-by-ssa-after-poison-plot-20210126.

Newton-King, Susan, and V. C. Malherbe. 1981. *The Khoikhoi Rebellion in the Eastern Cape (1799–1803)* (No. 5). Cape Town: Centre for African Studies, University of Cape Town.

Ngcobo, Duke. 1958. "No Drinking When Khotso Is Around." *Drum: East Africa*, September 1958.

Ngcukana, Lubabalo. 2019. "Homes Torched, Hundreds Displaced as Eastern Cape Villages Fight over Boundary." *City Press*, April 8, 2019. https://www.news24.com/citypress/news/homes-torched-hundreds-displaced-as-eastern-cape-villages-fight-over-boundary-20190408.

Ngonini, Xola A. 2007. "Anxious Communities: The Decline of Mine Migration in the Eastern Cape." *Development Southern Africa* 24, no. 1: 173–85.

Ngubane, Harriet. 1977. *Body and Mind in Zulu Medicine. An Ethnography of Health and Disease in Nyuswa-Zulu Thought and Practice*. London: Academic.

Ngwane, Zolani. 2003. "'Christmas Time' and the Struggles for the Household in the Countryside: Rethinking the Cultural Geography of Migrant Labour in South Africa." *Journal of Southern African Studies* 29, no. 3: 681–99.

Nhleko, Musa. 2011. "Cops Called in as Angry Pupils Attack Principal." *Times of Swaziland*, May 19, 2011. http://www.times.co.sz/News/64769.html.

Niehaus, Isak. 2001. "Witchcraft in the New South Africa: From Colonial Superstition to Postcolonial Reality?" In *Magical Interpretations, Material Realities: Modernity, Witchcraft, and the Occult in Postcolonial Africa*, edited by Henrietta Moore and Todd Sanders, 184–205. London: Routledge.

Nkiru, Jenn. 2017. "Black Star: Rebirth Is Necessary." *Nowness*, September 20, 2017. https://www.nowness.com/series/black-star/rebirth-is-necessary-jenn-nkiru.

Nontsizi, Mgqwetho. 2007. "The Stream of Despair." In *Nations's Bounty: The Xhosa Poetry of Nontsizi Mgqwetho*, edited by Jeff Opland, 212–15. Johannesburg: Wits University Press.

Northern Natal News. 2017. "Hundreds Confess to Eating Human Remains as Shocking Cannibalism Comes to Light in Escourt and Possibly Ladysmith, KZN." *Northern Natal News*, August 22, 2017. https://northernnatalnews.co.za/187427/hundreds-confess-eating-human-remains-shocking-cannibalistic-rituals-come-light-estcourt-possibly-ladysmith-kzn.

Ntombana, Luvuyo, and Siphiwo Meveni. 2015. "Spiritual or Social Phenomenon: A Cultural Analysis of Amakhosi Possession in the Eastern Cape, South Africa." *Pharos Journal of Theology* 96. https://www.pharosjot.com/uploads/7/1/6/3/7163688/article_10_vol.96_2015.pdf.

Ntombela, Sithabile. 2011. "The Progress of Inclusive Education in South Africa: Teachers' Experiences in a Selected District, KwaZulu-Natal." *Improving Schools* 14, no. 1: 5–14.

Ntsebeza, Lungisile. 2011. "Resistance in the Countryside: The Mpondo Revolts Contextualized." In *Rural Resistance in South Africa: The Mpondo Revolts after Fifty Years*, edited by Thembela Kepe and Lungisile Ntsebeza, 21–42. Leiden, NL: Brill.

Nunn, Cedric. 1986. "A Sugar Cane Cutter in the Sugar Farms of KwaZulu Natal, iNyoni, 1986." *Africa South Art Initiative*. Accessed June 15, 2022. https://asai.co.za/artist/cedric-nunn/.

Nyanende, Abner. 1996. "Regional Variation in Xhosa." *Stellenbosch Papers in Linguistics Plus* 26: 202–17.

Nyanzi, Stella. 2013. "Dismantling Reified African Culture through Localised Homosexualities in Uganda." *Culture, Health and Sexuality* 15, no. 8: 952–67.

Offen, Karl. 2003. "Narrating Place and Identity, or Mapping Miskitu Land Claims in Northeastern Nicaragua." *Human Organization* 62, no. 4: 382–92.

Ombagi, Eddie. 2019. "Nairobi Is a Shot of Whisky: Queer (Ob)scenes in the City." *Journal of African Cultural Studies* 31, no. 1: 106–19.

Ong, Aihwa. 1988. "The Production of Possession: Spirits and the Multinational Corporation in Malaysia." *American Ethnologist* 15, no. 1: 28–42.

Oruka, Henry Odera. 1997. "Part I: Essays by H. Odera Oruka." In *Sagacious Reasoning: Henry Odera Oruka in Memoriam*, edited by Anke Graness and Kai Kresse, 23–138. Nairobi: East African Educational.

Osinubi, Taiwo Adetunji. 2014. "Hostile Witnesses and Queer Life in Kenyan Prison Writing." *Eastern African Literary and Cultural Studies* 1, no. 3–4: 152–66.

Oswin, Natalie. 2005. "Researching 'Gay Cape Town' Finding Value-Added Queerness." *Social & Cultural Geography* 6, no. 4: 567–86.

Parish, James. 2001. "Black Market, Free Market: Anti-witchcraft Shrines and Fetishes among the Akan." In *Magical Interpretations, Material Realities: Modernity, Witchcraft, and the Occult in Postcolonial Africa*, edited by Henrietta Moore and Todd Sanders, 118–35. London: Routledge.

Peires, Jeffery B. 1982. *The House of Phalo: A History of the Xhosa People in the Days of Their Independence*. Vol. 32. Berkeley: University of California Press.

Peires, Jeffery B. 1989. *The Dead Will Arise: Nongqawuse and the Great Xhosa Cattle-Killing Movement of 1856–7*. Bloomington: Indiana University Press.

Penn, Nigel. 2004. "Wild Coast: Shipwreck and Captivity Narratives from the Eastern Cape." *Kronos: Journal of Cape History* 30, no. 1: 201–21.

Pereira, Charmaine, and Dzodzi Tsikata. 2021. "Extractivism, Resistance, Alternatives." *Feminist Africa* 2, no. 1: 14–48.

Peterson, Bhekizizwe. 2000. *Monarchs, Missionaries and African Intellectuals: African Theatre and the Unmaking of Colonial Marginality*. Johannesburg: Wits University Press.

Peterson, Bhekizizwe. 2019. "Spectrality and Inter-generational Black Narratives in South Africa." *Social Dynamics* 45, no. 3: 345–64.

Pickens, Therí Alyce. 2019. *Black Madness: Mad Blackness*. Durham, NC: Duke University Press.

Pierre, Jemima. 2012. *The Predicament of Blackness: Postcolonial Ghana and the Politics of Race*. Chicago: University of Chicago Press.

Pieterse, Jimmy. 2011. "Reading and Writing the Mpondo Revolts." In *Rural Resistance in South Africa*, edited by Thembela Kepe and Lungisile Ntsebeza, 43–65. Leiden, NL: Brill.

Pitcher, Gemma. 2020. "The Xhosa Cattle Killing." *Siyabona Africa*. Accessed June 15, 2022. http://www.siyabona.com/eastern-cape-xhosa-cattle-killing.html.

Plaatje, Sol T. (1915) 1982. *Native Life in South Africa: Before and Since the European War and the Boer Rebellion*. Johannesburg: Ravan.

Povinelli, Elizabeth A. 2011. *Economies of Abandonment: Social Belonging and Endurance in Late Liberalism*. Durham, NC: Duke University Press.

Prins, Frans E. 2009. "Secret San of the Drakensberg and Their Rock Art Legacy." *Critical Arts* 23, no. 2: 190–208.

Prins, Frans E., and Hester Lewis. 1992. "Bushmen as Mediators in Nguni Cosmology." *Ethnology* 31, no. 2: 133–47.

Puar, Jasbir K. 2017. *The Right to Maim*. Durham, NC: Duke University Press.

Putuma, Koleka. 2017. "Water." In *Collective Amnesia*, 96–100. Cape Town: Uhlanga.

Puwar, Nirmal. 2004. *Space Invaders: Race, Gender and Bodies Out of Place*. New York: Berg.

Quijano, Aníbal. 2000. "Coloniality of Power, Eurocentrism and Latin America." *Nepantla: Views from South* 1, no. 3: 533–80.

Quinn, Ben. 2016. "Migrant Death Toll Passes 5,000 After Two Boats Capsize Off Italy." Guardian, December 23, 2016. https://www.theguardian.com/world/2016/dec/23/record-migrant-death-toll-two-boats-capsize-italy-un-refugee.

Rappaport, Julian. 1987. "Terms of Empowerment/Exemplars of Prevention: Toward a Theory for Community Psychology." *American Journal of Community Psychology* 15, no. 2: 121–48.

Ratcliffe, Jo. 2010. *As terras do fim do mundo*. Cape Town: Michael Stevenson.

Ratele, Kopano. 2013. "Subordinate Black South African Men without Fear." *Cahiers d'études africaines* 53, no. 209–210: 247–68.

Ratele, Kopano. 2016. *Liberating Masculinities*. Cape Town: HSRC Press.

Ratele, Kopano. 2019. *The World Looks Like This from Here: Thoughts on African Psychology*. Johannesburg: Wits University Press.

Ricco, John Paul. 2019. "Mourning, Melancholia, Moonlight." CR: *The New Centennial Review* 19, no. 2: 21–46.

Richter, Marlise. 2009. "Bread, Baby Shoes or Blusher? Myths about Social Grants and 'Lazy' Young Mothers." SAMJ: *South African Medical Journal* 99, no. 2: 94.

Rifkin, Mark. 2017. *Beyond Settler Time: Temporal Sovereignty and Indigenous Self-Determination*. Durham, NC: Duke University Press.

Riley, Charles A. 2005. *Disability and the Media: Prescriptions for Change*. Hanover, NH: University Press of New England.

Robinson, Cedric J. 2000. *Black Marxism: The Making of the Black Radical Tradition*. Chapel Hill: University of North Carolina Press.

Ross, Robert. 2017. *These Oppressions Won't Cease: An Anthology of the Political Thought of the Cape Khoesan, 1777–1879*. Johannesburg: Wits University Press.

Roy, Arundhati. 1999. "The Greater Common Good." *Frontline* 16, no. 11: 4–29.

Rumsey, Alan. 1994. "The Dreaming, Human Agency and Inscriptive Practice." *Oceania* 65, no. 2, 116–30.

SABC1. 2017. "Cutting Edge: Vampires—Vondos." *YouTube*, May 23, 2017. https://www.youtube.com/watch?v=jwWGBmBEgJk.

SAHO (South African History Online). 2017. "Timeline of the Marikana Massacre 2012–2013." Accessed June 15, 2022. https://www.sahistory.org.za/article/timeline-marikana-massacre-2012-2013.

SAHO. 2019a. "Pondoland Revolt—1950–1961." Accessed June 15, 2022. https://www.sahistory.org.za/article/pondoland-revolt-1950-1961.

SAHO. 2019b. "Nontetha Nkwenkwe." Accessed June 15, 2022. https://www
.sahistory.org.za/people/nontetha-nkwenkwe.

SAHO. 2021. "Sharpeville Massacre, 21 March 1960." Accessed June 15, 2022. https://
www.sahistory.org.za/article/sharpeville-massacre-21-march-1960.

Samuelson, Meg. 2005. "Remembering the Nation, Dismembering Women? Stories of the South African Transition." PhD diss., University of Cape Town.

Samuelson, Meg. 2010. "(Un)settled States: Indian Ocean Passages, Performative
Belonging and Restless Mobility in Post-apartheid South African Fiction."
Social Dynamics 36, no. 2: 272–87.

Samuelson, Meg. 2013. "Sea Changes, Dark Tides and Littoral States: Oceans and
Coastlines in Post-apartheid South African Narratives." *Alternation* 6: 9–28.

Sanders, Todd. 2001. "Save Our Skins: Structural Adjustment, Morality and the
Occult in Tanzania." In *Magical Interpretations, Material Realities: Modernity,
Witchcraft and the Occult in Post-Colonial Africa*, edited by Henriette Moore and
Todd Sanders, 160–84. London: Routledge.

SAPS (South African Police Service). 2021. *Crime Statistics: Fourth Quarter 2020–21.*
https://www.saps.gov.za/services/fourth_quarter_2020_21_crimestats.pdf.

Savage, Michael. 1986. "The Imposition of Pass Laws on the African Population in
South Africa 1916–1984." *African Affairs* 85, no. 339: 181–205.

Senna, Danzy. 1998. "The Mulatto Millennium: Since When Did Being the
Daughter of a WASP and a Black-Mexican Become Cool?" *Salon*, July 24, 1998.
https://www.salon.com/1998/07/24/24feature_10/.

Serote, Pethu. 1992. "Solomon Mahlangu Freedom College: A Unique South African
Educational Experience in Tanzania." *Transformation* 20: 47–60.

Sexton, Jared. 2008. *Amalgamation Schemes: Antiblackness and the Critique of Multi-
racialism.* Minneapolis: University of Minnesota Press.

Sexton, Jared. 2011. "The Social Life of Social Death: On Afro-Pessimism and Black
Optimism." *InTensions* 5, no. 1: 1–47.

Sexton, Jared. 2016. "The Vel of Slavery: Tracking the Figure of the Unsovereign."
Critical Sociology 42, no. 4–5: 583–97.

Sharp, Lesley A. 1990. "Possessed and Dispossessed Youth: Spirit Possession of
School Children in Northwest Madagascar." *Culture, Medicine and Psychiatry* 14,
no. 3: 339–64.

Sharpe, Christina. 2014. "Black Studies: In the Wake." *Black Scholar* 44, no. 2:
59–69.

Sharpe, Christina. 2016. *In the Wake: On Blackness and Being.* Durham, NC: Duke
University Press.

Shaw, Martin. 2016. "Book Review: Genocide as Social Practice: Reorganizing
Society under the Nazis and Argentina's Military Juntas." *Genocide Studies and
Prevention* 9, no. 3: 183–87.

Shaw, Rosalind. 2001. "Cannibal Transformations." In *Magical Interpretations, Material Realities: Modernity, Witchcraft, and the Occult in Postcolonial Africa*, edited by
Henrietta Moore and Todd Sanders, 50–70. London: Routledge.

Shell, Sandra Rowoldt. 2018. *Children of Hope: The Odyssey of the Oromo Slaves from Ethiopia to South Africa*. Athens: Ohio University Press.

Sibomana, André. 1999. *Hope for Rwanda: Conversations with Laure Guilbert and Hervé Deguine*. Translated and with a postscript by Carina Tertsakian. Foreword by Alison Des Forges. Sterling, VA: Pluto.

Siisiäinen, Lauri. 2013. *Foucault and the Politics of Hearing*. New York: Routledge.

Simons, Harold Jack, and Ray E. Simons. 1969. *Class and Colour in South Africa, 1850–1950*. Johannesburg: Penguin African Library.

Simpson, Leanne Betasamosake. 2017. *As We Have Always Done: Indigenous Freedom through Radical Resistance*. Minneapolis: University of Minnesota Press.

Siwila, Lilian Cheelo. 2014. "Tracing the Ecological Footprints of Our Foremothers: Towards an African Feminist Approach to Women's Connectedness with Nature." *Studia Historiae Ecclesiasticae* 40, no. 2: 131–47.

Sletto, Bjørn. 2009. "'Indigenous People Don't Have Boundaries': Reborderings, Fire Management, and Productions of Authenticities in Indigenous Landscapes." *Cultural Geographies* 16, no. 2: 253–77.

Sletto, Bjørn. 2012. "Indigenous Rights, Insurgent Cartographies, and the Promise of Participatory Mapping." *Portal* 7: 12–15.

Smith, Linda Tuhiwai. 1999. *Decolonizing Methodologies: Research and Indigenous Peoples*. London: Zed Books.

Smith, Linda Tuhiwai. 2007. "The Native and the Neoliberal Down Under: Neoliberalism and 'Endangered Authenticities.'" In *Indigenous Experience Today*, edited by Marisol de la Cadena and Orin Starn, 333–52. New York: Berg.

Soga, J. Henderson. 1927. "Aba-Mbo Genealogical Tables." *Bantu Studies* 3, no. 1: 49–53.

Somer, Eli. 2006. "Culture-Bound Dissociation: A Comparative Analysis." *Psychiatric Clinics* 29, no. 1: 213–26.

Somers, Margaret R. 1994. "The Narrative Constitution of Identity: A Relational and Network Approach." *Theory and Society* 23, no. 5: 605–49.

Southall, Roger. 1983. *South Africa's Transkei: The Political Economy of an "Independent" Bantustan*. New York: Monthly Review Press.

Spillers, Hortense. 1987. "Mama's Baby, Papa's Maybe: An American Grammar Book." *Diacritics* 17, no. 2: 65–81.

Spivak, Gayatri. C. 1999. *A Critique of Postcolonial Reason: Toward a History of the Vanishing Present*. Cambridge, MA: Harvard University Press.

Stapleton, Timothy J. 2001. "Faku, the Mpondo and Colonial Advance in the Eastern Cape, 1834–53." In *Agency and Action in Colonial Africa*, edited by Christopher P. Youé and Timothy J. Stapleton, 12–33. London: Palgrave Macmillan.

Stapleton, Timothy J. 2006. *Faku: Rulership and Colonialism in the Mpondo Kingdom (c. 1780–1867)*. Waterloo, CA: Wilfrid Laurier University Press.

Statistics South Africa. 2016. *Quarterly Labour Force Survey. Quarter 1: 2016*. Pretoria: Stats SA. https://www.statssa.gov.za/publications/P0211 /P02111stQuarter2016.pdf.

Statistics South Africa. 2020. *Quarterly Labour Force Survey. Quarter 1: 2020*. Pretoria: Stats SA. https://www.statssa.gov.za/publications/P0211 /P02111stQuarter2020.pdf.

Steinberg, Jonny. 2008. *Three-Letter Plague: A Young Man's Journey through a Great Epidemic*. Johannesburg: Jonathan Ball.

Sterne, Jonathan. 2012. "Sonic Imaginations." In *The Sound Studies Reader*, edited by Jonathan Sterne, 1–18. London: Routledge.

Stoller, Paul. 2014. *Yaya's Story: The Quest for Well-Being in the World*. Chicago: University of Chicago Press.

Takemoto, Tina. 2016. "Queer Art/Queer Failure." *Art Journal* 75, no. 1: 85–88.

Tallie, T. J. 2019. *Queering Colonial Natal: Indigeneity and the Violence of Belonging in Southern Africa*. Minneapolis: University of Minnesota Press.

Tamale, Sylvia. 2020. *Decolonization and Afro-Feminism*. Ottawa: Daraja.

Taylor, Stephan. 2004. *The Caliban Shore*. London: Faber & Faber.

Teather, Elizabeth Kenworthy. 2001. "The Case of the Disorderly Graves: Contemporary Deathscapes in Guangzhou." *Social and Cultural Geography* 2, no. 2: 185–202.

Terrefe, Selamawit, and Christina Sharpe. 2016. "What Exceeds the Hold?: An Interview with Christina Sharpe." *Rhizomes: Cultural Studies in Emerging Knowledge* 29. http://www.rhizomes.net/issue29/terrefe.html.

Tewolde, Amanuel Isak. 2019. "'What Is Your Race?' Eritrean Migrant Encounters with Racial Identification Questions in South Africa." *African Studies Quarterly* 18, no. 3: 29–45.

Theal, George McCall. 1886. *Kaffir Folk-Lore: A Selection from the Traditional Tales Current among the People Living on the Eastern Border of the Cape Colony*. 2nd ed. No. 34341. London: Swan Sonnenschein, Le Bas & Lowrey.

Theal, George McCall. 1902. *The Beginning of South African History*. London: Unwin.

Thomas, Deborah. 2011. *Exceptional Violence: Embodied Citizenship in Transnational Jamaica*. Durham, NC: Duke University Press.

Thomas, Deborah. 2019. *Political Life in the Wake of the Plantation: Sovereignty, Witnessing, Repair*. Durham, NC: Duke University Press.

Thomas, Jerry. 2017. "Queer Sensibilities: Notes on Method." *Politics, Groups, and Identities* 5, no. 1: 172–81.

Thomas, Kylie. 2013. *Impossible Mourning: HIV/AIDS and Visuality after Apartheid*. Lewisburg, PA: Bucknell University Press.

Thrift, Nigel. 2008. *Non-representational Theory: Space, Politics, Affect*. Oxfordshire: Routledge.

Tinsley, Omise'eke Natasha. 2008. "Black Atlantic, Queer Atlantic: Queer Imaginings of the Middle Passage." *GLQ* 14, no. 2–3: 191–215.

Tinsley, Omise'eke Natasha, and Matt Richardson. 2014. "From Black Transgender Studies to Colin Dayan: Notes on Methodology." *Small Axe* 18, no. 3 (45): 152–61.

Titlestad, Michael. 2008. "'The Unhappy Fate of Master Law': George Carter's A Narrative of Loss of the *Grosvenor*, East Indiaman (1791)." *English Studies in Africa* 51, no. 2: 21–37.

Titlestad, Michael, and Mike Kissack. 2005. "'I Have Always Known Shipwreck': Whiteness in Sheila Fugard's *The Castaways*." ARIEL: *A Review of International English Literature* 36, no. 1–2: 135–55.

Tlale, Mpho Tsepiso. 2020. "Conflicting Levels of Engagement under the Interim Protection of Informal Land Rights Act and the Minerals and Petroleum Development Act: A Closer Look at the Xolobeni Community Dispute." PER: *Potchefstroomse Elektroniese Regsblad* 23, no. 1: 1–32.

Tolsi, Niren, and Paul Botes. 2013. "Marikana: One Year after the Massacre." *Mail and Guardian*. Accessed June 15, 2022. https://marikana.mg.co.za/.

Tugli, A. K., and K. G. Morwe. 2013. "Sexual Risk Behaviours among Rural Learners at Mdutshane Senior Secondary School, Eastern Cape Province, South Africa." *African Journal for Physical Health Education, Recreation and Dance* 19, no. 42: 1025–36.

Twitty, Michael W. 2017. *The Cooking Gene. A Journey through African American Culinary History in the Old South*. New York: Amistad.

Van Laun, Bianca. 2018. "Bureaucratically Missing: Capital Punishment, Exhumations, and the Afterlives of State Documents and Photographs." *Kronos* 44, no. 1: 123–44.

Vinson, Robert Trent. 2012. *The Americans Are Coming! Dreams of African American Liberation in Segregationist South Africa*. Athens: Ohio University Press.

Vizenor, Gerald. 2010. "American Indian Art and Literature Today: Survivance and Tragic Wisdom." *Museum International* 62, no. 3: 41–51.

Vizenor, Gerald Robert. 1994. *Dead Voices: Natural Agonies in the New World*. Vol. 2. Norman: University of Oklahoma Press.

Vizenor, Gerald Robert, ed. 2008. *Survivance: Narratives of Native Presence*. Lincoln: University of Nebraska Press.

Wainwright, Joel, and Joe Bryan. 2009. "Cartography, Territory, Property: Postcolonial Reflections on Indigenous Counter-mapping in Nicaragua and Belize." *Cultural Geographies* 16, no. 2: 153–78.

Walcott, Derek. 1986. "The Sea Is History." In *Collected Poems 1948–1984*, 364–67. New York: Farrar, Straus and Giroux.

Walcott, Rinaldo. 2009. "Reconstructing Manhood; or, the Drag of Black Masculinity." *Small Axe* 13, no. 1 (28): 75–89.

Walcott, Rinaldo. 2015. "Genres of Human: Multiculturalism, Cosmo-politics, and the Caribbean Basin." In *Sylvia Wynter on Being Human as Praxis*, edited by Katherine McKittrick, 183–202. Durham, NC: Duke University Press.

Walcott, Rinaldo. 2021a. "The Black Aquatic." *Liquid Blackness* 5, no. 1: 63–73.

Walcott, Rinaldo. 2021b. *The Long Emancipation: Moving toward Black Freedom*. Durham, NC: Duke University Press.

Weheliye, Alexander G. 2014. *Habeas Viscus: Racializing Assemblages, Biopolitics, and Black Feminist Theories of the Human*. Durham, NC: Duke University Press.

Wekker, Gloria Daisy. 1994. *Ik ben een gouden munt, ik ga door vele handen, maar verlies mijn waarde niet: subjectiviteit en seksualiteit van Creoolse volksklasse vrouwen in Paramaribo*. Amsterdam: Feministische Uitgeverij VITA.

Wenzel, Jennifer. 2009. *Bulletproof: Afterlives of Anticolonial Prophecy in South Africa and Beyond*. Chicago: University of Chicago Press.

West, Cornel. 2007. "Niggerization." *Atlantic*, November 2007. https://www.theatlantic.com/magazine/archive/2007/11/niggerization/306285/.

Wicks, Jeff. 2017a. "Matric 2016—The Numbers You Should Know." News24, January 5, 2017. https://www.news24.com/news24/southafrica/news/matric-2016-the-numbers-you-should-know-20170105.

Wicks, Jeff. 2017b. "Bail Refused for Escourt 'Cannibals.'" *Sunday Times*, December 14, 2017. https://www.timeslive.co.za/news/south-africa/2017-12-14-bail-refused-for-escourt-cannibals/.

Wikipedia. n.d. "Clara Germana Cele." Accessed June 9, 2022. https://en.wikipedia.org/wiki/Clara_Germana_Cele.

Wildcat, Daniel R. 2005. "Indigenizing the Future: Why We Must Think Spatially in the Twenty-First Century." *American Studies* 46, no. 3–4: 417–40.

Willan, Brian P. 1978. "The South African Native Labour Contingent, 1916–1918." *Journal of African History* 19, no. 1: 61–86.

Wilson, Monica. 1959. "The Early History of the Transkei and Ciskei." *African Studies* 18, no. 4: 167–79.

Winters, Joseph R. 2016. *Hope Draped in Black: Race, Melancholy, and the Agony of Progress*. Durham, NC: Duke University Press.

Wood, Felicity, and Michael Lewis. 2007. *The Extraordinary Khotso: Millionaire Medicine Man of Lusikisiki*. Johannesburg: Jacana.

Wright, Michelle. 2015. *The Physics of Blackness*. Minneapolis: University of Minnesota Press.

Wylie, Diana. 2011. "The Shock of the New: Ngquza Hill 1960." In *Rural Resistance in South Africa*, edited by Thembela Kepe and Lungisile Ntsebeza, 191–208. Leiden, NL: Brill.

Wynter, Sylvia. 2001. "Towards the Sociogenic Principle: Fanon, Identity, the Puzzle of Conscious Experience, and What It Is Like to Be 'Black.'" In *National Identities and Sociopolitical Changes in Latin America*, edited by Mercedes Duran-Cogan and Antonio Gomez-Moriana, 30–66. New York: Routledge.

Wynter, Sylvia. 2003. "Unsettling the Coloniality of Being/Power/Truth/Freedom: Towards the Human, After Man, Its Overrepresentation—An Argument." *CR: The New Centennial Review* 3, no. 3: 257–337.

Wynter, Sylvia. 2006. "On How We Mistook the Map for the Territory, and Reimprisoned Ourselves in Our Unbearable Wrongness of Being, of *Desêtre*: Black Studies toward the Human Project." In *A Companion to African-American*

Studies, edited by Lewis R. Gordon and Jane Anna Gordon, 107–18. Oxford: Blackwell.

Young, Francis. 2016. "Exorcism in an Age of Doubt: The Nineteenth and Twentieth Centuries." In *A History of Exorcism in Catholic Christianity*, 181–207. London: Palgrave Macmillan.

Yuval-Davis, Nira. 2006. "Intersectionality and Feminist Politics." *European Journal of Women's Studies* 13, no. 3: 193–209.

worlding, 104–5, 124–26, 222n2. *See also*
    ukukhupuka izizwe
World War I, 76–78
Wrath of the Ancestors, The (Jordan), 173
Wright, Michelle, 80, 143, 222n7
written form, 11, 61. *See also* narratives
Wylie, Diana, 186, 228n23
Wynter, Sylvia, 13, 23, 48, 51, 54, 58, 162,
    174, 181

Xhosa, 1, 44, 62, 64, 72, 80, 150, 213n1
Xolobeni, 102
Xolobeni Mineral Sands Project, 98–99

Young, Francis, 127–28

Zimbabwe, 154
Zulu, 75, 80, 213n1
Zuma, Jacob, 175, 206